184801

David W. Swift
University of Hawaii

35-67

IDEOLOGY AND CHANGE IN THE PUBLIC SCHOOLS:

Latent Functions of

Progressive Education

CHARLES E. MERRILL PUBLISHING COMPANY
A Bell & Howell Company
Columbus, Ohio

Merrill's Sociology Series
Under the Editorship of **Richard L. Simpson**
University of North Carolina

LA
217
S9

International Standard Book Number: 0-675-09229-9

Library of Congress Catalog Card Number: 70-143439

1 2 3 4 5 6 7 8 9 10 — 75 74 73 72 71

Printed in the United States of America

To Lois
and my parents

PREFACE

While much has been said about progressive education, this study examines it from a new perspective, focusing upon its consequences for the *school* rather than for the *child*. I've written this book because, as an elementary teacher and now a sociologist specializing in education, I have found no adequate explanation for some of the most frustrating characteristics of our public schools. In spite of Sputnik, programmed learning, black militancy and the like, progressive (or "progressivistic") education is far from dead, and I've attempted to explain why it persists.

David W. Swift

Honolulu, Hawaii

ACKNOWLEDGMENTS

I am indebted to Charles Glock; without his encouragement and sug-gestions this book would not have been written. I also appreciate the assistance of professors Kenneth Bock, Jack London, Tamotsu Shibutani and Richard Simpson. Burton Clark's studies offered models for this analysis, and the work of Lawrence Cremin, Raymond Callahan, Myron Lieberman and James Koerner supported key points of my book.

My own experiences in public schools have been supplemented by the observations of several career teachers, particularly Harry and Irene Dyarman and William Nolan. My wife, Lois, taught for ten years in elementary schools; her insights have been most helpful. My father, D. W. Swift, Sr., reviewed this manuscript and contributed considerably to its clarity. I'd also like to thank Chrys Cotting for her careful editing.

The Houghton-Mifflin Company, Prentice-Hall, Random House and the University of Chicago Press have granted permission to quote from their books.

D.W.S

CONTENTS

IDEOLOGY AND CHANGE IN THE PUBLIC SCHOOLS

one

INTRODUCTION

VARIOUS EXPLANATIONS HAVE BEEN GIVEN FOR THE POPULARITY OF PRO-
gressive education in the United States. The most familiar point of view
credits — or blames — John Dewey and his colleagues at Columbia
Teachers College.[1] Other observers, most notably Lawrence Cremin,
have gone beyond a review of key figures in the progressive education
movement to tie in threads from the larger society, examining the impact
of such factors as municipal reform, vocational training, agricultural
education, political progressivism, and psychological tests and measure-
ments.[2]

This study takes a third approach, examining progressive education
with respect to public school systems as organizations. It attempts to link
progressive education, as an idea in the minds of a few visionaries or
even as a broad social movement, to the actual problems and everyday
experiences of public schools and their employees. It is my contention
that progressive education was virtually forced upon public schools, not
by John Dewey, nor by idealistic laymen and educators concerned with
the welfare of the child. Rather, it arose of necessity out of the endless
attempts of teachers and administrators to cope with recurring problems,
many of which had little direct connection with education. While a few
of these problems had been present in earlier times, they became increasingly oppressive in the latter decades of the nineteenth century and unbearable during the first part of the twentieth. Progressive education
offered a means of coping with these problems. Thus, it was more than
an ideal and more than a pedagogical philosophy. It was also an adaptive

3

mechanism, facilitating the operation of the public schools, and enhancing the working conditions and the security of school personnel.

In fact, progressive education may be viewed as an ideology: a set of ideas justifying and helping to maintain a particular social system.[3] Although the term *ideology* often carries a derogatory connotation, it is also used in a neutral sense. The study of ideologies is a method of analysis employed in the sociology of knowledge. This field is concerned with the relations between ideas and situations; between theories, doctrines, intellectual movements and ways of thinking, on the one hand, and the interests and purposes of specific groups on the other. The sociological approach to ideas maintains that they are not immanent; they do not occur by themselves, but have an existential basis in the "real" world, in a particular social stratum, ethnic group, power structure or organization.[4] In this study, the existential base of progressive education is the individual American public school and school district, consisting of the teachers, administrators and other employees under the direction of the local board of education.

Thus, the two main threads of this study are progressive educational philosophy and organizational problems confronting the school. The former has been examined in considerable detail but the latter have been largely ignored. The relations between progressive education and actual organizational exigencies have received little, if any, attention.[5]

Progressive education, according to a former president of the Progressive Education Association, holds that "the child rather than what he studies should be the center of all educational effort."[6] As we shall see in the next chapter, progressive education first attracted serious notice in the United States during the decades following the Civil War. By the beginning of this century many educators were discussing it, some were advocating it, and a few were even attempting to practice it. The movement gathered momentum during the 1910s and 1920s and reached its greatest popularity immediately before World War II. After the war, and especially following the Soviet Union's spectacular successes in space technology, progressive education fell from favor, and is now seldom mentioned.[7]

These stages in the popularity of progressive education are familiar to students of American educational history, particularly since the appearance of Lawrence Cremin's definitive study, *The Transformation of the School*. Along with the waxing and waning of progressive philosophy, however, other more concrete developments were exerting a profound influence upon the school and its staff. Control and retention of students, administration, relations with the community, and the working conditions and aspirations of personnel were all affected by changes which occurred during the half-century between the Civil War and the end of World War I. Previously, traditional methods had sufficed in coping with the difficulties encountered by the small, simple schools of the colonial and early national eras. But the period extending roughly from 1870 to 1920 brought such a transformation in the aims and the structure of the school that time-honored solutions were no longer satisfactory. These changes set the stage for the wholesale adoption, during the twenties, thirties and forties, of what was popularly known as progressive education.

Although reference to these changes may be found in many books on American education, most accounts are lacking in two respects. First, they underestimate the impact of these changes upon the school and its personnel. Secondly, they have not examined the relationship between organizational problems and progressive pedagogy; there has been little recognition that educational policy might be affected by non-educational considerations.[8] This neglect is due, in large part, to the manner in which public schools are usually viewed: as rational instruments for attaining officially stated goals. Most, if not all, of the school's activities are presumed to be directed toward the achievement of these goals. The focus is upon the formal, planned aspects of the organization; little attention is paid to other factors, such as control over personnel or the demonstration of administrative efficiency.

Guided by this perspective, educators and laymen, supporters of progressive curriculum and proponents of traditional subject matter, theorists and administrators alike have been inclined to assume that the school's main problem is simply one of deciding what its formal objective should be and then figuring out the best way to achieve it. While they may be aware that other problems exist, they seldom fully appreciate the degree to which these problems may affect the attainment of the school's formal goals.

Consequently, another approach seems more promising for our purposes here. It leads us to look at a school as an interrelated whole, a natural system attempting to maintain its equilibrium in the face of internal tensions and pressures from the environment. The rational pursuit of the organization's formal goal — in this case, the education of children — is seen as only one of several factors influencing the school's behavior. Other forces, such as organizational survival or the personal interests of employees, may also be operative, resulting, at times, in the neglect or distortion of the official goal and perhaps even leading to competition with it. This approach does not claim that official goals are irrelevant; rather than accepting them at face value, however, we will try to discover how they may be affected by various non-educational concerns of the school.

This study examines four major areas of tension: *clientele, administration, autonomy,* and *personnel.* Each of these is analyzed in a temporal sequence divided into three periods. The first may be called the traditional period, extending over two centuries from the early days of the American colonies up through the Civil War. During this time there was little impetus for change. The old, established ways of doing things generally seemed satisfactory. Many problems which later became troublesome did not yet exist, or if they did, time-honored responses were usually adequate for coping with them. On occasions when these traditional methods did not work, it was up to each individual teacher to improvise his own solution as best he could because there was little or no communication with other teachers. Consequently, even if someone had developed new approaches, there was really no way in which such innovations could be disseminated to others who might have used them.

The next period, from 1870 to the end of World War I, was a time of transition in the public schools. During this half-century, a number of profound changes raised problems for which traditional responses were no longer adequate. At the same time, interaction among educators increased, facilitated by technological improvements in transportation and communication, and also by teachers' organizations. Improved roads, telegraphy, railways, radio, automobiles and rapid, inexpensive printing made it possible to learn what other educators were doing. Furthermore, professional associations, teachers' institutes, normal schools and governmental agencies provided focal points for the development and dissemination of new educational ideas.

During the third period, approximately 1920 to 1950, these changes led to the widespread adoption of new procedures. These practices were legitimated by the popular new pedagogical philosophy. Thus, by mid-century, progressive practices had become institutionalized as an integral part of the public school, so firmly established that the ideology which facilitated their adoption was no longer needed. This situation in American education resembled Max Weber's description of the relationship between religion and capitalism: Protestantism was helpful in getting capitalism started but, after capitalism became strongly established, it no longer required the support of Calvinist theology.[9]

From a more general perspective, this is an example of social change in an industrializing society, focusing particularly upon the interplay between ideology and social structure. The relationship among these elements is complex. Although ideology may play an important part in change, it is not sufficient, by itself, to bring about this change. In addition, there must also be strains in the system which encourage receptivity to new ways of thinking. Thus, the fundamentals of progressive education had been formulated, in some detail, by the end of the eighteenth century but did not attract much interest until more than a hundred years later, when tensions in the rapidly developing American school system had become intolerable and traditional solutions no longer sufficed. It should also be noted that, after the new ideology became institutionalized, it facilitated further changes, setting up a complex pattern in which cause and effect were often intermingled.

Because this is an unfamiliar approach to progressive education, and since feelings about progressive education are likely to run high, several points should be made clear from the start. First, this study augments, rather than contradicts or replaces, the other explanations for the rise of progressive education. It does not, for example, deny the contributions of individual pioneering philosophers and practitioners, nor does it minimize the importance of broad social movements. What it does is to say that these factors, significant though they may have been, provide only a partial explanation. In addition, the problems of the school itself must also be considered.

Thus, Dewey and his colleagues played a major role, perhaps an essential one, by further conceptualizing progressive education and by giving it its initial impetus in the United States. Furthermore, public concern for industrial training, social uplift, and agricultural education helped to popularize it and gain it public support.

But, these forces alone would not necessarily have been sufficient to implant progressive education in the schools. It is possible that an institution may resist change in spite of the existence of a recipe for reform and considerable public support. In other cases, organizations might be ahead of the times, ready to change before there is a fully developed formula for change and before there is much public support. Consequently, the acceptance of a new idea or mode of thought depends in part on conditions within the organization. This study suggests that American public schools, faced with serious problems, were quite ready to accept the new philosophy of education — or at least some aspects of it — and did not have to be prodded along by public opinion or by the exhortations of progressive philosophers.

A second point to keep in mind is that this study is not concerned with the educational effectiveness of progressive education. Educational efficacy is certainly important, but we needn't get embroiled in this controversial issue here. Instead, we will examine other, latent consequences of progressive education, looking for ways in which it may have alleviated problems which were not primarily educational in nature. For public schools are not merely educational institutions, concerned solely with pedagogical issues. They are also organizations and, as such, are beset by problems similar to those found in various types of organizations: problems of controlling clientele, of large scale operations, of autonomy and finance, and of the status and security of personnel. Progressive education, whatever its instructional advantages or disadvantages may have been, played a vital role in coping with these issues — issues which, in spite of their non-educational nature, were nevertheless very real and could not be ignored.

A third admonition, perhaps the most important one of all, concerns the definition of progressive education itself. Progressive education as it was actually practiced in American public schools was often a far cry from what its originators had in mind. In fact, the discrepancies were so pronounced that John Dewey turned from propounding progressive education to criticizing it. He attacked some of its manifestations as "stupid" — an exceptionally harsh term for one whose writing was usually so mild — and, for ten years, he boycotted the Progressive Education Association, the organization supposedly devoted to the cause he had formerly advocated.[10] It is probable, in spite of the popularity which progressive education eventually attained, that few truly progressive schools have ever existed. This contention is not inimical to the thesis of this study, for there is often a vast gulf between the stated, original aims of an ideology and its actual application in everyday life. Christianity, for example, has millions of adherents but relatively few may really be practicing it in the spirit that its founder intended. In short, the subsequent embodiment of an ideology may be very different from its original intent; exalted ideals may be used for mundane ends. This seems to have been true of progressive education in American public schools.

This study involves two steps. First, it traces the emergence of strains in the social structure, of urgent non-pedagogical problems facing the public school and its personnel. Secondly, it suggests ways in which attempted solutions to these problems were facilitated by an ideology, namely, progressive education.

The next chapter is devoted to a discussion of progressive education, first contrasting it with traditional education and then presenting some of the major points in its history. The third chapter examines the problem of controlling a vast, heterogeneous, and often recalcitrant student body. Chapter four investigates difficulties of operating large complex organizations. The fifth chapter describes the school's attempts to maintain its autonomy in spite of local control and financing. Chapter six turns from problems at the organizational level to consider progressive education's impact upon the status and working conditions of school employees. Chapter seven points out that some groups within the school had more to gain from progressive education than others, and therefore were presumably more apt to support it. The final chapter discusses, among other things, the means by which progressive education was adopted by the schools, its greater acceptance in the United States in comparison with other countries, and its probable continuing influence in the future.

REFERENCES

[1] For example, Max Rafferty, *Suffer Little Children,* p. 15; and *What They Are Doing to Your Children,* pp. 18, 59, 66, 84.

[2] Cremin, *The Transformation of the School.* Merle Curti has also been especially concerned with the social context of American education: *The Social Ideas of American Educators;* and *The Growth of American Thought,* 3rd. ed.

[3] Broom and Selznick, *Sociology,* 2nd. ed., p. 304.

[4] Mannheim, *Ideology and Utopia,* pp. 2-3, 265-67.

[5] A recent bibliography of more than eight hundred studies of formal organizations listed only a handful which dealt with elementary or secondary schools, and even those few were not directly concerned with the issues to be examined in the present study. Blau and Scott, *Formal Organizations, A Comparative Approach,* pp. 258-99. For other summaries, dealing specifically with education, see Neal Gross, "The Sociology of Education," pp. 128-52, in Merton, Broom and Cottrell, Jr., *Sociology Today;* Brim, *Sociology and the Field of Education;* Hansen and Gerstl, eds., *On Education: Sociological Perspectives.* Ronald M. Pavalko's *Sociology of Education* provides a good cross-section of sociological approaches to education. The two sociologists who came closest to my concerns in this book are Ronald Corwin and Burton Clark. Corwin develops a general organizational perspective for educational institutions in his *A Sociology of Education,* and Clark provides valuable case studies of a junior college and an adult education program in California: *The Open Door College;* and *Adult Education in Transition.*

[6] Fowler, "President's Message," cited in Cremin, *Transformation of the School,* p. 258.

[7] Cremin, *Transformation of the School,* p. ix.

[8] An exception is Callahan's *Education and the Cult of Efficiency* which will be discussed in Chapter 4.

[9] The two studies are similar in another respect. Like Weber's analysis, which concentrated on the *rise* of capitalism rather than on its mature, contemporary stage, this study deals primarily with the *development* of American schools rather than with their present form (Weber, *The Protestant Ethic and the Spirit of Capitalism,* trans. Talcott Parsons).

[10] Cremin, *Transformation of the School,* pp. 142, 234-35. See also Dworkin, "John Dewey: A Centennial Review," in Dworkin, ed., *Dewey on Education,* p. 10.

two

PROGRESSIVE
EDUCATION

WHAT IS PROGRESSIVE EDUCATION? BASICALLY, IT IS *education which emphasizes the pupil rather than the subject matter.* However, as soon as we try to define progressive education in more detail, we encounter difficulties. As Cremin stated in the preface to his study:

> The reader will search these pages in vain for any capsule defini-
> tion of progressive education. None exists, and none ever will; for
> throughout its history progressive education meant different things
> to different people, and these differences were only compounded by
> the remarkable diversity of American education.[1]

The situation is complicated by the fact that John Dewey, perhaps the most influential progressive educator in the United States, was not always precise in his statements about progressive education. At times his inconsistencies and lack of clarity left considerable doubt as to what he really meant.[2] For example, he claimed that the apparent antagonism between subject matter and a concern for the pupil was illusory; both shared a place in the ideal form of education. Nevertheless, his reitera-tion of the necessity to consider the pupil did convey the impression that this was more important to him than the material which was to be learned.[3] At any rate, Dewey himself complained that many of his fol-lowers, and especially educators, either did not understand his ideas or garbled them just enough to use for their own purposes.[4] A recent review of his work observed, "Dewey's followers have continually bickered among themselves over their certainties about his meaning."[5]

In explaining why Dewey became and remained a controversial figure in education, Berger listed three factors:

> First, the obscurity of some of his writing led many to misunderstand him. Second, . . . many . . . , sincerely believing they were following the ideas of Dewey, brought forth new conceptions that contradicted or went far away from Dewey's own belief. . . .Finally, there are many who have attacked Dewey but never bothered to read and examine his meanings.[6]

Fortunately, these problems of definition do not present insurmountable obstacles for this study. For our purposes here it is enough to realize that something called progressive education did appear in America around the end of the nineteenth century and that its critics, as well as its supporters, agreed that it differed fundamentally from traditional education. Traditional education had emphasized subject matter, seeing it as the knowledge of the ages which would provide information, discipline and guidance for the present and the future. In contrast, progressive educators centered upon the child, hoping that, by development of his physical, psychological and social needs, the child would develop his personality, initiative and spontaneity.[7]

Before turning to the history of progressive education it may be helpful to consider briefly the two forms of education in terms of ideal types.

TRADITIONAL EDUCATION

The dominant aim of the traditional school was the development of character and intellect through the acquisition of long-established knowledge. Mastery of this basic heritage of human learning was likely to be hard and disagreeable, but the strict application required for this task was the best preparation for the rigors of adult life. The knowledge to be acquired in school was viewed as a fixed, known entity remaining basically the same throughout the ages. Although classic languages and literature were found less and less as time went by, they provided models for what was believed to be the ideal education.[8]

By present standards, curriculum of the traditional school was narrow. It emphasized reading, writing, spelling, arithmetic, and gave some attention to history, English, grammar, and geography. Each of these subjects was presented according to the logical divisions inherent in the discipline itself, with no attempt to correlate one subject with another. The resulting courses of study remained unchanged year after year and were to be followed down to the last detail. The same material was given to all pupils, without regard for individual differences.

Pupils were perceived as passive recipients of information—receptacles into which knowledge was poured. Because all children were considered to be basically alike in their needs and abilities, their rate of progress supposedly depended upon the amount of effort they expended upon their studies. Differences in their ultimate achievement were attributed simply to the fact that some children remained in school longer than others and therefore were able to climb higher on the educational ladder. Promotion occurred only upon mastery of the standardized prescribed material. As a result, unsuccessful pupils might remain in the same grade for several years.

Lectures, drill, memorization, recitation, and examinations were the principal methods of instruction. Pupils usually studied by themselves. Whispering and conversation were prohibited. Approved interaction among schoolmates was limited to formalized competition rather than cooperation. Play was considered a distracting frivolity; it had no place in the curriculum, and was supposed to occur only during recess or outside of school hours.

Emphasis was on learning facts and rules. Textbooks were the only source of information other than the teacher. These books, when available, had few pictures, often discussed material outside of the child's experience, and contained long lists of facts to be memorized. Homework was not only necessary to complete assignments which had not been finished during school hours, but also was often specifically assigned as such.

In the traditional classroom, pupils who were not occupied in formal recitations and drills with the teacher were expected to keep quiet. To maintain silence and other desired behavior, harsh punishments were meted out. When misbehavior occurred it merely gave further support to the assumption that children were naturally unruly and had to be kept under control by corporal punishment, ridicule or punitive assignments.

The teacher was a drill master and disciplinarian. He assigned lessons, heard recitations and kept order. It was not considered his duty to help pupils in the actual learning of their lessons. He maintained an aloof, superior attitude, and relations with his pupils were, at least in theory, reserved and austere.

The formality of lessons and of teacher-pupil relations was reflected in the appearance of the classroom. Desks, benches and chairs were kept in straight, orderly rows, and were often bolted or nailed to the floor. The walls were drab, with few pictures or spots of color to distract the pupils from their lessons.

Concentration upon the "three Rs" and the remnants of classical heritage separated the school rather sharply from other aspects of the child's life. The essentials of daily existence were to be learned else-where, outside the classroom. Consequently, the pupil and his parents viewed schooling as something of a luxury, of secondary importance after home or work or church, with the result that the school term was comparatively short, taking those seasons of the year when children were not needed elsewhere. This does not mean that schools were, in fact, isolated from community life. Far from it. Supporters of the schools variously considered them to be essential agents for religious orthodoxy, moral training, civic responsibility, ethnic survival, or practical voca-tional preparation. Without such functions the school would not have received the support it did. These expectations permeated the atmos-phere of the traditional school. Pupils memorized passages from the Bible, read from textbooks filled with such maxims as "Procrastination is the thief of time,"[9] and were admonished at the close of the school day to "Go straight home and be civil to everybody [you] might meet."[10] Nevertheless, the school's role was a passive one. It did not make a con-scious attempt to relate itself to the community, but instead accepted almost automatically the tasks assigned to it. Contacts between the teacher and the community occurred as a matter of course; there was no need to seek them deliberately as an adjunct to the educational program.

PROGRESSIVE EDUCATION

In marked contrast to traditional instruction, progressive education emphasizes the whole child rather than merely concentrating upon his intellect. Mastery of subject matter is less important than the develop-ment of personality, social attitudes and physical well-being. According to progressives, pupils are best prepared for life when the teacher pays attention to their present needs and encourages the full realization of their potentialities.

Education is not preparation for life; it is life itself. Education should be interesting, exciting and enjoyable. The curriculum, instead of presenting a standardized body of knowledge inherited from the past, should be based upon the child's own interests, with the students them-selves selecting the material they want to study and the skills they wish to learn. Pupils' experiences are enriched by a wide range of expressive, creative, physical and social activities. Music, manual arts, home eco-nomics, dramatics, recreation, and physical education are an integral part of the curriculum.

The traditional subjects as such are discontinued. When instruction is given in subjects like reading, writing, geography, or mathematics, it is not compartmentalized but is incorporated into an on-going activity of interest to the students. Moreover, no material is introduced before the pupil is physiologically and psychologically ready for it. The flexible progressive curriculum, recognizing the enormous range of individual differences between pupils, provides options to suit the needs and interests of every pupil. Courses of study are not stated in terms of subject matter but rather in terms of the educational objectives sought. Moreover, these courses of study are not to be followed literally but are only indications of the possibilities contained within each suggested activity.

Various learning methods are used as the pupils engage in the real-life experiences which will prepare them for the larger problems of living. Activity, rather than intellectual pursuit, is emphasized. Memorization and drill are replaced by leading the pupils to discover general principles and by creative expression. Information is no longer obtained only from textbooks or from the teacher. Pupils also build models, make scrapbooks, paint pictures, go on field trips, and utilize a variety of audio-visual aids. Instead of studying silently at their desks or drilling in formal groups under the close supervision of the teacher, pupils are free to move about the room and to converse with their classmates. Ample opportunities for learning are provided in class and it is felt that the student, spending many hours each day in school, should have some time for himself and his family. Therefore, homework has been omitted. Examinations and promotions are informal and flexible, and are evaluated in terms of the pupils' overall needs rather than merely his academic achievements.

In contrast to the traditional assumption that children were inherently sinful and therefore had to be rigidly disciplined, the progressive views children as potentially good creatures whose goodness is nurtured by kindness, reason and love. Discipline is self-imposed. On the rare occasions when punishment is needed at all, it is mild, with classmates and teacher offering sympathetic constructive suggestions in an effort to help the miscreant avoid repetition of his unfortunate act.

The teacher is democratic, friendly and permissive. His training in child development and psychology enables him to understand the complex factors which may be impinging upon his pupils. Rather than giving information and assigning specific lessons, he suggests possibilities for investigation and tries to stimulate pupils to think clearly and to develop other potential abilities they might have.

The progressive classroom is bright, cheerful and informal. Desks and chairs are movable, and are shifted and regrouped throughout the day into circles, clusters or lines, according to the changing activities in which the pupils are engaged. The walls are painted in pastel hues and are decorated with colorful pictures. Models, murals and exhibits provide additional stimulation for pupil interest.

Distinctions between school and other spheres of pupils' lives are minimized. The school, as an extension of home, continues activities with which the children are already familiar. To talk in terms of the pupils' interests is to deal with events which happen outside of the classroom in the family and the community. These are a meaningful part of the students' lives. Family and community are encouraged to minimize the artificial separation between education and the rest of life by keeping in close contact with school affairs.

These are the major differences between the two types of education. Now we can place them in historical perspective, examining some of the highlights of the transition from traditional education to progressivism.

The History of Progressive Education

A new conception of human nature emerged during the seventeenth and eighteenth centuries, attacking the traditional view which held that people are inherently sinful. Instead, argued the Enlightenment philosophers, man is born neither bad nor good; it is only his environment which makes him one or the other. If this environment would be consistently favorable, there would be virtually no limit to the heights which men might achieve, because humans are born neutral and are infinitely perfectable.[11]

This concept of man provided the base for a new philosophy of education, which Rousseau publicized in *Emile*. Education was viewed as a process of normal growth during which the child developed naturally. The trouble with orthodox education, Rousseau believed, was that the parents and teachers were thinking in terms of the accomplishments and abilities of adults, and were attempting to force these upon children. He further felt that, instead of making pupils absorb preformulated facts and ideas, education should be a process of growth in which the potentialities endowed us at birth are permitted to develop naturally in a healthy environment. The child was best prepared for life by experiencing the things which had meaning for him. Moreover, he had a right to enjoy his childhood.[12]

Rousseau also incorporated another concept which had emerged during the enlightenment: *sense realism*. This concept differed from the traditional belief that ideas were present in the mind at birth or that they existed independently from man and were waiting to be grasped by the mind. Instead, sense realism held that people learned through their senses, through the experiences received by touch, sight, hearing, smell, and taste. Therefore, Rousseau argued, schools should be conducted in a way that would utilize the senses; children should be learning from real objects which they could see and feel rather than trying to absorb the elusive abstractions found in books.[13]

Rousseau's writing did much to popularize the new pedagogy. However, he was primarily concerned with ideals and general theories. It remained for Pestalozzi and Froebel to reduce Rousseau's ideas to the actual details of classroom work. They took the vague concept of natural development and translated it into precise steps which teachers could use from day to day. Pestalozzi developed methods which became widely used in elementary education. He applied them in his own schools in Switzerland, and they were soon adopted by the primary schools in Prussia. Froebel adapted these principles for use in kindergartens, a new type of school he had established for children who were too young to attend regular primary schools.[14]

In the United States, these new educational ideas found several proponents in the pre-Civil War era. In 1808, for example, Joseph Neef published a treatise on Pestalozzi's ideas, calling for a wealth of experiences with which to develop pupils' individual potentialities. The three Rs were to be centered around materials drawn from the everyday life of the children. Books, Neef believed, should not be introduced until children were older. Similar suggestions were made by William MacClure in 1826.[15]

Perhaps the most influential proposal appearing in America before the Civil War was put forward by Horace Mann in 1843. Mann was the first secretary of the newly formed Massachusetts Board of Education. His recommendations did not contain anything really new, but they stirred up a heated controversy. He criticized what he believed to be the degeneration of public schools, attacked the poor teaching that occurred there, and called for basic, far-reaching reforms. In suggesting improvements, he praised the Prussian school system, especially its methods based on sense realism, and its new approach to discipline based on love rather than on authoritarianism.[16]

Mann's report was attacked not only by ministers and laymen, angered over his concepts of human nature, but also by a committee of thirty-one Boston schoolmasters. The schoolmasters issued a 144-page refutation of his proposals. Mann replied, and again the teachers put forth a rejoinder. The ultimate result of this controversy was to draw considerable attention to Mann's report and to the new educational methods he advocated.[17]

The rise of progressive education in the United States followed the earlier movement to establish a system of universal education. By 1860, the principle of free instruction for all, at least at the elementary level, had gained general acceptance. A majority of the states had public school systems, and half of the nation's children were receiving some formal education.[18] As the ideal of universal education came closer to realization, there emerged subsequently a concern for the quality of the education being provided. Many Americans who had misgivings about traditional teaching practices were impressed by the idea that education should be centered around the pupil and that the various parts of the curriculum should be interrelated in order to be more meaningful to the child. Also intriguing were Froebel's suggestions of kindergartens for children three or four years of age, and Herbart's belief that history and literature could form a core around which other subjects could be unified.[19]

As early as 1873 some of these principles were put into practice in the public schools of Quincy, Massachusetts. Under the direction of Francis Parker, the Quincy schools had abandoned the rigid curriculum and the usual divisions into spelling, reading, grammar, and the like. Instead of the alphabet learned by rote, reading began on words and sentences. Magazines, newspapers, and informal material prepared by the teachers replaced traditional textbooks. Geography was introduced by trips through the countryside and arithmetic began inductively rather than through rules.[20]

Another departure from traditional pedagogy involved manual training. The Philadelphia Centennial Exposition of 1876 had introduced Russian vocational methods which demonstrated how mechanical processes could be analyzed, systematized and effectively taught. Instruction consisted of graded exercises in which the pupil, following a definite method, gradually surmounted tasks of increasing difficulty until he eventually attained a requisite level of skill. Various Americans, including the president of the Massachusetts Institute of Technology, saw this method as a way of combining mental and manual training to provide more balanced schooling than the narrowly intellectual education usually offered in public schools. In 1884 manual training was established in three cities and homemaking was introduced shortly afterward. By 1890, thirty-six cities were offering some instruction in metal work, carpentry, cooking, sewing and drawing. Most of this instruction was at the secondary level.[21]

In spite of such exceptions, however, widespread interest in educational reform remained fragmentary until the 1890s, when a series of muckraking articles by Joseph Rice appeared in the monthly *Forum*. Rice attacked inadequate programs, political corruption, and professional backwardness in the schools, stated that the problem was national in scope, and called for a unified movement of progressively oriented people to rectify these conditions. These articles set off a tremendous controversy, and were credited by Cremin with marking the start of the progressive movement in education.[22]

About this time, John Dewey founded the Laboratory School at the University of Chicago for the purpose of testing his educational theories. The activity program he developed there was based on the principle that life itself should furnish the basic experiences of education. However, he denied that there was an inherent division between subject-centered and child-centered education. He claimed that differences between the two were only a matter of emphasis; there need not be a real gap between them.[23]

Perhaps Dewey's most important contribution to progressive education was the synthesis of his pedagogical ideas with his concern for democracy and social reform. He believed that the school must take a central role in the improvement of society. This was the basis on which curricula should be evaluated. Because traditional education had not prepared citizens for the problems they would face in the rapidly changing world, a new curriculum was needed.[24]

Other foundations for progressive education were being developed, around the turn of the century, by Edward Thorndike. While previous theories of learning had stressed repetition and practice, Thorndike's experiments with animals suggested that the results of a particular behavior were crucial in determining whether that behavior would be learned. If a specific act were successful—if, for example, an animal placed in a box was rewarded with food or freedom after pressing a lever—that act would be learned. On the other hand, if there were no reinforcement of the connection between behavior and its consequences, learning would not occur. These experiments undermined traditional methods of drill and practice by suggesting that sheer repetition was not in itself the key to learning.[25]

Thorndike's further investigations emphasized specificity in learning: acquisition of knowledge and skills is not general; specific learning is required for specific behavior. This finding shook the venerable concept of transfer of training and cast doubt upon the value of traditional subjects in developing the mind. In another area, Thorndike's study of heredity led him to a concern for individual differences. Still other interests included the application of quantitative methods to psychological study, and the hope that a science of education would eventually be established.[26]

Although Dewey and Thorndike were influential figures, they were not the only ones contributing to progressive education during the early part of this century. Others, including G. Stanley Hall and William

James, were also preparing the theoretical base for a new philosophy of education, while James Stout's philanthropies in Wisconsin and Marietta Johnson's work at the Organic School in Alabama were providing actual models for educational reform.[27]

A particularly interesting development was the introduction of a new principle for utilizing school rooms. In 1907 the public schools of Gary, Indiana, adopted a plan set forth by the new superintendent, William Wirt. While using many innovations incorporated in other progressive schools, the really novel feature of Wirt's plan was the *platoon system* of organization. Instead of the usual procedure of assigning each pupil to a permanent desk in a regular classroom, the auditorium, laboratory, shop and playground also became integral parts of the school, in constant use throughout the day. While half of the students were in the regular classrooms, the others were using these new facilities.[28]

Whatever its instructional merits, the Gary Plan also seemed to offer the advantage of housing twice the number of pupils in the same amount of space, resulting in large savings in the cost of school construction and maintenance. Within a few years this concept was put into practice in many school systems, largely because of its apparent economy. It was heralded for its presumed educational merits in the same rhapsodic prose which characterized other pedagogical innovations of that period. For example, "Those who follow Professor Dewey's philosophy find in the Gary schools—as Professor Dewey does himself— the most complete and admirable application yet attempted, a synthesis of the best aspects of the progressive 'schools of tomorrow'."[29]

News of these innovations spread across the nation. In some cases, as in Dewey's, the educator himself wrote at length about his own work. In other instances, support came from enthusiastic journalists like Randolph Bourne, whose articles about the Gary Plan brought it to the attention of many readers. In still other cases, educational innovations came to the attention of an audience through political notoriety. For example, the Gary Plan was a major issue in the 1917 campaign for mayor of New York. Wirt had been brought there, with the incumbent mayor's approval, to supervise the installation of his system in the city schools, but the Tammany candidate attacked it as an attempt to economize on the education of slum children. In addition to the feelings aroused by this contention, the religious issue also flared up because Wirt had introduced into the Gary schools the idea of release time for religious instruction.[30]

Thus, through various channels, the general outlines of progressive education were fairly well-known by the time of the First World War.

Familiarity with its detail may have remained sketchy, but at least many people were aware that there was an alternative to traditional education. Nevertheless, most schools still held the position that their first responsibility was to uphold academic standards. In the average elementary school, according to Butts and Cremin, ". . . traditional methods persisted in great force, and rote or textbook learning was the rule. . . ."[31] "At the secondary level the college preparatory program still predominated."[32]

The period from the end of the First World War to the middle of the century marked the widespread adoption of progressive education by American public schools. By 1929 over two hundred cities had adopted the Gary Plan, in whole or in part, and at least 15 percent of all high school students were taking typing, general science, or physical education. By the late thirties, school superintendents and state commissioners of education felt free to use the ideas of progressive education in public announcements regarding their plans for revising the educational system, and in 1938 an advocate of progressive education stated that it was no longer a rebel movement but had become respectable.[33]

In 1919 the schools in Winnetka, Illinois, adopted a plan developed earlier at San Francisco State Normal School. Under the Winnetka Plan each child proceeded at his own pace through a series of assignments. When he completed his parcel of individual work he asked for a test. If he passed it, he went on to a new assignment. If he did not succeed, he returned to work on the material until he did master it. Thus, a great variety of work went on in each classroom, and the same pupil might be doing third-grade work in one subject and sixth-grade work in another.[34]

Many other communities, while hesitant to go this far, used a modification of the Winnetka Plan, *ability grouping,* in which a regular class was subdivided into smaller groups according to ability as indicated by tests of achievement, intelligence, or by previous performance. This method became so popular that by 1926, 247 cities with populations over ten thousand were employing some type of ability grouping in elementary schools. The *individual system* was also introduced into the high schools of Dalton, Massachusetts, and subsequently spread to other secondary schools.[35]

In colleges, too, pedagogical developments continued. At Columbia Teachers College, William Kilpatrick, a student of Dewey, became a leading proponent of progressive education. He had been impressed by Dewey's search for a problem-solving method applicable to all social issues. Kilpatrick developed this into the *project method,* which reorganized the curriculum into a series of projects or assignments combining the "purposeful activity" emphasized by Thorndike and the "social setting" Dewey had advocated as a means of sensitizing pupils to the concerns of other people. In 1918 Kilpatrick's article on the project method drew national attention and eventually 60,000 reprints were distributed. His views on progressive education were also transmitted directly to his students; over 35,000 attended his classes at Columbia.[36]

Three organizations helped to disseminate news of these developments in progressive education. The Progressive Education Association was formed in 1919 to provide a focus to the scattered and disjointed attempts at educational reform. In 1924 it began publishing a journal, *Progressive Education.* Some of its early issues became standard reference works. These emphasized "the child's own modes of self-expression through all of the creative arts, as opposed to more adult standards of finish and perfection." In 1926 the association hired a paid executive director. In 1928 it had six thousand members and an annual budget of $35,000, and by 1938 its membership reached ten thousand.[37]

The organization was founded as "an association of parents and others;" although teachers were eligible, the organization was not intended to be professional. Only one of the leading progressives took an active part in its founding, and Dewey refused to join. By the late twenties, however, a shift in its character occurred as many professional educators became members, and even Dewey accepted an honorary position.[38]

The most significant single accomplishment of the Progressive Education Association was the Eight Year Study. Begun in 1932, its purpose was to explore ways in which progressive education might be brought successfully to the secondary school. Twenty-nine high schools, public and private, participated and more than three hundred colleges agreed to waive their entrance requirements for pupils graduating from these schools during the period of the experiment. The study encouraged many changes in the participating schools, attracted widespread attention, and brought the Progressive Education Association over a million and a half dollars in foundation grants.[39]

Another organization which furthered the spread of progressive education was the National Education Association. Although founded some years earlier, it became a potent force between the two world wars, as its membership grew from 10,000 in 1918, to 210,000 by 1941. The N.E.A.'s power was limited to persuasion, but it used this effectively to disseminate information and ideas on progressive education through its research bulletins and its journal. Along with its own members, the N.E.A. reached other teachers through its many state and local affiliates.[40]

A third organization facilitating the spread of progressive education was the United States Office of Education. It accomplished this in two ways. By its effective administration of the *Smith-Hughes Act,* the office hastened the adoption of vocational programs in many schools which might otherwise have remained traditional for some time to come. However, it was probably more influential through its dissemination of information. The Office of Education published a steady stream of pamphlets about new teaching methods and new curricula, and provided information on a variety of topics, ranging from achievement tests to school-house construction. Like the National Education Association, the Office of Education's perspective was progressive. This may have been partly due to conscious intent, but it also resulted from the fact that the new educational materials, the new ideas coming forth in the twenties and the thirties, were overwhelmingly progressive. The dissenters, if they existed, were hardly noticeable in the flood of fresh ideas.[41]

Another force operating during the twenties and thirties was centralization. As small school systems consolidated into larger districts, individual schools could afford much richer programs and were, therefore, able to consider seriously the suggestions of progressive educators. On the state level, too, departments of education distributed lesson plans and instructional materials, and held institutes, seminars and conferences to disseminate the latest educational ideas to previously isolated districts. Centralization was facilitated by improved transportation. Busses became common in the decade following the First World War, making it feasible to transport children many miles to school. Better transportation also meant that teachers from outlying districts could assemble to hear new ideas, and that representatives of the state departments of education could maintain closer contact with the personnel under their jurisdiction.[42]

By mid-century, the more concrete manifestations of progressive education were visible across the nation. For example, in 1948, 40 percent of urban school systems reported some form of individualized instruction. This trend was even more pronounced in larger cities: more than half of those with over thirty thousand people had such programs. Ability grouping was being used in half the cities, and again, was more extensive in the larger metropolitan districts. Similarly, remedial classes, particularly in arithmetic and reading, were offered by more than half the cities; here too, the tendency was most pronounced in larger cities.[43]

The statistics for schools using social promotion were especially interesting. While only 17 percent of the districts actually reported a "no failure" policy, it was undoubtedly far more common than these figures suggest. Formal policies are one thing; actual practices may be something else. Few people object to the recognition of individual differences, and grouping on the basis of ability may be approved as being one aspect of achievement. In contrast, promoting pupils regardless of their progress may not seem fair, so school administrators are reluctant to admit that this practice exists in their districts. At any rate, at least one-sixth of the urban school systems, and probably many more, were using this aspect of progressive education in 1948.[44]

Movement away from a narrow curriculum toward new teaching methods and concern for pupils' overall development is indicated by the growth in special services. By 1948, 89 percent of city school systems provided audio-visual education and 84 percent had library services. Seventy-four percent of the city districts had guidance departments, 73 percent had school lunch programs and 72 percent had school health departments. Recreation departments were provided by 65 percent, 44 percent had adult education departments, 37 percent had work experience programs, and 29 percent offered summer classes.[45]

Perhaps most significant of all was a change in attitude. By the end of World War II, progressivism had become the conventional mode of educational thought, the standard approach to pedagogical issues. As Cremin noted:

> Discussions of educational policy were liberally spiced with phrases like "recognizing individual differences," "personality development," "the whole child," "social and emotional growth," "creative self-expression," "the needs of learners," "intrinsic motivation," "persistent life situations," "bridging the gap between home and school," "teaching children, not subjects," "adjusting the school to the child," "real life experiences," "teacher-pupil relationships," and "staff planning." Such phrases were a cant, to be sure, the peculiar jargon of the pedagogues. But they were more than that, for they signified that Dewey's forecast of a day when *progressive* education would eventually be accepted as *good* education had now finally come to pass.[46]

From mid-century onward, however, opinion was turning against progressive education. A host of writers, including Bernard Bell, Mortimer Smith, Robert Hutchins, Albert Lynd, and H. G. Rickover, bitterly attacked progressive practices in the public schools. Their criticisms were exemplified by those of Arthur Bestor. In *Educational Wastelands* and *The Restoration of Learning,* he viewed intellectual training as the prime task of the school. Bestor claimed that the ability to think is achieved by systematic training in science, mathematics, history, English and foreign languages. These basic academic disciplines evolved historically as effective methods for problem-solving. Far from being the perquisites of a privileged few, these basic disciplines should be imparted to people in all walks of life.[47]

The problems of American education, according to Bestor, could be traced to the schools' abandoning scholarship and to the separation of teacher training from the other disciplines of the college. The blame for these actions lay with an "interlocking directorate" of education professors, the school administrators trained by them, and the state departments of education which required education courses for teaching credentials. To rectify this situation, Bestor proposed a coalition of liberal arts professors and parents to take control of the schools away from the "interlocking directorate;" revision of credential requirements to bolster academic subjects and reduce emphasis on methods; and placement of teacher training under the control of the whole university.[48]

While criticisms such as these were becoming increasingly frequent, other developments were occurring within the schools. For example, in 1951 the superintendent of the Pasadena school system was fired on charges that he spent too much time and money on "frills" and not enough on the three Rs. Although this was not the first instance in which a progressive administrator had lost his job, the case attracted national attention. In subsequent years, protests against progressive education came from many sources, ranging from extremist patriots through harried taxpayers to people concerned with academic standards and the schools' failure to teach the fundamentals.[49]

At the same time, the Progressive Education Association was in its final stage. From its zenith in the late 1930s, it had declined because of financial difficulties, loss of members, change of name, and, perhaps most of all, lack of interest and vitality. In 1955 the president of the Association formally disbanded it and two years later the journal *Progressive Education* stopped publication.[50]

In 1957 the spectacular success of Sputnik drew attention to Russia's educational system, and criticism of American public schools grew even stronger.[51] There soon emerged a flood of attempts to revise curriculum and teaching methods. Foreign language in elementary schools, stress on the three Rs, programmed learning, closed-circuit television, special classes for gifted pupils, legislative action by the state to tighten teacher certification requirements, federal funds for curriculum study, and special science units were among the many suggestions proposed and often put into practice.

These educational developments occurred in the broader context of profound changes in American society. The years between 1870 and 1920 witnessed the transformation of the United States from a predominantly agricultural nation into a major world power. As the population grew from forty million to one hundred million, the effects of change were especially pronounced in the cities. At the beginning of the era, the rural population had been three times larger than the urban population. By World War I, however, cities and towns had as many inhabitants as the rural regions. Migration from farms and natural increase were sharply augmented by unprecedented floods of immigrants from the Old World. From 1870 on, a third- to a half-million settlers poured into the United States each year, and between 1905 and 1914 the annual influx often exceeded one million persons. Unlike previous newcomers, many of these came directly to the cities. In addition, a much larger proportion was coming from central and eastern Europe, and they encountered more difficulty adjusting to their new surroundings than did their predecessors from the northwestern parts of the continent.[52]

Growth and change continued during the following decades. By 1950 the population had reached 152 million. Although immigration from abroad decreased sharply in the 1920s, internal migration continued the process of urbanization. This long term trend received added impetus from the "dustbowl" refugees in the mid-thirties, and soon afterward the war industries provided additional incentive for movement to the cities. By 1950, two-thirds of the population lived in urban areas.[53]

Along with population increase, America was also experiencing phenomenal growth in industry, transportation, and communication. By 1900 there were 200,000 miles of railroad track, and networks of telegraph lines traversed the country. United States Steel, already worth a billion dollars, heralded the advent of the giant corporations. By the start of World War I the nation was producing half of the world's mechanical power. A fraction of this power, in the form of farm machinery, was also revolutionizing agriculture.[54]

Material progress was not without its social problems. The late-nineteenth century and the beginning of the twentieth witnessed a growing concern over the less pleasant aspects of industrialization and urbanization. Pressures for social reform were generated by awareness of the pitiful conditions confronting many working men, slum dwellers, immigrants, small farmers, women and children. Attempts were made to establish settlement houses in the blighted areas of large cities. In another sphere, reformers were attacking corruption and intransigence at all levels of government, from local to national. While some reform attempts were the work of a few individuals or of small philanthropic groups, other concerns were manifested in larger movements, like those of the Populists and Progressives. The beginnings of trade unions were also apparent, and the struggle for womens' right to vote came to a successful climax in the form of a constitutional amendment in 1919.[55]

Thus, as Cremin observed, progressive education was one facet of this more general concern for social reform. In addition, however, it was also a direct response to concrete problems confronting the public schools—problems analyzed in detail in the next chapters.

REFERENCES

[1]Cremin, *Transformation of the School*, p. x.

[2]Dworkin, *Dewey on Education*, p. 13.

[3]According to Dworkin, Dewey is ". . . continually ambivalent on the basic intellectual issue of the value of traditional knowledge. Sometimes a single article is truly a 'witch's mirror' wherein we see reflections of two faces: the one demanding study of history and of the learning of the past as vital for understanding the present; the other calling for liberation from all old ideas and knowledge, in order to be untrammeled in developing new ideas and knowledge" (Dworkin, *Dewey on Education*, p. 15).

[4]*Ibid.*, p. 14.

[5]*Ibid.* For further discussions of Dewey, see Oscar Handlin, *John Dewey's Challenge to Education*; and Reginald Archambault, ed., *John Dewey on Education*.

[6]Berger, "John Dewey and Progressive Education Today" in Brickman and Lehrer, eds., *John Dewey: Master Educator*, p. 83.

[7]*Ibid.*, p. 84.

[8]These descriptions of traditional and progressive education were obtained from the following sources: Butts and Cremin, *A History of Education in American Culture*, pp. 118-27, 267-80; Cubberly, *Public Education in the United States*, rev. ed., pp. 40-76, 512-35; Dewey, *Experience and Education*; Dewey, "My Pedagogic Creed," in Mayer, ed., *Introductory Readings in Education*, pp. 182-91; Eby and Arrowood, *The Development of Modern Education*, pp. 895-97; Johnson, *Old Time Schools and Schoolbooks;* Parker, *A Textbook in the History of Modern Elementary Education*, pp. 90-92.

[9]Johnson, *Old Time Schools*, p. 111.

[10]*Ibid.*, p. 114.

[11]Butts and Cremin, *History of Education*, p. 218.

[12]*Ibid.*

[13]*Ibid.*, p. 219.

[14]John Dewey and Evelyn Dewey, *Schools of Tomorrow*, pp. 45-46; Cubberly, *Public Education*, rev. ed., pp. 350-52.

[15]Butts and Cremin, *History of Education*, p. 219; Cordasco, *A Brief History of Education*, p. 91.

[16]Butts and Cremin, *History of Education*, pp. 219-20.

[17]Cremin, *The American Common School*, pp. 146-47.

[18]Cremin, *Transformation of the School*, p. 13.

[19]Butts and Cremin, *History of Education*, pp. 379-82; Cubberly, *Public Education*, rev. ed., pp. 449-59.

[20]Cubberly, *Public Education,* rev. ed., pp. 472-75; Cremin, *Transformation of the School,* pp. 129-30.

[21]Cremin, *Transformation of the School,* pp. 32-33.

[22]*Ibid.,* p. 22.

[23]*Ibid.,* pp. 135-41.

[24]*Ibid.,* pp. 118-19.

[25]*Ibid.,* pp. 110-12.

[26]*Ibid.,* pp. 113-15, 185-86.

[27]*Ibid.,* pp. 101-09, 143-46, 148-50, 170.

[28]*Ibid.,* pp. 155-57.

[29]Bourne, *The Gary Schools,* p. 144, as cited in Cremin, *Transformation of the School,* p. 155.

[30]Cremin, *Transformation of the School,* p. 158.

[31]Butts and Cremin, *History of Education,* p. 439.

[32]*Ibid.,* p. 440.

[33]Cremin, *Transformation of the School,* pp. 160, 276, 291.

[34]*Ibid.,* pp. 295-97.

[35]*Ibid.,* pp. 298-99.

[36]*Ibid.,* pp. 215-18.

[37]*Ibid.,* pp. 240-44, 257.

[38]*Ibid.,* pp. 245-50.

[39]*Ibid.,* pp. 251-57.

[40]*Ibid.,* pp. 272, 275-76.

[41]*Ibid.,* p. 275.

[42]*Ibid.,* pp. 274-75.

[43]Butts and Cremin, *History of Education,* p. 590.

[44]*Ibid.*

[45]*Ibid.,* pp. 590-91.

[46]Cremin, *Transformation of the School,* p. 328.

[47]*Ibid.,* pp. 339-47; and Bestor, *Educational Wastelands.*

[48]Cremin, *Transformation of the School,* pp. 344-46.

[49]*Ibid.,* pp. 341-42.

[50]*Ibid.,* pp. 269-70.

[51]*Ibid.,* p. 347.

[52]United States Bureau of the Census, *Historical Statistics of the United States, Colonial Times to 1957,* pp. 7, 14; Cremin, *Transformation of the School,* p. 66.

[53]U. S. Bureau of the Census, *Historical Statistics of the United States,* pp. 7, 14.

[54]Butts and Cremin, *History of Education,* pp. 300-03.

[55]Cremin, *Transformation of the School,* pp. 58-89.

three

THE PROBLEM
OF CONTROL

WHEN CONSIDERING THE PROBLEMS WHICH PUPILS POSE FOR PUBLIC
schools, we are likely to think first of educational problems, such as
remedial instruction for slow learners, more effective methods for average children, and stimulation of gifted students to the full utilization of
their potentialities. In addition, however, pupils also present problems
of a custodial nature. On one hand, the school must try to keep all
children in school, preferably until they graduate from the twelfth grade.
At the same time, it is imperative that they be kept under control. Taken
separately, these custodial tasks are not easy, and together they become
formidable.

The public school has been delegated the responsibility of educating all children. Regardless of their background, ability or inclination,
the school must keep them almost until they reach adulthood. If they
drop out before that time, it is considered to be a failure not merely of
the individual pupil but also of the school. Therefore, the motivation of
pupils is a major concern of the school. It must do everything in its
power to encourage them to remain, at least until they receive a high
school diploma and, preferably, even longer. This task is complicated
by the tremendous diversity among pupils. Universal compulsory education brings into the schools a student body characterized by an extremely
broad range of social origins, motivations and abilities. Many of these
pupils lack the willingness to learn the traditional skills and, in fact,
resent having to come to school at all. If given a choice, they would
stay home, work, or engage in other activities more pleasurable than

those involved in formal education. But, they have little choice in the matter. Whether they want to or not, they must attend school, and it is the school's responsibility to see that they do.

Keeping all youngsters in school, however, is only one part of the job. Pupils also pose problems in control. This is a crucial problem, and its consequences extend far beyond educational issues. When, for one reason or another, a pupil fails to learn, it is regretable, but it is primarily an individual misfortune, in the sense that it does not have an immediate disruptive effect upon other students, the teacher, or the school. Overt misbehavior is a different matter. One mischievous boy or girl can upset an entire class, interrupting the education of other pupils and interfering with the instructor's attempts to teach.

If pupils get too far out of hand there is the danger of physical injury or property damage. In addition, teachers are expected to keep their classes under control; their inability to do so may cast doubts upon their competence and can lead to dismissal. Perhaps the most general reason for wanting to avoid disorder is simply that the work of teachers and administrators is easier when the school is running smoothly. At any rate, while the education of all pupils is certainly desirable, a modicum of law and order is considered to be essential.

The essence of the problem of control lies in the fundamental conflict between the aims of the pupils and those of the teacher. This conflict was aptly described by Waller:

> Teacher and pupil confront each other in the school with an original conflict of desires, and however much that conflict may be reduced in amount, or however much it may be hidden, it still remains. The teacher represents the adult group, ever the enemy of the spontaneous life of groups of children. The teacher represents the formal curriculum, and his interest is in imposing that curriculum upon the children in the form of tasks; pupils are much more interested in life in their own world than in the desiccated bits of adult life which teachers have to offer. The teacher represents the established social order in the school, and his interest is in maintaining that order, whereas pupils have only a negative interest in that feudal superstructure. Teacher and pupil confront each other with attitudes from which the underlying hostility can never be altogether removed.[1]

This chapter, then, deals with custodial problems of attendance and behavior. The next section discusses the situation in traditional American schools. Section three views the changes which raised problems that could not be handled satisfactorily under traditional methods.

The fourth section discusses the responses to these problems and the ways in which progressive education facilitated these responses.

THE TRADITIONAL ERA

Misbehavior was a prevalent problem in the traditional American school, and it often attained serious proportions. In 1837, for example, over three hundred schools in Massachusetts alone were broken up by rebellious pupils.[2] Disruption of ten percent of the schools in the state[3] during a single year is especially notable in view of the fact that Massachusetts had been a leader in education since earliest colonial times, and was still, in many respects, ahead of the rest of the nation. Therefore, these figures may present an unduly optimistic picture of the country as a whole. We can assume that conditions in other states were not much better and frequently were considerably worse.[4]

In addition to minor mischief, which undoubtedly went on much of the time, two more serious forms of misbehavior directly challenged the teacher's authority: locking the teacher out of the school, and physically assaulting him. At the least, either of these would disrupt the school for several hours, if not the rest of the day. Frequently, however, these episodes led to the dismissal of the teacher and the closing of the school until a replacement could be found.

The first of these two types of rebellion was known as "putting out" or "turning out" the teacher. He was removed from the classroom either by subterfuge or by force, and then was prevented from getting back in. This process was discussed by Horace Greeley:

> At the close of the morning session of the first of January, and perhaps on some other day that the big boys chose to consider or make a holiday, the moment the master left the house in quest of his dinner, the little ones were started homeward, the doors and windows suddenly and securely barricaded, and the older pupils, thus fortified against intrusion, proceeded to spend the afternoon in play and hilarity. I have known a master to make a desperate struggle for admission, but the odds were too great. If he appealed to the neighboring fathers, they were apt to advise him to desist, and let matters take their course. I recollect one instance, however, where a youth was shut out who, procuring a piece of board, mounted from a fence to the roof of the schoolhouse and covered the top of the chimney nicely with his board. Ten minutes thereafter, the house was filled with smoke, and its inmates, opening the doors and windows, were glad to make terms with the outsider.[5]

The other serious type of rebellion involved physical interference with, or attacks upon, the teacher. Sometimes these confrontations evolved out of a situation which the rebels felt to be grossly unfair, as in unreasonable punishment administered to a classmate. Mild and just chastisement was not likely to stimulate other pupils to attack the teacher.

> If, however, the whipping was continued beyond what was considered by the older boys as reasonable, and the boy happened to be a favorite with his fellows, some protest on the part of the big boys might be made; and if that did not effect the object, forcible, if not indeed armed, intervention might be the result.[6]

Castigation of a big boy was particularly crucial because it ". . . required greater effort, the punishment was usually more severe, and the chances of interference were materially enhanced."[7]

On other occasions, trouble might even grow out of a seemingly innocuous, good-humored contest between teacher and pupils. For example, one account of a nineteenth-century school related:

> In the school were several bad boys who were good wrestlers, and prided themselves on athletic sports and feats. [The teacher] was a pretty good wrestler himself, or thought he was. Indulging in the sport with some of them he was downed successively by two or three and soon, as a result, lost control of the school, as they found they could handle him, and so concluded to have their own way.[8]

The seriousness of such incidents resided in the possibility that they might lead to a permanent loss of control. A teacher who had been defeated in these encounters was likely to have difficulty restoring and maintaining order. If the situation got too far out of hand, as it sometimes did, his usefulness at that school was at an end, and the loss of his job was apt to follow. For instance, the teacher who engaged in the wrestling matches and subsequently lost control over his class consulted the trustees of the school:

> . . . it was thought best that he should resign as the signs were unmistakable that an insurrection was brewing; and if he had insisted on staying, in all probability he would have been thrown out with little ceremony. . . .[9]

Johnson noted that when pupils had "put out" two or three teachers in succession, the school got the reputation of being "hard," with the result that the school authorities might have to offer liberal wages and seek out a teacher who could subdue the young rebels.[10]

For such reasons, the basic task of the traditional teacher was considered to be *schoolkeeping* rather than *school teaching.* "The teacher's job was to maintain order—to keep the class intact. In the upper grades, as often as not, this meant that the teacher had to be able physically to subdue the larger members of the class."[11] Severity in a teacher was considered to be a virtue. Unless he made frequent and forceful use of the rod, many parents felt uneasy and doubted that the children could be learning much.[12] The average schoolmaster used extremely primitive methods for controlling his pupils. He relied mainly on a three-foot ruler, known as a *ferule,* and the *heavy gad,* a flexible sapling about five feet in length. These implements were applied "with force and frequency" to boys and girls, to young and old alike.[13] Cubberly aptly summed up the situation when he commented, "There was little 'soft pedagogy' in the management of either town or rural schools in the days before the Civil War."[14]

American schools were not alone in their use of severe discipline. In centuries past, schools everywhere had relied upon harsh methods of control. However, this general tendency may have been further accentuated by material conditions prevalent in the American colonies and on the frontier. As historian Bernard Bailyn has pointed out, these difficult conditions undermined the authority of parents. Their traditional ideas and customs were of little help in facing unfamiliar problems posed by the wilderness. Instead, such conditions put a premium upon youthful strength and originality. Moreover, abundant land coupled with a scarcity of labor offered young adults opportunities to become economically independent. The elders, attempting desperately to prevent what they interpreted to be the disintegration of their families and the decay of the entire culture, threatened to impose severe sanctions against disobedience. In Massachusetts and Connecticut, for example, the death penalty was authorized as a suitable punishment for disobeying one's parents.[15] Although it is unlikely that many rebellious children were subjected to this extreme penalty, its existence does suggest that control was considered to be a serious problem and that severe measures were thought to be appropriate.

Subsequent generations witnessed some amelioration of punishment, but harsh discipline persisted throughout the traditional period. A schoolhouse constructed in Sunderland, Massachusetts, in 1793, contained a whipping post set firmly in the floor of the schoolroom.[16] Descriptions of nineteenth-century schools indicate, ". . . the walls of the schoolroom were marred by the dents made by ferules hurled at misbehaving pupils' heads with an aim that sometimes proved untrue."[17]

By the middle of the nineteenth century, some attempts were being made to curb brutal disciplinary procedures, but these efforts did not necessarily meet with immediate success. In 1844, for example, the Boston Board of Education passed a rule requiring a full report of every case in which flogging was used. This ruling, however, apparently had little effect. During inspection tours the following year, the board members found that whippings in a "representative" school of four hundred pupils averaged sixty-five per day. In their subsequent report, the committee mentioned "severe injuries" following corporal punishment of pupils, and stated that in most cases the offense was "very trifling."[18]

Because of the importance of classroom control, it will be helpful to get a clear picture of the methods used in traditional schools. Johnson's description of typical disciplinary practices in the middle of the nineteenth century will enable us to appreciate the contrast with the much milder progressive methods to be discussed later and, insofar as harsh punishment may actually aggravate discipline, may give us some idea of the genesis of many traditional behavior problems:

> "Spare the rod and spoil the child" was a Bible text which received the most literal acceptance both in theory and practice. Even the naturally mild-tempered man was an "old-fashioned" disciplinarian when it came to teaching, and the naturally rough and coarse-grained man was as frightful as any ogre in a fairy tale.
>
> In summer, unless the teacher was an uncommonly poor one, or some of the scholars uncommonly wild and mischievous, the days moved along very harmoniously and pleasantly. In winter, when the big boys came in, some of them grown men, who cared vastly more about having a good time than getting learning, an important requisite of the master was "government." He ruled his little empire, not with a rod of iron, but with a stout three-foot ruler, known as a "ferule," which was quite as effective. The really severe teacher had no hesitation in throwing this ruler at any child he saw misbehaving, and it is to be noted that he threw first and spoke afterward. Very likely he would order the culprit to bring him the ferule he had cast at him, and when the boy came out on the floor would further punish him. Punishment by spatting the palm of his hand with a ruler was known as "feruling." The smarting of blows was severe while the punishment lasted, but this was as nothing to a "thrashing." The boy to be thrashed was himself sent for the apple-tree twigs with which he was to be whipped. Poor fellow! Whimpering, and blinded by the welling tears, he slowly whittles off one after the other of the tough twigs. This task done, he drags his unwilling feet back to the schoolroom.
>
> "Take off your coat, sir!" says the master.

The school is hushed into terrified silence. The fire crackles in the wide fireplace, the wind whistles at the eaves, the boy's tears flow faster, and he stammers a plea for mercy. Then the whip hisses through the air, and blows fall thick and fast. The boy dances about the floor, and his shrill screams fill the schoolroom. His mates are frightened and trembling, and the girls are crying. . . .

The list of milder punishments was a varied one. If the master saw two boys whispering, he would, if circumstances favored, steal upon them from behind and visit unexpected retribution upon them by catching them by the collars and cracking their heads together. Frequently an offender was ordered out on the floor to stand for a time by the master's desk, or he was sent to a corner with his face to the wall, or was asked to stand on one leg for a time. In certain cases he was made to hold one arm out at right angles to his body— a very easy and simple thing to do for a short time, but fraught with painful discomfort if long continued. Sometimes the punishment was made doubly hard by forcing the scholar to support a book or other weight at the same time. When the arm began to sag, the teacher would inquire with feigned solicitude what the trouble was, and perhaps would give him a rap on his "crazy bone" with the ruler to encourage him to persevere. This process soon brought a child to tears, and then the teacher was apt to relent and send him to his seat.

Making a girl sit with the boys, or a boy with the girls, was another punishment. The severity of this depended on the nature of the one punished. For the timid and bashful it was a terrible disgrace. . . .

Some of the punishments produced very striking spectacular effects to which the present-day mind would feel quite averse. Fancy the sight of a boy and girl guilty of some misdemeanor standing in the teacher's heavy armchair, the girl wearing the boy's hat and the boy adorned with the girl's sunbonnet. Both are redfaced and tearful with mortified pride. They preserve a precarious balance on their narrow footing with difficulty, and every movement of one causes the other to grasp and clutch to prevent inglorious downfall.

To sit on the end of a ruler, which the teacher presently knocked from under the boy, was considered by some pedagogues an effective punishment. One teacher used to have the offending boy bend over with his head under the table. Then the teacher whacked the culprit from behind with his heavy ruler, and sent him shooting under the table and sprawling across the floor. Among the most ingenious and uncomfortable in the varied list of punishments was the fitting a cut from a green twig, partially split, to the offender's nose. In cases of lying, this rude pair of pinchers was attached to the scholar's tongue.[19]

In short, life in the traditional school was often harsh and hectic, for master and pupils alike. It remained this way, with few fundamental changes, for more than two hundred years, from the early colonial period to the middle of the nineteenth century. Only in the final few years before the Civil War was there any hint of the forces which, during the following decades, would transform the nature of American public education.

A number of factors contributed to the stability of this traditional pattern: prevailing attitudes regarding public education, the isolation of one-room rural schools, the characteristics of the teacher's job, the homogeneity of the student body, the low economic investment in the schools, and the marginal place of the school in the activities of the community.

During the traditional era the public school was not expected to educate everyone. Compulsory education as we know it today did not exist. Before the Civil War only one state had enacted compulsory attendance laws — Massachusetts made schooling mandatory in 1852.[20] In most parts of the country, free public schools were just being established on a broad scale during the 1840s and 1850s. Many districts had only the most rudimentary educational facilities, and other communities, especially in the South, had none at all.

Consequently, education was mostly a matter of individual choice, with the decision left to the pupil and his family. If he came to school, it was mainly because his parents wanted him to, and he was more or less willing to do so. As far as the school was concerned, it didn't really matter whether or not he attended but, if he did come, he had to abide by the teacher's demands or accept the frequently severe consequences. If school became intolerable, he was free to leave. In the case of a backward or unruly pupil this was all to the good, from the teacher's point of view, because the class would be easier to manage without him. Pupils who returned after an interlude of truancy might be punished by the schoolmaster, but basically the responsibility for attendance rested with the pupil and his parents.

Thus, the traditional public school, when it existed at all, was a selective institution, accommodating only those hardy souls who were able to adapt to its inflexible demands. Those who could not, or would not, dropped out. It should be noted that this applied to teachers as well as to pupils. Usually it was the pupils who left, one by one, as punishment or study reached the point of being unbearable, but occasionally, as we have seen, when several students joined forces, it was the schoolmaster who was compelled to leave. However, the sporadic disruptions and closings of the school by rebellious pupils did not generate enough pressure to alter the traditional patterns of the school or to encourage critical reappraisals of its methods.

Although school closings may not have been welcomed — except by the pupils, who received an unscheduled holiday — the closing of a school apparently worked no great hardship on anyone except the teacher, and he was not in a position to do much about it. His duties were simple and it was easy to replace him. Because his instructional effectiveness was defined, in large part, by his capacity to maintain order, his inability to do so was interpreted as evidence that he was incompetent and therefore should not be teaching. He had no colleagues to whom he might turn for support. Most schools before the late-nineteenth century were in the country and the majority had only one teacher. School administrators did not appear until the 1840s and '50s.[21] This isolation gave little chance even for communication with other teachers, from whom the embattled schoolmaster might have learned of similar problems and of possible solutions. There were few teacher-training institutions, educational journals, and no occupational associations through which to take concerted action. Thus, for the great majority of teachers, the struggle to maintain control was a solitary one, and there would be few to mourn those who failed.

Moreover, the economic consequences of student revolts were far less serious than they are today. In fact, school districts actually saved money when the school was closed. The lone teacher was the only paid employee. There were no other personnel — no superintendents, secretaries, principals, custodians, counselors, or coordinators — who would also have to be paid, or laid off, if the teacher left. Shutting down the school did not mean a waste of money. Quite the contrary: there was actually a saving because not even the meager salary of the teacher had to be expended.

In addition, the financial investment in the school plant was small. Most schoolhouses were crude, one-room structures, furnished with a few rough benches and a stove. They were devoid of equipment; there were no free textbooks or supplies, and blackboards did not become common until well into the nineteenth century. Thus, even the more rambunctious students could do little material damage and there was nothing worth stealing when the school was closed.

Pupils who left school early were not seriously handicapped by their lack of formal education in their endeavors to earn a living. As for the more general benefits of universal education, the public was far from unanimous in its support, and even members of the school board were sometimes ambivalent about it, especially when they considered the expenses it involved. When students dropped out, or when the school closed down for a while, it was not generally viewed as a calamity because education itself was not considered to be of paramount importance.

Acceptance of the idea of education for all had been delayed by factional fears that one group might gain control of the schools and impose its beliefs and customs upon others. In addition, universal education had to await the development of stable methods of financial support. While many people agreed in theory to the principle of education for everyone, they were less prepared to pay the taxes needed to support such education, especially for the benefit of other people's children. Even after some public support was available, students often had to pay partial tuition fees. These assessments, known as *rate bills* because parents were charged according to the number of children they had in school and the length of time they attended, were not entirely abolished until after the Civil War.[22] Charges for textbooks and supplies often provided a further barrier.

Even where adequate and completely free schools existed, other factors prevented many children from attending. America was still a rural nation. As late as 1870, seventy-two percent of the people were living outside of cities and towns.[23] Transportation was a common problem. The miles of poor roads and open country which separated some farms from the district school made attendance difficult for many children, even under the best of circumstances, and poor weather presented an almost insurmountable obstacle. In addition, many youths were kept at home to work around the house or in the fields.

Consequently, in 1850, less than half of the nation's youth between the ages of five and nineteen were enrolled in public schools. Moreover, education at that time was limited to whites; less than two percent of the non-Caucasians in the five-to-nineteen age group were attending school.[24] Furthermore, even the white population was predominantly of northwest European stock; the waves of immigrants from central and southern Europe had not yet arrived. Thus the student body of the traditional school was relatively homogeneous, and most pupils were thought to have some chance of success in the same simple, undiversified curriculum that had sufficed in their grandparents' day.

To sum up, awareness of individual differences in pupil ability did not emerge until late in the nineteenth century. In earlier times, it was not considered to be a reflection on the school when a pupil dropped out but was, instead, attributed to laziness or a similar deficiency in the character of the child. Education was still seen as somewhat of a luxury, though not necessarily an enjoyable one, to be experienced only under a fortuitous configuration of circumstances. The education of everyone was not considered to be the responsibility of the traditional school.

Under such conditions the traditional school could be a selective enterprise, offering a simple curriculum to a relatively homogeneous student body. Harsh discipline may have frightened many children into submission, but it also forced others to leave school entirely.

THE TRANSITIONAL ERA

After the Civil War, traditional patterns of attendance and discipline were shattered by a number of profound changes in American society. These changes, associated to a considerable degree with urbanization, industrialization and immigration, transformed the character of the student body, increased the school's responsibility toward pupils, made control more urgent, and rendered unusable the orthodox, time-honored methods of discipline.

One of the most obvious changes was the spectacular population increase. In 1850 there were twenty-three million people in the United States. By the end of the century the population had more than tripled, to seventy-six million, and by 1950 it had doubled again.[25] Growth in itself, however, would not have so changed the character of everyday life if the increase had merely consisted of the establishment of more communities like those which already existed. But this was not the case; urbanization brought profound alterations. In 1830, ninety-one percent of the population lived in rural areas. In 1870, three-fourths of the population was still rural but, by 1920, half of the people were living in cities.[26]

Industrialization and urbanization were accompanied by changes in family structure. The extended family, common in agrarian societies, was broken up as some of its members moved to the cities, leaving behind friends, relatives and neighbors. The family in the city often found itself in an unfamiliar milieu where few others knew them or cared about them.

As a result of these changes, a new role emerged for the child. In a rural setting he had been a useful member of the family, contributing to its maintenance by working directly in the production of food and marketable goods, or by assisting with household chores. This changed drastically, however, under the impact of urbanization and industrialization. City children were no longer assets; they had become liabilities. There was a brief transitional period during which children could still work in factories or in home industries but, as sentiments against child labor were followed by legislation outlawing the practice, even this opportunity for contributing to family support was eliminated.

Consequently the urban youth, in comparison to his rural counterpart, had less productive work to occupy his time, and had fewer adults or older siblings around to supervise his increased leisure. In addition, crowded metropolitan conditions, especially in tenement areas, provided few opportunities for wholesome recreation, or for harmless dissipation of youthful energy. Moreover, there were many others in the same situation living within a block or two. The stage was set for juvenile delinquency. As early as 1870, the annual report of the Philadelphia schools estimated that ". . . upwards of 20,000 children not attending any school, public, private or parochial, are running the streets in idleness or vagabondism. . . ."[27]

The desire to forestall youthful mischief, concern of working men over competition from cheap child labor, and genuinely altruistic regard for child welfare probably all contributed to the rising demand for universal compulsory education. Following Massachusetts' pioneer legislation of 1852, Vermont made education mandatory in 1867. By 1919, all of the states had enacted compulsory education laws.[28] Although this legislation did not mean that every young person was actually attending school, it does at least give some indication of the situation.

More important, however, the enactment of these laws signified that a new burden had been placed upon the school, vastly complicating its work and requiring a radical change in its treatment of pupils.[29] Now that a large share of the responsibility was in the school's hands, motivation for attending school shifted from being solely the concern of the pupil and his family to also being a concern of the school. This meant that the school's previous operating principles had become inapplicable. Teachers and administrators could no longer employ a "take it or leave it" attitude toward their students. Under the traditional pattern it had been up to the pupil to adjust to the school. If he was unable or unwilling to do so, the school could expel him, if he did not leave voluntarily. Now, however, the shoe was on the other foot; the school had to adapt itself to the pupils. If pupils were unwilling to cooperate with traditional expectations, a new system had to be devised which they would be willing to tolerate.

The school's responsibility for encouraging all pupils to continue their schooling as long as possible was increasingly accepted by educators as well as laymen. For school personnel themselves, it became a fact of life which they seldom questioned. Even when individual teachers complained about the policy of keeping every pupil in school, they nevertheless accepted it as inevitable. Of course, many pupils still dropped out before they graduated, but the school now had the responsibility of doing all it could to keep them in.

The rapid growth of cities and the obligation to educate all children confronted metropolitan schools with the difficult problem of providing for the deluge of pupils.[30] Urban districts were seldom able to keep up with their soaring enrollments. Costs of construction increased, and less land was available for building additional rooms or for enlarging playgrounds. The result was that city schools became increasingly crowded,[31] and this in turn increased tensions among pupils, and aggravated problems of control. The more congested the classroom became, the more difficult it was for pupils to study or even to remain relatively quiet. In addition, behavior in the classroom was also affected by the inadequacy of playground facilities. A spacious yard would give pupils the opportunity to work off tensions built up in class. They could release their energy through physical activity or, if they preferred, they could find a quiet corner in which to relax. In this respect, rural schools, with their almost unlimited space, held a big advantage. Life inside the little country schoolhouse may have been grim but at least, during recess or at noon, the whole out-of-doors was a playground. The urban pupil was less fortunate in this respect. His yard was smaller and he had to share it with hundreds of others. Because of such crowding his activities were further limited by rules and adult supervision. The urban pupil had less opportunity to release tension and, therefore, was probably more inclined to be a restless, potential behavior problem.

Furthermore, if disturbances did occur, they could have more serious consequences in the larger, urban schools than in small, isolated rural schools. There were more pupils who might participate in the disorder. There were other personnel, other teachers and administrators whose work might be made more difficult by the outbreak. Also, the disruptions would be immediately noticed, and perhaps feared, by residents and shopkeepers whose homes and businesses adjoined the school. Finally, there was a greater financial investment in the buildings, equipment, supplies, and grounds of the urban school. In these respects, crowding of city schools gave a new urgency to the maintenance of law and order. Control over pupils in the urban school was far from being the solitary concern of one lone teacher. There were other people who also had an interest in the maintenance of discipline and the smooth operation of the school.

To complicate things further, the student body became considerably more varied, and consequently more difficult to handle. Not only were there more pupils, but also they were more heterogeneous than in traditional times, varying more widely in age, ability, religion, social and economic status, place of birth, race, and language. The previous differences among the earlier settlers from northwestern Europe were dwarfed by the entry of heretofore unfamiliar groups from southern and eastern Europe, not to mention Orientals, Negroes and Latin-Americans. The age-range broadened, with more younger pupils and also more older pupils in their late teens. In 1871, ninety-one percent of the nation's seven million public school pupils were in elementary schools.[32] By 1920, ten percent of all public school pupils were enrolled in high school or postgraduate courses.[33]

The percentage of non-white pupils, infinitesimal during the traditional era, began to rise very rapidly during the Civil War decade. In 1860, less than two percent of the non-white children, aged five to nineteen, were in public schools. By 1870 the proportion had increased to ten percent, and by 1920, fifty-four percent of the non-white school-age population was actually enrolled.[34]

As the age of compulsory attendance rose, there were more likely to be full grown men and women in school. These older students were less inclined than were the younger ones to submit to traditional methods of discipline. If nothing else, their size alone would be a deterrent to the frequent whippings given to smaller students. And, increasingly, there were pupils whose poor scholastic performance was clearly not the simple consequence of laziness. Some of these students came from unsettled or impoverished families, others were handicapped physically or mentally, and still others did not speak English. By 1909, fifty-eight percent of the pupils in thirty-seven of the nation's largest cities had foreign-born parents. In New York, the percentage was seventy-two, in Chicago, sixty-seven, and in Boston, sixty-four. In Chelsea, Massachusetts, and Duluth, Minnesota, the percentage reached seventy-four.[35] Of course, there had been pupils with similar handicaps in traditional times, but, as their numbers increased toward the end of the nineteenth century, the shortcomings of orthodox methods of instruction and control became more and more obvious. The inadequacy of such time-honored methods as meting out a sharp rap with a ruler for a poorly prepared recitation was more apparent than ever before.[36]

On one hand, then, the advent of universal compulsory education brought a far more heterogeneous group of pupils into the schools and forced a fundamental change in the school's responsibilities. This, in turn, necessitated modification of the school's attitudes toward its pupils. On the other hand, traditional methods of control were rendered unusable by at least two changes. First, a gradual softening of attitudes regarding acceptable methods of child treatment meant that neither the public-at-large nor school personnel were as willing to use the harsh punishments of the past. Prohibition of corporal punishment was written into the codes of most school districts, and the possibility of lawsuits by parents provided a further restraint.

Second, changes in the composition of the teaching staff meant that corporal punishment was less practical than before, even in districts where it was still permitted. During the eighteenth and early-nineteenth centuries most teachers were men, but in later times the majority of American public school teachers have been women. It is possible that the advent of industrialization offered educated men other opportunities which were more appealing than public school teaching. Perhaps, too, there was increasing desire by school boards to hire women rather than men. Women could be paid less than men, a point which became more important as the number of teachers in a school district increased. There also emerged the belief that women were better attuned to children, better able to understand them and to establish satisfactory relations with them.[37]

The change began around 1830[38] and by 1870 the majority of teachers were women. The ratio of male teachers continued to drop steadily. In 1920, only fourteen percent of the teaching staff were men. The proportion still has not climbed much above this level.[39]

This radical change in the teaching staff undoubtedly had some effect upon methods of control. Women, for various reasons, are less likely than men to rely on brute force. In the first place, women seldom have the size and the physical strength needed to control obstreperous pupils by sheer force. Many sixth-grade boys, for example, are as tall as their teachers, and even younger pupils may match an adult's strength. Of course, there are exceptions to these generalizations. We need not look far to find mild-mannered men of slight build or robust women who would be capable of thrashing almost every pupil in the school. All things considered, however, women's assets in the problem of maintaining control consist less of physical strength than of gentle inducements to cooperation.

Female capacities and limitations became increasingly important as women assumed a larger and larger share of teaching positions in public schools. This, along with a general softening of cultural attitudes regarding the treatment of children, rendered traditional reliance on corporal punishment unacceptable and pointed the way to new methods of control, which will be discussed in the next pages.

In sum, four major changes made the school's task more difficult after 1870. First, a large part of the responsibility for pupil attendance shifted from the pupil to the school. Second, pupils were more varied than before. Third, traditional methods of control were no longer practical or acceptable. Finally, the consequences of disorder became more serious.

THE PROGRESSIVE ERA

As a result of these changes, public schools in the twentieth century, and especially city schools, have been confronted with custodial problems quite different from those of the traditional era. The age-old task of maintaining order is still present, but former methods of coping with it can no longer be used. To make matters even more difficult, a new burden has been placed upon the schools in the form of the obligation to educate all of the nation's youth.

By 1920, 77.8 percent of the population between the ages of five and seventeen were receiving some sort of formal education, and by 1940, the proportion had risen to 85.3 percent. The vast majority of these pupils were attending public schools.[40] Although the flow of immigrants from abroad was stemmed by restrictive legislation in the 1920s, internal migration continued to supply the schools with challenging problems. The depression and drought of the 1930s and the booming war industries and manpower shortages of the 1940s brought to the cities many people from the Midwest and South whose differences from the mainstream of middle-class American culture were only slightly less pronounced than those of earlier immigrants from foreign countries.

Consequently public schools were attempting to accommodate a student body characterized by a very wide range of social origins, motivations and abilities. In earlier times, pupils who were not scholastically inclined dropped out after a few years, while children from poor families were not likely to attend at all. The relatively select group of students who remained had some chance to succeed in the traditional academic program. In the last few decades, however, there have been many pupils who are unable or unwilling to learn under those conditions.

In addition to these problems, resulting from the greater variety of students, there was also a very significant shift in the responsibility for the students. The school was expected to educate them or, at least, to keep them in school until they graduated from the twelfth grade. As a result, dropouts could no longer be shrugged off merely as "misfits;" the school was sharing the blame for their failure. The school could not continue as a selective institution, forcing its students either to accept its rigid demands or to leave. It now had to adapt its ways to fit the students, in an effort to encourage them to remain. Keeping all pupils in school was not an easy task. In spite of many attempts to persuade them to remain, many youngsters were still dropping out.

The handling of these pupils is complicated by the American tradition of equality. Not only must every child be educated but, in addition, it is believed that he should receive the same kind of education as everyone else. Although this tradition is in part responsible for many pupils being in school in the first place, it discourages the establishment of separate schools and makes it difficult to set up clearly distinct curricula for different types of pupils. Differentiation does appear in junior and senior high school, but it is somewhat covert and is not carried to the degree that characterizes some European systems. Consequently, all pupils, representing virtually the entire spectrum of human ability, must ideally be accommodated within the same schools.

There is a vital relationship between the school's responsibility for pupil attendance and methods of control. When pupils attend voluntarily they are more apt to comply with the school's expectations regarding behavior. They have some desire to remain in school, even if it is only a half-hearted desire, prompted largely by their parents. Therefore they are more willing to tolerate its rules. On the other hand, when pupils are forced to attend, regardless of their own inclinations or their parents' wishes, they may be less likely to cooperate with the teacher and are more apt to create disciplinary problems.

Thus, along with this newer problem of retention, the school still faced the age-old problem of control. The one-room country school was rapidly fading into the past but the possibility of losing control still confronted public school teachers. As a study of Chicago's schools observed, "One of the teacher's basic work problems is that of maintaining constant control over the actions of her pupils."[41] Moreover, "it is important to remember that the problem of discipline is one that is always present for the teacher. Even where a solution seems to have been reached, the teacher fears the possibility of an outbreak of disorder."[42] Even well-behaved classes are aware of the possibility of breaking the teacher's control. The teacher of one such class said: "There's the whole roomful of them sitting on the edge of their seats with their eyes gleaming, waiting to see how much this one is going to get away with."[43]

Most breaches of school rules would seem mild and inconsequential to laymen and even to some administrators. Talking or whispering, for example, or chewing gum, making faces, leaving one's seat without permission, and many similar actions may not seem serious when indulged in by only a few pupils. However, the danger lies in the possibility of escalation. Many teachers fear that if these minor infractions are allowed to continue unchecked, they may lead to more serious disturbances. There seems to be practically no limit to the kinds of problems which may arise in public schools. For example, another Chicago

study provided some illustrations of the things which actually had
occurred in elementary schools:

> The reports which these teachers gave of what *can* be done by a
> group of children are nothing short of amazing. A young white
> teacher walked into her new classroom and was greeted with the
> comment, "Another damn white one." Another teacher was
> "rushed" at her desk by the entire class when she tried to be ex-
> tremely strict with them. Teachers report having been bitten, tripped
> and pushed on the stairs. Another gave an account of a second-
> grader throwing a milk bottle at the teacher and of a first-grader
> having such a temper tantrum that it took the principal and two
> policemen to get him out of the room.
>
> In another school following a fight on the playground, the prin-
> cipal took 32 razor blades from children in a first grade room. Some
> teachers indicated fear that they might be attacked by irate persons
> in the neighborhoods in which they teach. Other teachers report
> that their pupils carry long pieces of glass and have been known to
> threaten other pupils with them, while others jab each other with
> hypodermic needles. One boy got angry at his teacher and knocked
> in the fenders of her car.[44]

While incidents like these are less frequent in schools outside of
urban slums, they nevertheless occur often enough to keep alive in the
minds of school personnel the spectre of insurrection. Most teachers,
even if they have escaped the experience themselves, know of colleagues
who have lost control of their classes, at least momentarily, or who,
because of their inability to maintain order, were transferred to undesirable positions or were fired.[45] Threats to the teacher's control may be
more obvious in the lower class school, but they are also present in
middle class and well-to-do schools. The difference is that more privileged pupils are usually more subtle in their defiance of school rules.
The relative rarity of spectacular incidents in middle and upper class
schools is offset, to a considerable degree, by more serious repercussions
which these incidents may have on the occasions when they do occur.
Parents of higher social status are more likely to take an interest in
occurrences in the school. They are more apt to be disturbed by events
which would pass unnoticed in a lower class school. They are more
inclined to protest to school officials, and their protests generally carry
more weight.

For example, when a slum child falls to the floor as a result of
being tripped by a classmate, the incident is likely to end there, at
least as far as the teacher is concerned. However, when this happens
to a pupil from a middle class or upper-middle class family, there is a

higher probability that the parents will complain to the principal or even to the superintendent about it, and in turn, the teacher may have to explain why such things were allowed to happen in her class. Or, the parents may threaten the school and the teacher with a lawsuit because of alleged negligence and incompetence. Teachers and other school personnel are quite vulnerable to such pressures and threats, and their desire to forestall such unpleasant possibilities provides added incentive to maintain control of the classroom. Again, it is not that loss of control happens often, but rather the grim possibility that it *can* happen, anywhere, which causes teachers to be concerned with the problem.

The general effect of this continuing struggle was described by a high school teacher:

> ... there's that tension all the time. Between you and the students. It's hard on your nerves. Teaching is fun if you enjoy your subject, but it's the discipline that keeps your nerves on edge, you know what I mean? There's always that tension. Sometimes people say, "Oh you teach school. That's an easy job, just sitting around all day long." They don't know what it's really like. It's hard on your nerves.[46]

The Functions of Progressive Education

Thus, faced with problems of retention and control, and unable to use traditional methods of maintaining order, new procedures were necessary. Instead of using force and coercion, public schools now sought the pupils' willing participation. This was done by minimizing pressures, especially those of an academic nature, and, in general, by making school as pleasant as possible. Whatever the pedagogical merits or shortcomings of this approach might have been, it did enable the school to win the cooperation of many pupils who would have resisted a more traditional program.

It may be helpful, therefore, to consider several aspects of the progressive school from the standpoint of pupil retention and control. First, punishment is much milder. Second, attention is given to the psychological needs of pupils. Third, many subjects are offered in place of a single academically oriented course of study. Fourth, counseling and testing guide marginal pupils to classes in which chances of failure or frustration are minimized. Fifth, teaching methods take into account the interests of pupils. Sixth, standards of grading and promotion are more flexible. Finally, extracurricular activities appeal to some pupils who would find little else of interest in the school. In short, every effort is made to make the modern school as pleasant as possible, and these efforts are facilitated by various aspects of what is commonly called progressive education.

Milder Discipline. The relaxing of discipline has removed much of the sting from education. Harsh punishments of a bygone era have all but disappeared. Where not explicitly forbidden by law, corporal punishment is discouraged by public sentiment, educational theory, school district policies, and the feelings of school personnel. Some teachers and principals still, on occasion, wield a paddle, give a quick spat with a ruler, twist an ear or in some other manner inflict momentary pain, but this happens with far less frequency and ferocity than before.

Even traditional sanctions not involving physical punishment are used with restraint: ridicule, sarcasm, detention, extra assignments, or suspension for a few days are generally avoided whenever possible. Permanent explusion is relatively rare.[47] Although compulsory education laws may provide loopholes for use in extreme cases, the schools are reluctant to resort to them. These procedures for expulsion are troublesome. Furthermore, it may be perceived as an indication of failure on the part of the school. In addition, many teachers and administrators are restrained by humanitarian considerations; they are reluctant to cast the erring youth into society, especially when they know that his next step will be into juvenile hall or that, at best, he will have difficulty getting a job without a high school diploma.

Thus, the conscious motivation for the repudiation of harsh punishment was largely a concern for the well-being of the pupil. In general, people today have more compassion for children's feelings than their forefathers did. This sympathy has been strengthened by the emergence of pedagogical and psychological theories advocating the elimination of harsh punishment, on the grounds that it adversely affects the child's natural development. Again, the emphasis has been upon the welfare and happiness of the pupil. As Dewey put it, "The child has a right to enjoy his childhood."[48]

At the same time, the abolition of severe disciplinary measures also has had custodial consequences. It lessens the possibility of kindling pupil resentment, a resentment which might even lead to overt retaliation against the teacher and the school. The pupil who has been severely chastised is likely to feel angry about it, no matter how much it might seem that he deserved it. A description of a typical incident in a mid-nineteenth-century school observed that the boy who had just been whipped ". . . in his heart vows vengeance, and longs for the day when he shall have the age and stature to thrash the teacher in return."[49]

The culprit himself was not the only one disturbed by severe castigation. It affected his classmates, too, and these effects were not always those which the teacher would have wanted. Harsh punishment, whatever its chastening effects might have been, also promoted an increased consciousness of the existence of two separate groups, teachers and pupils, and it made very clear the subordination of the latter to the former. The more obvious the differences between the two, the more likely were conflicts between them. When people think of themselves as relatively similar, pursuing the same general goals together, they are less likely to clash than if they perceive themselves as members of sharply differentiated groups, struggling for mutually exclusive ends. Speaking of the incident referred to in the previous paragraph, the chronicler of the nineteenth-century punishment observed, "When the sobbing boy is sent to his place, whatever his misdemeanor may have been, the severity of the punishment has won him the sympathy of the whole school, and toward the master there are only feelings of fear and hate."[50]

Sensitivity to Pupils' Needs. Second, the progressive school facilitates control by recognizing the psychological needs of the pupil, especially in showing greater concern for him as an individual. According to progressive ideology, each child should be approached as a unique human being whose personal characteristics must be thoroughly understood. Nothing, not even subject matter, should obscure this aim.

This concern is not intended merely to locate the pupil's strengths and weaknesses so that he may be helped toward mastery of his school work. Instead, it is a concern for the pupil himself, for his happiness and his physical, social and psychological well-being. By treating each pupil as an individual, the child-centered school tries to build his self-respect and to give him a sense that he is valued in his own right. The teacher, therefore, deemphasizes the status gap between herself and her students and plays the role of a friendly parent or sibling, providing the warmth and security of a primary relationship. Most pupils would respond to such treatment anyway, but it is especially important for those whose home life is not very satisfying.

Here, too, the basic motivation behind the recognition of individual needs was concern for the welfare of the child. Its usefulness as a mechanism of social control has rarely been considered. Nevertheless, it does have important custodial consequences for the school. The more content the child is, the less likely will he be to cause disciplinary problems for the teacher. Even though the origins may lie outside the school —within his family, for example—his frustrations may erupt at school, upsetting routine in the classroom, in the hallways, on the playground, or on the way to and from school. Giving the pupil the feeling that he is respected and liked by the teacher lessens the possibility that his unhappiness will upset the operation of the school. An elementary school principal observed:

> At home, their parents ignore them or curse and whip them. But here at school we treat them as individuals, build them up, give them self-respect. They have to be really worked up before they'll turn their backs on this.[51]

Sensitivity to individual needs also helps to prevent the formation of a united front against the teacher. One rebellious pupil can be disruptive enough, but control becomes even more difficult when several students join forces. If pupils feel little connection with the school, if they do not believe that their teacher really knows them or cares about them, they are more likely to get into mischief or to support other pupils who create trouble. On the other hand, the more they like their teacher, the more satisfaction they receive from her in friendship, praise, and encouragement, the less apt they are to be uncooperative, or to support rebellion against her. Thus, it behooves the teacher to establish positive relations with her pupils. One of the best ways to do this is to give each one the feeling that she believes he is important and that no one else could take his place.

Of course, this goal is difficult to achieve even under the best of circumstances, and teaching conditions are rarely ideal. However, even if the teacher does not succeed in reaching every pupil, her partial success is nevertheless worthwhile because class control is not an all-or-nothing matter. If the teacher can reduce the number of active troublemakers to two or three, it is still an improvement over opposition by the entire class. There are usually a couple of pupils in each room who would be hard to handle in any situation, but the others, the "uncommitted majority," may hold the balance of power in the struggle for class control. At the least, the teacher may dissuade them from joining in mischief against her. And, if she can win the majority to her side, their disapproval of the rebellious behavior may be a more effective restraint upon the culprits than any sanction the teacher herself could impose. The teacher's ability to reach out into the masses of pupils and to give each one a feeling that he means something to her not only gives the pupil a sense of satisfaction but is also essential for the teacher.[52] Her sensitivity to individual pupils, her college training in psychology, and her experience in human relations can be powerful tools for maintaining control over her class.[53]

Diversified Curriculum. A third way in which progressive education has eased problems of control is by offering a variety of courses in place of a single, academically oriented program. This reduces intellectual pressures to the point where they are tolerable to many marginal students. Because academic subjects require mental effort and the restriction of bodily activity, they are less apt to be enjoyed than are courses like shop, art, homemaking, or physical education. When an academic, "solid" course is required of all public school students, regardless of their ability or motivation, serious disciplinary problems may occur. On the other hand, pupils are more likely to enjoy courses which do not require concentration or the prolonged cessation of movement. A study of Chicago schools, for instance, observed, "Teachers of physical education report fewer problems of discipline and lack of motivation. They say that children like their classes and are cooperative in them because they like to play."[54] Waller aptly summed up the situation when he stated that, "It is only because teachers wish to force students to learn that any unpleasantness ever arises to mar their relationship."[55]

The variety of courses ameliorates a problem which is particularly acute in the United States. Egalitarian values in this country discourage the establishment of completely separate schools or courses of study, but differences of ability and motivation between one pupil and the next are nevertheless so pronounced that they cannot be ignored. Broadening the curriculum and reducing the number of academic courses required of all students offers a workable compromise. This compromise presents the appearance of offering the same educational opportunities to everyone, yet it allows a considerable degree of flexibility in the assignment of pupils. It is especially useful in handling troublemakers and potential dropouts, many of whom would encounter difficulties in compulsory academic courses.[56]

Counseling and Testing. A fourth point, related to the previous one, involves counseling and testing programs. Because it is no longer necessary for everyone to follow the same path to graduation, the selection of courses for each pupil has become an important aspect of American secondary education. In fact, it is so important, for the school as well as for the student, that it cannot be left to chance. Aptitude testing, counseling, and detailed records of health, behavior, scholastic progress, and home conditions facilitate the placement of students in classes where they are least likely to encounter frustration. Youths who might not get along in academic work are guided away from it and assigned to courses where mental effort is presumably not imperative. For example, an art teacher in a California high school complained:

> All I get in here are the rejects from other classes. Most of them are really sad; they're practically human vegetables. I have six classes and it's the same thing all day long. I probably don't have more than three or four kids with an I.Q. above 90.
> Art classes are a dumping ground for clods who can't do anything else. They think that if a kid can't work with his head, he can do work with his hands. If a kid screws up in an English class, they throw him in here.[57]

Guiding potential discipline problems into non-academic courses is only part of the problem. Because these classes often require extra equipment and special supplies, they are more expensive than regular classes. Therefore, only a minimal number are usually provided and space in them is limited. In order to insure enough room for potential troublemakers or dropouts, the average and good students are likely to be steered away from these non-academic courses. The same art teacher, quoted above, commented wistfully:

> The other day after school a couple of girls came into my room to work on decorations for the senior prom. You could see they were alert youngsters, the kind you'd really like to work with. They saw the projects my classes were working on and one of them said that she wished she could take art. She said she had asked her counselor about it several times but he always told her they were full, there wasn't any room.
> That's not true. I have empty seats in here, but they're being saved for the clods who can't make it anywhere else.[58]

Thus, one result of counseling is the reduction of pressures on pupils who might otherwise cause problems of control.[59] Of course, this is not the justification usually given for counseling programs, but these services do minimize haphazard or "mistaken" assignments which might make retention and control more difficult. The development of these services was encouraged by progressive education.[60] It is possible that counselors, aptitude tests, and detailed records covering many phases of the pupils' school and family life might have evolved anyway, out of the sheer necessity for organizational survival, but they have received further support from progressive beliefs that individual differences are important and should be the focus of scientific study.

New Teaching Methods. Fifth, tensions which might lead to custodial problems have been relieved by progressive teaching methods. These methods reduce intellectual demands and, instead, emphasize learning through meaningful activity. Many children and adolescents would find it difficult to sit quietly for several hours a day, puzzling over a problem in long division, analyzing sentences, or memorizing long lists of facts. As Dewey stated, "Nature has not adapted the young animal to the narrow desk, the crowded curriculum, the silent absorption of complicated facts. His very life and growth depend upon motion, yet the school forces him into a cramped position for hours at a time."[61] The progressive approach permits and even encourages students to leave their desks and to engage in a variety of interesting projects, even to the point of working with other pupils.

Interest in school work may also be maintained by the use of a variety of teaching methods and equipment. Such devices as plays, murals, dioramas, models, projects, games, tape recorders, movies, committees, television, and field trips are more palatable to most pupils than the limited instructional techniques used in previous times, and are less likely to arouse frustration and resentment. An indication of the effectiveness of such methods appeared in a newspaper near the end of summer vacation. When a reported asked, "Are you eager for school to start?" a ten-year-old boy replied:

> I sure am! There's nothing to do in the summer but hang around
> the parks. At school I like the movies in the auditorium and the field
> trips. School is more of a vacation than vacation is.[62]

Flexible Standards. Sixth, lenient policies of grading and promotion have removed the threat of failure, which otherwise would have been a source of anxiety for many pupils and their parents. As an English observer of comparative education has noted:

> . . . the common school principle behind American education, which
> makes it automatic for every boy and girl to pass from the primary
> school to some form of secondary education in the high school,
> frees both parents and children from the anxiety neuroses which
> abound in Europe [where there is an examination hurdle which
> determines their educational future].[63]

With an extremely heterogenous student body it is difficult to maintain standards which will guide the intellectually capable pupils to better performance, but which will not discourage pupils with less ability. By reducing emphasis upon grades and by virtually eliminating the danger of failure, the school maintains the cooperation and interest of most pupils, especially those whose motivation and ability are low. American students learn relatively early in their school careers that the path to promotion and graduation presents few intolerable demands. They know that, with minimum effort, they will receive passing grades and will be promoted at the end of the year and, as long as they don't create too many disturbances, they will eventually receive a high school diploma. Pupils are occasionally expelled for extremely bad behavior, but no matter how little studying one does, it is almost impossible to "flunk out" of elementary or high school.[64]

Again the dual aspects of progressive education are evident. Besides preventing damage to the pupil's self-image, social promotion averts a potentially serious custodial problem for the school by avoiding disturbances which are likely to occur when a larger, older pupil is put back into a classroom with younger children. Occasionally pupils who cause a lot of trouble, instead of being demoted or held back, are skipped ahead a grade or two, "kicked upstairs" in order to rid the school of them a year or so earlier. For example, in one such instance known to the writer, an aggressive boy who had been held back a year in elementary school was moved forward an extra grade as soon as he entered junior high. At the end of the year he was skipped again, missing the last year of junior high and going on to senior high school. In this way, the junior high had to put up with him for only one year instead of the usual three.[65]

Thus, progressive education's emphasis upon the needs of the whole child rather than merely his intellectual development provides a useful rationale for the promotion of inept pupils who might otherwise cause serious problems of control and retention.

Extracurricular Activities. Finally, extracurricular activities offer incentives to remain in school and to obey its rules. These activities appeal to many pupils who would not be interested in intellectual endeavors. Baseball games, dances, carnivals, football, rallies, hobby clubs, assemblies, basketball, talent shows, and track meets can be powerful inducements for cooperation, offering to otherwise apathetic adolescents pleasures which would not be available outside the school. Though some of these activities may have existed on a smaller scale before the advent of progressive education, they now occupy a much more important place in the school program.[66] Mallison writes:

> One marked feature of the American high school is the emphasis placed on extra-curricular and out-of-school activities. . . . There are schools at which something is going on every night, and on Saturdays as well, organized by the pupils on an often extremely elaborate scale. The fact that most of the drive behind these activities comes from the pupils themselves is evidence that they are genuinely interested.[67]

Such activities have contributed to a reversal of the former pattern of sanctions: instead of behaving in order to avoid corporal punishment, pupils today are more likely to behave and to stay in school because they don't want to miss the fun which school offers. For example, the principal of a large high school in a California ghetto remarked:

> The worst thing that could happen to many of these kids is suspension. I can paddle the daylights out of them and they'll just laugh at me. But kick 'em out for a few days and that usually brings them around. It gets pretty dull and lonely at home. Suspension puts them away from their friends and school activities. That really hurts.[68]

The custodial potentialities of athletics are especially noteworthy. Competitive sports provide an outlet for some of the very pupils whose size, energy, and aggressiveness would almost inevitably have embroiled them in mischief in the traditional school. Now, however, instead of bullying weaker students, attacking the teacher, or otherwise causing trouble, their energies are diverted away from the school and are dissipated against each other, or ultimately, against rivals from another school. The highly structured nature of these contests provides further control over the release of potentially destructive energies; practice sessions and the actual games are held at certain times in specified places, and are conducted according to detailed rules under the watchful eyes of peers, adults and official referees. Even if violations of these rules occur, in the form of "unnecessary roughness" or "unsportsmanlike conduct," for example, they are far less disruptive there, on the athletic field, then they would be in the classroom.

The custodial benefits of competitive sports are not limited to redirecting youthful energy into relatively harmless areas. In addition, the athlete actually becomes dependent upon the school, because it is the means by which he achieves his pleasure and his status. Thus, he is put in the position of staying in school and conforming to most of its expectations so that he can enjoy its rewards. He may not like everything about it but he must tolerate it in order to receive the benefits it offers. Without the school there would be no team, no games, no rallies, no sweaters, no throngs of admirers, no cheering sections chanting his name, no mention of him on the sports page of the local newspaper.

Perhaps the alchemy of athletics is best exemplified by the new meanings associated with the school's name. Of course, not all athletically capable pupils would have been unsuccessful in a traditional setting. Nevertheless, for many of them, the name of the school would have signified frustration, unhappiness and failure. For the present-day athlete, however, the school's name has taken on more pleasant connotations, as a symbol of his success and prowess in sports. The school's initial, displayed on his sweater or jacket, is one of the most coveted awards the high school student can receive.

Thus, athletics, whatever its other functions might be, is also an instrument of social control.[69] It does not solve all custodial problems faced by contemporary public schools but it does forestall many of them, especially with regard to some of the pupils who are potentially most troublesome. Perhaps the main drawback of sports, from a custodial point of view, is that not all of the problem pupils are big enough or agile enough to qualify for the team. As one observer points out, however, the progressive school provides other possibilities for success:

> Inadequacy in the most glamorous sports is not by any means total failure in the bid for popularity, because all kinds of opportunities are provided for each child to be at least in something the king of the hour.[70]

A variety of other positions are available, ranging from team managers and yell-leaders to monitors responsible for student behavior. Thus, in one form or another, extracurricular activities do much to simplify the school's problems of retention and control.

CONCLUSION

The advent of mass compulsory education created custodial as well as educational problems. The necessity for accommodating a large and varied student body which could not be controlled by traditional methods of corporal punishment, segregation, failure, or expulsion forced American public schools to seek new solutions. Controversial phenomena like "pupil-centered" curriculum and the relaxing of academic standards, whatever their educational value might have been, alleviated urgent problems confronting the schools.

It may be illuminating to compare the school with another institution whose custodial function is more obvious: the prison. The comparison between the two is not as far fetched as it might at first seem, especially if we consider progressive, minimal security prisons. Both the prison and the school have a non-voluntary clientele, and both face custodial problems of retention and control. Of course, there are differences. Pupils are younger than prisoners, they go home every night, they attend coeducational institutions, and so forth. Basically, however, both the school and the prison must retain within their walls large numbers of "clients" who are forced, regardless of their own wishes, to spend time there. Thus, both institutions are confronted with problems of control.

It is worth noting that a prison's custodial problems, like those of the school, are also affected by its orientations. A recent study, for example, found that the prisons' general outlook had a noticeable effect upon the attitudes of its inmates.[71] Two contrasting orientations were observed, which were analogous to the traditional and progressive approaches in education. The "traditional" prison's main concern was containment, with little effort directed toward rehabilitation. There were many regulations, discipline was strict, and prison personnel remained aloof from the inmates. In contrast, the "progressive" prison was oriented toward treatment. There were maximal provisions for guidance and counseling, considerable interaction between staff and inmates, and a sincere effort toward constructively changing the prisoner.

The study revealed that inmates' attitudes toward prisons, staff, and treatment programs were most hostile in the institutions whose primary goal was containment, without much effort toward rehabilitation. Convicts' attitudes were more favorable in other prisons where there was considerable interaction between staff and inmates, where there was maximal opportunity for counseling and guidance, and where guards and administrators made a sincere effort to help the inmates.[72] The harsh conditions in the custodial prison led inmates to view the prison itself as the source of many of their problems, so they were more likely to unite against it. In contrast, the humane atmosphere of the progressive institution reduced deprivations to the point where inmates were unlikely to join forces against the prison and its staff.

The similarity between this and the contemporary public school is striking. In neither institution was the progressive orientation introduced officially as a means of control. Instead, the welfare of the inmate or the pupil was the reason given for adopting the new system. Nevertheless, in both the prison and the school, the progressive approach has softened the sting of compulsory attendance, alleviating critical problems of retention and control.

There is an old saying that "even the tyrant must sleep;" a progressive ideology makes it easier for him to do so.

REFERENCES

[1]Waller, *The Sociology of Teaching*, pp. 195-96.

[2]Johnson, *Old Time Schools*, p. 121.

[3]*Ibid.*, p. 129.

[4]Where not otherwise indicated, the sources for historical details in this and subsequent chapters are Cubberly's *Public Education in the United States*, rev. ed., and Butts and Cremin's *A History of Education in American Culture.*

[5]Horace Greeley, in Clifton Johnson's *Old Time Schools*, pp. 123-26.

[6]Ruth S. Freeman, *Yesterday's Schools*, p. 77.

[7]*Ibid.*

[8]*Ibid.*, pp. 78-79.

[9]*Ibid.*

[10]Johnson, *Old Time Schools*, p. 121.

[11]Butts and Cremin, *History of Education*, p. 286.

[12]Johnson, *Old Time Schools*, p. 121.

[13]*Ibid.*, pp. 121-22.

[14]Cubberly, *Public Education*, rev. ed., p. 328.

[15]Bailyn, *Education in the Forming of American Society*.

[16]Cubberly, *Public Education*, rev. ed., p. 57.

[17]Johnson, *Old Time Schools*, p. 123.

[18]Caldwell and Curtis, *Then and Now in Education: 1845:1923*, pp. 20-21.

[19]Johnson, *The Country School in New England*, pp. 47-52.

[20]Butts and Cremin, *History of Education*, p. 357. A compulsory education law had been enacted two centuries earlier. Although it eventually fell into disuse, it is worth noting. The Massachusetts law of 1642 heralded the first occasion, at least in the English-speaking world, that a legislative body representing the state had ordered that all children should be taught to read. Town officials were directed to see that all parents and masters of apprentices were training their children "in learning and labor and other employments profitable to the commonwealth" and that they were learning "to read and understand the principles of religion and the capital laws of the country." Fines were to be imposed on those who neglected to give adequate instruction.

However, the results were unsatisfactory, so five years later the "Old Deluder Satan" Act ordered the establishment of elementary and secondary schools, under penalty of fines for failing to do so. Thus, by the middle of the seventeenth century, the idea of compulsory attendance in publicly supported schools had appeared in legislation and was, for a while, being enforced in the courts (Cubberly, *Public Education*, rev. ed., p. 17-18).

[21]Cubberly, *Public Education*, rev. ed., p. 320.

[22]Wisconsin was one of the first states to abolish the *rate bill,* in 1848. Other midwestern states followed suit during the 1850s (Indiana, 1852; Ohio, 1853; Illinois, 1855; and Iowa, 1858). However, rate bills were not eliminated in New York until 1867, in Connecticut until 1868, and in Michigan until 1869 (Butts and Cremin, *History of Education*, pp. 247, 249, 252).

[23]U. S. Bureau of the Census, *Historical Statistics . . .*, p. 14.

[24]*Ibid.*, p. 213. "In some of the districts near to the reservations, Indian children were sometimes sent to school, but not very regularly" (Freeman, *Yesterday's Schools*, p. 64).

[25]U.S. Bureau of the Census, *Historical Statistics . . .*, p. 7.

[26]*Ibid.*, p. 14.

[27]*Report of the Commissioner of Education . . . for the Year 1870*, p. 273.

[28]After the 1954 Supreme Court decision, several states repealed their compulsory education laws or adopted other means for avoiding racially integrated schools.

[29]See Cremin's statement, *Transformation of the School*, pp. 127-28.

[30]There had been a few large schools before, with sixty or more pupils jammed into a single-room rural school, and some of the Lancastrian monitorial schools

held several hundred students. These, however, had been the exception rather than the rule.

[31]The reduction of the class size to sixty pupils per teacher was often considered an unattainable ideal (Cremin, *Transformation of the School*, p. 21).

[32]U.S. Bureau of the Census, *Historical Statistics . . .*, p. 207.

[33]*Ibid.* In terms of actual numbers, the increase was more spectacular. There were only eighty thousand public school pupils in 1870, compared to 2,200,000 in 1920.

[34]*Ibid.*

[35]Cremin, *Transformation of the School*, p. 72.

[36]*Ibid.* As Cremin observed: "The mere fact that children in a single schoolroom spoke a half-dozen languages, none of them English, inevitably altered the life of that schoolroom. And the problem went far beyond language, for each language implied a unique heritage and unique attitudes toward teacher, parents, and school-mates — indeed, toward the school itself."

[37]Eby and Arrowood, *Development of Modern Education*, p. 719. By the middle of the nineteenth century, for example, Horace Mann was proclaiming women to be more sympathetic than men, and better adapted to elementary teaching. Therefore, he advocated the employment of more women teachers in common schools.

[38]Butts and Cremin, *History of Education*, p. 283.

[39]Research Division, NEA, in Lieberman, *Education as a Profession*, p. 242.

[40]U.S. Bureau of the Census, *Historical Statistics . . .*, p. 207.

[41]Becker, *Role and Career Problems of the Chicago Public School Teacher*, p. 60.

[42]*Ibid.*, pp. 62-63.

[43]*Ibid.*, p. 63. Another teacher explained ". . . the biggest problem you face in the public school is discipline. You have to get them in order and keep them that way before you can teach" (*Ibid.*, p. 61).

[44]Wagenschein, *Reality Shock*, pp. 58-59. For reports of similar problems in California, see James Herndon, *The Way it Spozed To Be*. Two Harlem teachers, Mary Frances Greene and Orletta Ryan, describe their situation in *The School-children*.

[45]Riesman observes that the teacher ". . . has been taught that bad behavior on the children's part implies poor management on her part" (Riesman *et al., The Lonely Crowd*, p. 84). Similarly, Brookover comments, ". . . in most communities, the adults, including the older teachers, expect the teacher to maintain authority over the children" (Brookover, *A Sociology of Education*, p. 233).

[46]Becker, *Role and Career Problems*, p. 63.

[47]For example, only four students were expelled from San Francisco's high schools during the 1968-69 school year, although principals had asked for the expulsion of sixty. The board of education permitted the other fifty-six to return to their schools (*San Francisco Examiner*, October 26, 1969).

[48]John and Evelyn Dewey, *Schools of Tomorrow*, p. 14.

[49]Johnson, *Country School*, p. 49.

[50]*Ibid.*

[51]A California elementary principal in a conversation with the author.

[52]In offering "Hints for New Teachers" on classroom control, the Richmond (California) Federation of Teachers suggested: "Work upon the ego of each student. Every individual is worth something — has some special talent or trait. The sooner you recognize and publicly acknowledge this worth, the sooner you will be on your way to winning the class" (R.F.T. *Newsletter*, October 8, 1969).

[53]The use of psychology in pupil control is mentioned by David Riesman. He speaks of teachers as "... young college graduates who have been taught to be more concerned with the child's social and psychological adjustment than with his academic progress. . . . This greater knowledge . . . prevents the children from uniting in a wall of distrust or conspiracy against the school. . . ." (Riesman *et al., The Lonely Crowd*, p. 80).

[54]Wagenschein, *Reality Shock*, p. 56.

[55]Waller, *Sociology of Teaching*, p. 355. Describing an early progressive school which emphasized manual training, a 1904 newspaper announced, "They need no truant officer at Menomonie." Cremin added, "Boys who might have become disciplinary problems elsewhere actually remained in school after hours to work in the machine and carpentry shops" (Cremin, *Transformation of the School*, p. 144).

[56]Although curricular diversity is not limited to progressive systems of education, and would probably emerge in any nation which is trying to educate all children, its appearance in American public schools was facilitated by progressive beliefs that individual differences among children should be recognized, and that pupils' interests and needs should shape the curriculum.

[57]From a conversation with the author.

[58]*Ibid.*

[59]This need of the school to minimize pupil frustrations may be a factor behind the complaints that counselors "discriminate" by their alleged readiness to assign minority-group pupils to vocational instead of college preparatory classes.

[60]Burton Clark has observed a similar process at the junior college level, whereby the pupil who appears to have little chance of success in academic endeavors is guided into an alternative curriculum more in keeping with his limited scholastic achievement (Clark, "The 'Cooling-Out' Function in Higher Education," pp. 569-76).

[61]John and Evelyn Dewey, *Schools of Tomorrow*, p. 15.

[62]*San Francisco Chronicle*, August 23, 1959.

[63]Mallinson, *An Introduction to the Study of Comparative Education*, p. 159.

[64]Expulsion because of low grades was so rare in California that even the threat of it, in a small high school a hundred miles away, was enough to make the front page of the *San Francisco Chronicle* in 1958. The article reported, "So far as local educators know, there have never been expulsions on such grounds in California.
" 'We don't feel this problem in San Francisco,' school superintendent Harold Spears said. 'I can't see anybody booted out just because he didn't have his grades up' " (*San Francisco Chronicle*, February 17, 1958).
To keep up appearances, administrators sometimes order a change in a pupil's grade, raising the mark given by the teacher (e.g., *San Francisco Chronicle*, March 5, 1958). In elementary schools, the principals often review report cards before they are sent home to the parents. High grades are rarely challenged; even when a child receives ten or twelve As, there is usually no question. A low grade, however, is more likely to be protested by the principal, and frequently it is not the pupil but the teacher who must defend the low mark she has given.

[65]During the 1959-60 school year, ninety-seven percent of all pupils in Los Angeles elementary schools received regular promotions both semesters, while only two percent were retained. One percent of the elementary pupils were accelerated, and half of these accelerations were due to over-age rather than to high ability or achievement. It is also interesting to note that the retention rate had dropped considerably during a period of approximately thirty years, from nine percent in 1927, to two percent in 1957-60 (Bowman, "Promotion, Retention, and Acceleration in

the Los Angeles City Elementary Schools," in *Educational Research Projects Reported by California County and District School Offices 1960-61*, C.T.A. Research Bulletin 153.

[66]One indication of their increasing importance is the change of terminology associated with them. Originally called *extra-curricular,* they are currently referred to as *co-curricular* activities.

[67]Mallinson, *Comparative Education,* pp. 182-83.

[68]From a conversation with the author.

[69]For example, following racial disturbances which closed a San Francisco high school, ". . . the only wholly 'normal' event on the Balboa campus was a lengthy football practice . . ." (*San Francisco Chronicle,* September 24, 1969).

[70]King, *Other Schools and Ours,* p. 117.

[71]Berk, "Organizational Goals and Inmate Organization," *A.J.S.,* March, 1966, pp. 522-34.

[72]These differences did not appear to be due to selective input of the inmates into various prisons, but rather to the differences between the prisons (*Ibid.,* p. 528).

four

THE PROBLEM
OF ADMINISTRATION

A SECOND PROBLEM INVOLVES ADMINISTRATION. THE CONTEMPORARY American public school system is a complex and often very large organization. Along with problems posed by exigencies of pupil retention and control, the school faces issues of quite a different nature. Teachers must be hired; books purchased; paper, pencils and other supplies ordered; heat and lights provided; buildings and grounds must be maintained. New schools must be planned, sites selected, construction contracts awarded, and so forth. Thus the school, in addition to being an educational institution, is also confronted by pressures generally characteristic of big organizations. In several respects it resembles a large commercial enterprise. As one observer noted:

> . . . education is a big business. It is concerned with fixed and circulating capital. It is concerned with budgets and the estimates of future capital requirements. There is a problem of depreciation, obsolescence, and replacement of equipment. There is the whole gamut of labor problems: recruiting, teachers' salaries, hours and conditions of work, pensions, teacher organization, and many more. In all of these phases, the school is like any other business establishment.[1]

This has not always been true. Schools of the traditional era were a far cry from those of today, administratively as well as educationally. The public school in its present form began to emerge in the years between the Civil War and World War I, and many of the school's

184801

administrative problems became even more intense in the second quarter of this century. The methods used in coping with these problems were comparable, in some respects, to those employed in other modern organizations, and their adoption was facilitated by progressive education.

Perhaps progressive education's most basic administrative contribution was flexibility. It gave school executives freedom to devise methods of coping with troublesome managerial problems. Faced with the mounting pressures of large, complex organizations, some adjustments had to be made. It was no longer possible to concentrate upon the clearly stated aims of the traditional school; other problems also had to be met, even though they were not specifically educational in nature. Something had to give, and room for adjustment was provided by the broad goals of progressive education, permitting the school to shift its emphasis away from scholarship, from mastery of subject matter, and even from education in any form, toward other urgent issues which confronted it.

In examining progressive education as a goal or guide for the school and its personnel, the crucial factor is not the specific substantive content of the school's goals but rather the precision or vagueness with which these goals are stated. Limited, clearly defined objectives can be readily translated into guides for everyday action, leaving little doubt as to what should be done in a given situation. On the other hand, goals which are broad and general have a greater chance of being misinterpreted or pushed aside in the face of other more concrete demands.

In a more narrowly defined, academic curriculum it would have been easier to decide which procedures would lead to the stated objectives of the school. Activities and decisions could be evaluated by considering their effect upon the scholastic achievement of the pupils. It was easier to assign definite grades and precise percentages to a pupil's work. A student, for example, who could repeat from memory the capitals of thirty-six states was obviously doing better than a classmate who could only remember thirty-three or thirty-four. Similarly, a class whose scores on such tests averaged, for example, 94 percent was better than a class whose average was only 82 percent. In short, these precise grades and clearly defined objectives provided definite indicators of the progress of the pupils and of the school. High grades demonstrated that all was well; low grades showed, in no uncertain terms, that improvement was needed in certain specific areas, improvement by the pupil, the teacher and the school. Thus, whatever the pedagogical value of traditional education might have been, it at least provided clearly defined criteria of success or failure, and established definite guides for decisions. There was relatively little uncertainty as to the proper action to be taken in any given situation.

Under progressive education, however, evaluation and decision making became more difficult because the organization's goals were more general. Progressive education broadened the school's objectives to such a degree that many kinds of work, including administration, could be interpreted as contributing to education. Since the avowed aim of the progressive school was the development of the whole child rather than of merely his intellectual powers, it became harder, if not impossible, to assess a decision in terms of its contribution to such an extremely board objective. For example, it may be acknowledged that a rally for the football team does little to improve knowledge of grammar or chemistry, but who can say with certainty that it does not contribute in some way to pupils' adjustment?

The consequences of progressive education were not limited merely to uncertainty over the best means of pursuing the school's goals. In addition, progressive education increased the possibility that these goals might sometimes be ignored altogether — either accidentally or intentionally — and that other matters would receive prior consideration. As Selznick observed: ". . . when guides are unrealistic, yet decisions must be made, more realistic *but uncontrolled* criteria will somehow fill the gap. Immediate exigencies will dominate the actual choices that are made."[2] Education, even in its broadest sense, could sometimes be overlooked entirely as administrators in progressive schools attempted to cope with more immediate, concrete problems.

Progressive education was administratively helpful in other ways, too, and these will be discussed later in the chapter. First, however, let's look at the origin and development of administrative problems.

THE TRADITIONAL ERA

Problems associated with large, complex organizations were virtually unknown during the traditional era, and did not begin to appear until the second half of the nineteenth century. There were few large schools or school systems, and where these existed, they remained simple and undifferentiated. As late as 1870, only the two biggest cities, New York and Philadelphia, had an average attendance of more than thirty-thousand pupils. Only eight other districts exceeded ten-thousand.[3] Public schools during most of the traditional period were small, scattered, or non-existent. The typical educational institution was the one-room, one-teacher school.

A number of factors delayed the development of big, complex educational systems. First, the principle of free public education was not generally accepted until the middle of the nineteenth century. Second, the United States was predominantly a rural nation, with few large cities or towns. Third, the prevailing method of school district organization consisted of forming entirely separate, new districts instead of enlarging the existing ones. Fourth, even where there were public schools, a relatively small proportion of eligible children attended them. Fifth, public education at the secondary level was almost non-existent. Additional factors were the traditional lack of provisions for beginning students, the housing of separate schools in the same building, and the monitorial school which required only one teacher for a large number of students. Finally, the concept of separate, fulltime administrators was virtually unknown.

The principle of free common schools for all children was not firmly established until the end of the traditional era and even then it was generally limited to elementary education. Although public education had been advocated in various quarters since early Colonial times, it remained relatively scarce and intermittent. Ethnic and religious factions feared that a state system of education might intrude upon their languages, beliefs and customs; many people felt that education was of little practical value; and still others believed that it was unfair to be taxed for the purpose of educating someone else's children.[4]

Gradually, however, the first organizations we would recognize as public schools began to appear. Cincinnati founded its public school system in 1825 and, during the following twenty years, public schools opened in a number of major cities and towns. In smaller communities, however, public schools were not established until later, after they had been required by state laws.[5] Even where public schools were provided, rate bills and other lesser expenses often continued for some years, discouraging the attendance of many children from poor families.[6]

A second factor limiting the development of large school systems was the small size of the communities served. During the traditional era the United States was still a rural nation. In 1860, four-fifths of the population lived outside of urban areas.[7]

A third factor delaying the growth of school districts during the traditional period was the prevailing pattern of district organization. Early school systems were extremely small and decentralized, usually consisting of one teacher in a one-room school. Wherever a few families lived close enough together to make organization feasible, the permissive early laws allowed them to form a school district and to establish their own school. Only those families or communities wanting schools had to be included in the district; those not wanting schools or unwilling to pay for them could be excluded. Consequently, districts of any size could be formed anywhere. When population pressures created a need for an additional teacher and another room, the usual procedure was to establish a completely new district rather than to enlarge the existing one. The new district, like its predecessor, formed its own governing board, devised its own system for raising money, supplied its own schoolhouse, and hired its own teacher.[8] This was true in cities as well as in the country, with the result that many school systems remained small even after the communities in which they were located began to grow rapidly.

By 1837 Buffalo, for example, had attained the respectable size of about fifteen-thousand people, but its public education system consisted of seven completely independent districts, each with one school and one teacher. Chicago's experience was similar. Its first public school opened in 1830, and by 1851 there were seven separate districts within the city, each with its own board of trustees and each employing teachers and levying taxes. It was not until 1853 that the city council appointed a superintendent to unify the work done in various districts. Finally, in 1857, the district system was abolished and a single board of education was placed in charge of all the schools in the city.[9]

A fourth factor retarding the growth of public schools into large complex organizations was the failure of many children to take advantage of available educational opportunities. Even where public schools existed, a small proportion of children attended them. Only a fraction of school-age boys and girls were enrolled in school, and even these enrollment figures were deceptively large because many children who were registered did not actually come to school regularly.[10]

A fifth factor delaying the emergence of complex organizational forms was that most of the growth in public education before the Civil War occurred in the lower grades. By 1850, as we have seen, the idea of providing a common elementary school education for every child had been accepted, at least in principle, by the Northern states and some steps in that direction were also being taken in parts of the South. But secondary education was another matter. High schools lagged far behind public elementary schools, and many of the factors which had earlier hindered the acceptance of free elementary education appeared again to resist the establishment of public secondary schools. Taxation was an especially crucial issue. The legality of forcing people to pay for the advanced education of others' children was often challenged in court, at times successfully, so that some proposed schools were prohibited before they were established and, in other cases, high schools which were already operating were forced to close down.[11] Public education was concentrated almost entirely at the elementary level.

A sixth factor was the size of the school buildings. Schoolhouses of the traditional period generally remained small and simple, regardless of enrollment. The one-teacher, one-room school building continued as the dominant pattern even after the first municipal systems appeared. Even in the largest city, New York, a typical nineteenth-century school building had only three rooms. Cubberly described a "model school," erected in 1843, at a cost, with site, of $17,000:

> A typical New York school building after 1830. The infant or primary school was on the first floor, the second floor contained the girls' school, and the third floor the boys' school. Each floor had one large room seating 252 children; the primary schoolroom could be divided into two rooms by folding doors, so as to segregate the infant class. This building was for long regarded as the perfection of the builders' art, and its picture was printed for years on the cover of the Society's Annual Reports.[12]

During this time the number of pupils accommodated in a building was likely to be large. "Nevertheless no matter how many [students] there was never any thought of providing more than a single teacher."[13] "Some schoolrooms not over thirty feet square accommodated a hundred pupils."[14]

Still another restraint upon the growth of large complex systems was the prerequisite of literacy for entry into elementary schools. Since colonial times there had been a tendency to restrict admission into public elementary schools (where they existed) to those children who were already well on their way to mastering the fundamentals of reading, writing and arithmetic.

To instruct beginners, "infant" or "primary" schools were introduced into the United States around 1816. These schools admitted children at four years of age and prepared them for the regular public schools. Often the management of these primary schools remained distinct from that of the grammar schools. Boston, for example, established primary schools in 1818, but not until 1854 were the two systems finally united under one board of education. In New York, also, primary schools were under separate management, being operated by the Public School Society.[15]

Growth was also delayed by the after-effects of the *Lancastrian* or *monitorial* school. This type of school had been very popular during the first part of the nineteenth century because it seemed so economical, allowing one teacher to instruct several hundred students. Under the Lancastrian system the teacher taught a prepared lesson to a small group of brighter pupils. In turn, each of these pupils or *monitors* instructed a group of younger students. By this method, one teacher could supervise two or three hundred pupils, instead of the several dozen which was the usual maximum class load.[16]

The building required for a Lancastrian school was simply one large study hall, with perhaps one or two smaller rooms attached. The teacher occupied the large hall, supervised the monitors, maintained order, and sometimes instructed one or two classes, while other pupils went to the classrooms to recite for the monitors. The monitorial school was able to absorb a large number of pupils without apparent signs of becoming overloaded. Because it required only one teacher and one room, there was little pressure for the development of an administrative superstructure.[17]

Still another factor was the *double-headed* school, consisting of two separate schools located in the same building. One of the schools was a grammar school, giving instruction in reading, grammar, and eventually one or two other subjects, such as geography. In the other school the writing master taught writing and arithmetic. The children were divided into two groups, each attending one school in the morning and switching to the other school, in the other room, in the afternoon. Each teacher had full authority over his class, or school, and was independent of the other teacher. If the teacher answered to anyone, it was directly to the governing board.

Variations of the double-headed school separated by subject included some divided by age or sex. While the schools were housed in the same building and usually taught the same students, they had no formal relation to each other, but were simple, one-celled organizations. They provided little necessity for coordination, supervision, or other problems which led to the emergence of an administrative superstructure. First appearing in the 1740s, some double-headed schools continued into this century.[18]

In view of these conditions it is not surprising that school administration as a separate function was slow to develop. The first city superintendents were appointed in Buffalo and in Louisville, Kentucky, in 1837. Twenty-nine cities and towns employed superintendents before 1870.[19] It is worth noting that the duties of these early administrators were clerical rather than executive; some of the first superintendents were not even educators. In Cleveland, for example, the first person to hold the office was actually the secretary of the school board. He acted as superintendent for twelve years until a real superintendent was finally hired. In Jersey City the office was unsalaried for some time, and was held by merchants and other businessmen, who merely performed nominal duties.[20] The principalship also emerged slowly. The early principal spent most of his time teaching. He had a small number of teachers to direct and his administrative duties were very simple.[21]

The absence of modern administration was not merely due to the small size and simplicity of early schools. In addition there was a lag in the concept of school administration itself. The idea of providing non-teaching personnel who would devote their full time to administrative tasks was virtually unheard of during the traditional era. For example, the New York City schools in 1869 had 237,000 pupils and 2,500 teachers but the superintendent's staff would seem infintesimal by today's standards.[22] He had four assistant superintendents, whose duties were to inspect schools and help examine candidates for teacher's licenses. Two clerks were also employed—and that was all. The 276 schools of the city were visited twice each year by one of the assistant superintendents. They were also inspected by the chief superintendent "as often as possible—at least once each year."[23] Clearly these early administrators were very active and covered a great deal of ground. It is surprising, then, to learn that the superintendent did not feel overburdened. To the contrary, when asked if his staff was adequate for the amount of work to be done, he replied: "It is."[24]

Some metropolitan districts lacked even the minute administrative services of the New York system. In 1869, Philadelphia was the second largest school system in the United States but it had no superintendent at all, even though the district had 380 schools, 1,515 teachers and 81,000 pupils. The expenditures for that year were $1,174,000.[25]

To summarize, most American school systems before the Civil War were small and simple, and even in the cities, where managerial assistance could have been useful, school districts were slow to appoint fulltime administrators.

THE TRANSITIONAL ERA

The half century following 1870 witnessed a profound change in public school organization. In earlier times the meager administrative tasks were performed either by teachers, in addition to their full-time classroom duties, or by part-time laymen whose major concerns lay outside the field of education. By World War I, however, school administration had emerged as a full-time activity, separate from teaching, and increasingly requiring advanced, specialized training. At least three factors contributed to the development of school administration: *size, complexity,* and the *emergence of a managerial ethos* in the larger society, especially in business.

The emergence of a school administrative staff began early in the transitional period. In 1870 there had been only twenty-nine cities with superintendents but, during the next six years, over a hundred more were added. Thus, by 1876 there were superintendents in 142 of the 175 cities whose population at that time was eight thousand or over.[26] The number continued to increase thereafter. By 1920 the United States Commissioner of Education listed 2,798 superintendents in towns of over 2,500 inhabitants.[27]

One major factor in this increase was the growing size of many schools and districts. By 1920 there were twenty-seven school systems whose average daily attendances were more than 30,000 and six of these had passed the 100,000 mark. New York City, for example, had 735,000 public school pupils, Chicago had 300,000 and Philadelphia had 200,000.[28]

Moreover, individual schools within these expanding districts were also growing. By 1920 some public high schools had reached immense proportions. The largest of all was Los Angeles' Polytechnic Evening High, where 7,380 boys were registered. The Manual Arts High School in Los Angeles had 3,586. The New York City system, which by this time included Brooklyn, had nine giant schools with enrollments over 2,500 each. The largest, Stuyvesant High, had 6,334. Three other New York City schools had more than five thousand pupils each and an additional three had over four thousand. Chicago, Minneapolis, Boston, and Washington, D.C. also had very large schools.[29]

But size alone could not have explained the rise of school administrators because even the smallest districts were hiring them. By 1920, for example, the six elementary schools of Wilkinsburg, Pennsylvania, with a total enrollment of 3,200 pupils, had thirteen supervisors, six principals and, presumably, a superintendent. The Meadville, Pennsylvania, elementary district had four principals and four supervisors for its 1,714 students. The ten elementary schools of Clinton, Iowa, with a total enrollment of 2,244 pupils had thirteen supervisors, in addition to eight principals.[30]

The same trend appears when statistics for all public schools in the United States are considered together. If administrative growth had been only a result of increasing size, we would expect the proportion of school personnel per pupil to remain about the same, regardless of the size of the school district, or to have increased somewhat disproportionately in the largest districts. For example, we would expect a system with 50,000 pupils to have twice as many administrators as a district with 25,000 pupils.

However, this was not the case. Medium-sized districts in 1920 had relatively more administrators than did the large districts, and the small systems had even more administrators per student than the middle-sized districts. Cities with a population over 100,000 averaged one superintendent or assistant superintendent for every 18,000 pupils. In towns with a population of 30,000 to 100,000, the average dropped to one superintendent or assistant superintendent for every 8,000 students, and in towns of 10,000 to 30,000, there was one superintendent for every 3,400 pupils.[31]

The same tendency applied to supervisors as well as to superintendents. Each supervisor in the largest districts had to cover about 4,000 pupils but in medium-sized districts the supervisors' workload diminished to 1,664 students apiece. In small towns the supervisor-pupil ratio was still less, with one supervisor for every 1,088 students.[32] Principals, too, were disproportionately more frequent in the smaller districts than in the large ones.

Thus, while all districts had more administrators and supervisors per pupil in 1920 than they had a half-century earlier, smaller districts had more than their share. This suggests that size alone was not responsible for the growth of school management. Other forces were also involved.

A second element in the emergence of modern administration was complexity. The business of public education had become much more complicated. The half-dozen or more academic courses which constituted the curriculum of 1870 had, by 1920, burgeoned into a profuse array of offerings. Special equipment and facilities were needed for vocational courses and for vastly expanded physical education and science programs. Auxiliary services, unheard of during the traditional era, were taken for granted by 1920: health, guidance, truant officers, etc. And, quite apart from the vital problems of raising money to operate the schools, which will be discussed in the next chapter, there remained the responsibility of accounting for funds received and of justifying their expenditure.

A number of factors led to this increasing complexity during the transitional period. The acceptance of the principle of universal compulsory education and the actual implementation of this principle brought a far wider range of pupils into American schools. The greater heterogeneity of the student body not only created custodial problems but also led to an increasingly intricate school structure. As the age-range expanded, as the curriculum became more diverse, as the spectrum of pupils' ability broadened to include the extremely capable and the severely retarded, these changes were felt not only within the classroom; they had administrative ramifications as well.

The idea of free secondary education for everyone was accepted during this period. The turning point came in 1872, when Michigan's supreme court, in the Kalamazoo decision, ruled that communities had the right to levy taxes for public high schools.[33] This decision set a precedent for a number of other states and removed a major obstacle to the extension of public education beyond the elementary level. By 1920, ten percent of all public school students were in secondary schools. Public secondary education, virtually non-existent in 1870, had grown in fifty years to the point where it involved over two million pupils.[34]

Schools also became more complex through combining different types of educational institutions which had previously remained independent of each other, even though they were often located in the same building. Double-headed schools, common during traditional times, disappeared by 1920.

School district consolidation further contributed to increasing size and complexity. In 1869 Massachusetts authorized the unification of school districts, and Ohio followed in 1892. By 1905, approximately twenty other states passed laws permitting school district consolidation. Although there were still about 200,000 independent systems in 1920, the movement toward consolidation had begun, with profound consequences for school administration.[35]

Consolidation not only enlarged districts but also introduced new functions which had hardly existed before. This becomes evident in Cubberly's description of what consolidation involved: abandoning three, four, five or more little district schools, erecting in their place a modern building in a central location, hauling children by wagon or automobile from their homes each day to this central place in the morning and back in the afternoon, and establishing graded instruction, a partial or complete high school, agriculture, manual and domestic work. An assembly hall, branch library room and playground should also be provided. A consolidated school included, in addition to classrooms, an assembly hall, library, manual-training room, domestic science room, an agricultural laboratory, toilets, and indoor play rooms in the basement.[36]

A third change affecting public schools was the emergence of an administrative ethos based upon the experiences of American industry. Two components of this ethos were particularly influential in the schools. One was an emphasis upon economic efficiency. The other involved the use of human relations in dealing with employees.

The organization of industry had been radically transformed since the beginning of the nineteenth century.[37] Like the schools, business enterprises also were becoming larger and more complex, resulting in, among other things, separation of ownership from control. As business became less the private property of those who established, inherited, or purchased it, as bureaucratic principles of competence rather than of nepotism or friendship became more widely accepted, there was more pressure for those who actually operated the organization to demonstrate their competence. "A manager was judged to be 'good' only if he produced."[38] A prime means of doing this was through money-saving operations. Since the goal of the business enterprise was profit, individuals who contributed most to it, who produced the most for the least cost, were considered most competent in the performance of their duties.

These developments in the business world had a marked effect upon the schools. As Bendix notes, "American businessmen and industrialists were the recognized elite of society."[39] If the captains of industry thought in terms of economic efficiency, people in other lines of work were likely to follow their example.

Interest in efficiency was further stimulated by reformers concerned with problems arising from industrialization and immigration. A popular antidote for such problems, especially those which seemed to be related to corruption and inefficiency, was the application of modern business methods in all sectors of society, public and private.

It was natural, therefore, whenever attention turned to the schools, to suggest that business methods should be used here as well.[40] In 1903, the *Atlantic Monthly* attacked politics in school administration and recommended the adoption of the practices which had worked so well in industry. The article warned that "school administrators should be economical" and that "peoples' money should not be wasted." In making this point clear, the author stated that: "The management of school affairs is a large business involving in a city of 100,000 inhabitants an expenditure of probably $500,000 annually; the same business principles adopted in modern industry should be employed here."[41]

Evidence that pressures to use business techniques were recognized by school personnel themselves was provided at the 1905 annual meeting of the National Education Association. The first speaker in a symposium on "Comparison of Modern Business Methods with Educational Methods" was the secretary of the Massachusetts State Board of Education. He observed, ". . . the contrast between modern business methods and the most modern methods in education is so great as to suggest some searching questions. In the comparison, educational processes seem unscientific, crude, and wasteful."[42]

Further evidence of business influence appeared in the 1907 textbook *Classroom Management*. It relied heavily on business concepts and terminology. Written for teacher training, it became so popular that it was reprinted more than thirty times.[43]

In 1911 a reform-minded economist expressed the matter of efficiency in terms which touched a basic concern of the school: its financial support. He demanded that schools give evidence of their contribution to society or have their budgets reduced: "The advocate of pure water or clean streets shows by how much the death rate will be altered by each proposed addition to his share of the budget. . . . Only the teacher is without such figures." Why should money be spent on schools rather than on other facilities and services? Why should the public ". . . support inefficient school teachers instead of efficient milk inspectors? Must definite reforms with measurable results give way that an antiquated school system may grind out its useless product?" He challenged the schools to produce results that could be "readily seen and measured."[44]

Although much of this criticism was directed at public schools in general, specific school districts were also being attacked by the public and by local newspapers. For example, the schools of Providence, Rhode Island, were castigated by the press because they gave students a four-day vacation by declaring a holiday on the Monday before Decoration Day. This action, it was claimed, cost the taxpayer $5,000. It was "poor business" and "not scientific economy."[45] That same year the Des Moines school board was ". . . found guilty, by the local press, of extravagance and loose business methods on a dozen or more counts."[46]

Agitation for economic efficiency was taken up by popular magazines like the *Saturday Evening Post* and the *Ladies Home Journal*. Illustrative of many articles was one in the *Post* entitled "Medieval Methods for Modern Children." It attacked school administrators with the claim that ". . . there is inefficiency in the business management of many schools such as would not be tolerated in the world of offices and shops."[47]

In sum, thrift became a major concern of boards of education and the public. It was something that the school executive could not ignore. Both the inexorable economic realities of large organizations and the pressure of public opinion forced him to devote much of his attention to frugal management procedures.

A second development in the business world which had an important effect upon school administration was the rise of human relations in handling personnel problems. The rapid expansion of American industry in the decades following the Civil War was accompanied by the formation of labor unions. By the beginning of the present century, unions were growing rapidly: in 1897 they had 447,000 members; by 1920 they numbered over five million.[48]

Even more alarming to employers were the increasing numbers of strikes. In 1900 there were 1,839 work stoppages, in which one-half-million workers participated, and in the years 1916 to 1920, there were three or four thousand strikes annually.[49]

At first, employers responded by an ever more rigorous assertion of their authority, campaigned for *open shops,* and organized for collective action against the rising tide of trade unionism. Eventually, however, it became evident that incentive wages, threats and instant dismissal were not providing enough control over the workers. As a result, employers were forced to look upon labor as a more complex problem which could not be "solved" simply by firing incompetent or intransigent workers. A new method was needed and the approach which emerged was human relations.[50]

Thus, by 1928 the *American Management Review* was reminding employers to "Treat workers as human beings. Show your interest in their personal success and welfare."[51] By the 1930s this view of workers as "human beings" became widespread among American employers, and placed a new type of demand upon the administrator.[52] The conception of "the manager" which developed after the First World War was of a man who was competent in his work, "half" of which consisted of the skillful handling of people.[53] As the *American Management Review* warned in 1924, managers were mistaken if they failed to see the importance of personality and of the ability to deal with people as factors contributing to better production. "Sympathetic supervison would result in better production and therefore it made 'sound business sense'."[54] A book written by Dale Carnegie in 1926, *Public Speaking and Influencing Men in Business,* was used as the "official" text by organizations like the American Institute of Banking, the New York Telephone Company, and the National Institute of Credit.[55] As one reviewer described it, the book embodied a combination of "Public Speaking, Salesmanship, Human Relationships, Personality Development and Applied Psychology."[56]

Thus, to industrial managers, human relations appeared to facilitate the control and coordination of a growing, increasingly specialized staff.[57] Here, too, as in the adoption of economic criteria for efficiency, schools followed the example set by business. Personnel practices in the schools had been quite primitive throughout the nineteenth century. As late as 1907 the textbook, *Classroom Management,* took a traditional hard line on relations between teachers and their superiors: "unquestioned obedience" was stressed as the "first rule of efficient service." The situation in the school was held to be ". . . entirely analogous to that in any other organization or system—the army, navy, government, great business enterprises (or small business enterprises, for that matter)."[58]

Developments in teacher-administrator relations followed the general pattern of industry, although somewhat more slowly. Large-scale disputes involving teachers did not occur until the eve of World War I. Previously, conflict had remained on an individual level, usually involving only a single teacher and her principal. The absence of militance among teachers was, to a considerable degree, a consequence of the ease of entry into the profession and the abundant supply of women who were willing to work for the low wages offered by most school districts. State certification requirements, when they existed at all, were so scanty that most small districts were able to find enough applicants to place an adult in each classroom.

Teachers' organizations were initially of little help. A National Teachers Association had been formed in 1857 but it remained weak, usually small, and never became seriously involved in the issue of teacher-management differences. In 1897, forty years after its founding, it had less than two thousand members and, though it grew to 5,044 by 1917, its membership consisted largely of administrators.[59] From its inception this association had been more interested in teaching methods and educational philosophy rather than in improved working conditions or personnel practices. As Butts and Cremin observed, "This type of neutrality was both demanded and expected of teachers during this period, and their associations tended to respect such boundaries."[60]

However, as schools grew larger and educational management became a fulltime function, distinct from classroom teaching, tensions between teachers and administrators became more evident. The most direct challenge to managerial authority was the emergence of teachers' *unions.* More militant than the associations, which they often derided as being "company unions," the unions viewed teachers and administrators as fundamentally different. The interests of the two groups, union teachers claimed, did not necessarily coincide, and might even conflict. Unions excluded superintendents, and granted membership to other administrative personnel only under conditions designed to protect the independence of classroom teachers.[61]

The legal right of teachers to form unions was established by the Lloyd-LaFolette Act of 1912. This act provided that membership in an employee organization, as long as it did not impose an obligation to strike against the government, was not justification for fine, demotion or dismissal. Encouraged by the Act, a national federation of teachers was formed in 1916 and, later that same year, it affiliated with the American Federation of Labor. The new organization grew rapidly. In 1919 it had one hundred sixty locals, with a total membership of about eleven thousand. For a while the A.F.T. was larger than the N.E.A.[62]

The response of school administrators and board members to the rising tide of unionism was the same as that of industrial management:

> The educational authorities became alarmed. They saw "the dig-
> nity of the teaching profession" threatened and its independence
> undermined through association with organized labor. They saw the
> discipline of the school system endangered through a classroom

teachers' movement which excluded supervisors. An antiunion campaign was launched directed by officials and influential members of the NEA, including prominent professors in the leading university schools of education. Deans, professors, state and local superintendents of schools toured the country, and with the prestige of their official connections and their relations with the NEA to add weight to their words, attacked the teachers' union movement before meetings of the state associations and local and county teachers' institutions. They wrote articles in the educational journals deploring the unprofessional character of unionization. They roused the teachers' prejudices, made effective appeals to their snobbery and played up the strike bogey. The campaign was greatly aided by the Boston police strike which took place about this time, and the open shop drive launched by employers' associations to counteract the rapid rise of labor organization in industry.

The climax of the campaign came in March 1920, five months after the Boston strike, when the affiliation of teachers with the labor movement was attacked at the annual meeting of the Department of Superintendence of the NEA, the real policy-determining board of the Association. Thereafter the opposition of the school authorities became universal.[63]

The growth of teachers' unions was an indication of tension between teachers and administrators and, as we have seen, was viewed with apprehension by the latter. In trying to retard the alarming increase of teacher unionism, school administrators turned again to industry, this time adopting the human relations approach to personnel problems. As a result, principals, superintendents and board members began to emphasize "teamwork," "participation" and "cooperation." Through the use of human relations, Lieberman observed, "Coercion has become more subtle, more refined." Consequently, ". . . it is difficult to locate the problem of coercion in a person who constantly preaches cooperation and participation."[64]

Even if administrators had been left completely on their own, the tremendous expansion and complexity of education would have given them plenty to do. As it was, public demands for economic efficiency and the need for "softer," more effective personnel practices pushed them into the direction taken earlier by business executives. Once there, school administrators had to justify their actions and, perhaps, even their existence.

THE PROGRESSIVE ERA

The school district which emerged after World War I was very different from its predecessors. The traditional system had been simple and undifferentiated. Even the largest districts had looked and behaved as if they were small. Increasing enrollment merely resulted in the addition of another segment similar to those already existing—another teacher, another classroom, or another school—but it did not bring about a more complex structure.

By the 1920s, however, even the smallest districts had taken on some of the characteristics of large, complex organizations. Especially notable was the growth of administration. For instance, in Middletown, during 1924 and 1925, the Lynds observed that the school was:

> ... adding fresh stories to its superstructure. If teaching is poor, supervisors are employed and "critic teachers" are added; in 1890 the only person in the entire school system who did not teach was the superintendent, while between superintendent and teacher today is a galaxy of principals, assistant principals, supervisors of special subjects, directors of vocational education and home economics, deans, attendance officers, and clerks, who do no teaching but are concerned in one way or another with keeping the system going; in 1924 the office of superintendent itself was bifurcated into a superintendent of schools and a business director.[65]

In the years that followed, administration became a still more prominent aspect of the schools, prompting the Lynds to comment, after their return to Middletown, about the "administrative horse" galloping off with the "educational cart."[66] This was not an isolated phenomenon. Administrative expansion was occuring across the nation, at a far more rapid rate than the increases of pupils or teachers. While student enrollment grew 16 percent between 1920 and 1950, the number of teachers rose 34 percent. During this same period, the number of principals increased 188 percent,[67] leading to additional complications. Although school administration came into being in response to certain problems, the new occupation, by its very existence, was itself the source of further problems. Along with their other concerns, school administrators were also trying to define their goals, establish their authority, enhance their security, and so forth.

At the same time the old pressures were continuing. By 1950 there were 3,500,000 more pupils than there had been in 1920,[68] and they were attending bigger schools in larger districts. During this thirty-year period, consolidation reduced the number of separate, independent school systems by more than half,[69] and two-thirds of the one-room schools closed down.[70] Public education became more complex in curricula, services and personnel, and problems of dealing with dissatisfied employees increased. Indeed, to the dismay of many administrators and board members, unions continued and grew stronger during this period. Although the actual percentage of teachers who belonged to the union remained small, rising from a little over one percent in 1920 to less than five percent by 1950, its rate of growth was almost ten times more rapid than that of the total number of teachers employed in the public schools.[71]

Such developments posed a number of problems for school administrators. Soaring enrollment was a prime example. Under the impact of rapidly increasing enrollment, other matters were subordinated to the housing and supervision of masses of pupils. Before everything else, there was the necessity of providing some place to put them and an adult who, if nothing else, would prevent them from running wild. Programs for gifted children, selection of supplementary materials, and revisions in curriculum became secondary considerations. The very concreteness of these problems produced by population pressures gave them precedence over other issues. Children might survive without knowledge of Latin or physics but they could not be left outside in the rain. As a result, a special type of knowledge was necessary for school personnel. Selecting locations for new schools, buying sites, arranging finances, hiring architects and building contractors, providing desks and chairs for the new classrooms—all of these required people with abilities unrelated to classroom teaching.

In addition to these problems there were other matters which demanded attention. As a school system grew into a large scale organization it encountered many problems common to non-educational structures of similar size and complexity. It had hundreds or thousands of employees and a budget of many millions of dollars. These, as well as educational issues, required attention so there came into being a number of roles, not directly connected with education, but concerned with meeting the day-to-day requirements characteristic of any large organization. Personnel had to be hired, bills paid, and buildings and equipment maintained.

In the face of such pressures many standard administrative procedures evolved. Along with principals, vice-principals, counselors, teachers and deans, school districts also employed special service men, coordinators, accountants and business managers as well as many secretaries and clerks. A modern high school might have two or three thousand pupils and more than a hundred teachers. Even when individual schools were much smaller, the large number of them within a given school system still created administrative difficulties. The resulting problems of coordination, supply and control required managerial rather than pedagogical skills. Buildings, books, grounds, supplies, custodians, secretaries, students and teachers were all segments of a larger totality.

Under such conditions education was only one of several elements which received attention.

The school had become a large, complex enterprise, with a number of administrative problems similar to those found in other types of organizations. Among these problems were those of demonstrating efficiency, bolstering managerial authority, enhancing control over personnel, reducing intra-staff tensions, and increasing employees' versatility. Progressive education made it easier for school administrators to cope with these problems. While its contribution in any one of these areas may have been minimal at times, its overall effect was to lighten the load of school management.

Functions of Progressive Education

The permissiveness sometimes ascribed to progressive education applied not only to pupils but to administrators as well. There no longer were strongly established goals of scholarship and academic excellence which might have hampered the school's attempts to cope with its managerial problems. The very broad objectives of progressive education virtually eliminated the possibility of obvious clashes between educational effectiveness and administrative expediency. Managerial actions which in traditional schools would have stood out clearly as being antagonistic to the school's official objectives now seemed, at worst, merely irrelevant. Consequently, human relations and economic criteria of efficiency, as well as other practices which might contribute to the management of large organizations, could be more easily brought into the school, simply because there was little to stand in their way.

Demonstrating Efficiency. In some organizations, the demonstration of efficiency is relatively easy. For example, a business which pays its stockholders high dividends may be considered to be well-managed. For public schools, however, the matter was not so simple. Confronted by the increasingly difficult educational problems emerging after the Civil War, attempts to prove competence in terms of academic achievement were doomed to failure. Nevertheless, some method of demonstrating efficiency was needed to justify continuing support for schools and their managers. Administrative practices used in the business world seemed to offer an answer, and the freedom of action provided by the broad, indefinite goals of progressive education facilitated the widespread adoption of these management procedures by the schools. The results were described by Callahan:

... the essence of the tragedy was in adopting values and practices indiscriminately and applying them with little or no consideration of educational values or purposes. It was not that some of the ideas from the business world might not have been used to advantage in educational administration, but that the wholesale adoption of the basic values, as well as the techniques of the business-industrial world, was a serious mistake in an institution whose primary purpose was the education of children.[72]

Callahan went on to suggest that the "tragedy" was not inherent in borrowing from business but rather in the manner in which these industrial concepts were applied:

It is possible that if educators had sought "the finest product at the lowest cost" — a dictum which is sometimes claimed to be a basic premise in American manufacturing — the results would not have been unfortunate. But the record shows that the emphasis was not at all on "producing the finest product" but on the "lowest cost." In all of the efforts which were made to demonstrate efficiency, it was not evidence of the excellence of the "product" which was presented, but data on per-pupil costs.[73]

Callahan concluded that this was primarily because school boards and the American people, when demanding efficiency, generally meant "lower costs" rather than "excellence of product." He stated, "This was so partly because of the difficulty of judging excellence."[74]

This difficulty in judging excellence was recognized at the time by school administrators themselves. The absence of precise standards for evaluation and the need for operational guidelines for routine decision making were mentioned, for example, by Frank Spaulding, superintendent of the Newton, Massachusetts, public schools. In his address to the 1913 annual meeting of the Department of Superintendence of the National Education Association, Spaulding began by saying:

Academic discussion of educational values is as futile as it is fascinating. Which is more valuable, a course in Latin or a course in machine shop? . . . There are, there can be, no permanent, no absolute and universal answers to such questions as these; but there are, and there must be, temporary, relative, and local assignments of value.[75]

The criteria for evaluation suggested by Spaulding were financial criteria. He felt that courses should be appraised in terms of their cost, and he pointed out that this was already being done, every day, by school administrators.

... so while we educational practitioners have been waiting on the educational theorist for an evaluation of the various subjects of actual or possible school curricula, we have been determining for our own schools definitely and minutely the relative values of every such subject. And we have done this, for the most part, without knowing it! The school administrator simply cannot avoid assigning educational values every time he determines the expenditure of a dollar.[76]

Spaulding then proceeded to describe the relative dollar values, or more precisely, the costs involved, in the various subjects taught in the Newton secondary schools. He reported that:

5.9 pupil recitations in Greek are of the same value as 23.8 pupil recitations in French; that 12 pupil recitations in science are equivalent in value to 19.2 pupil recitations in English, and that it takes 41.7 pupil recitations in vocal music to equal the value of 13.9 pupil recitations in art.[77]

Spaulding went on to assert that these costs should determine the curriculum; the values assigned to the various subjects should be monetary values rather than educational ones. Equating "local considerations" with "per-pupil costs" and "pupil-recitation costs," he stated:

Greater wisdom in these assignments will come, not by reference to any supposedly fixed and inherent values in these subjects themselves, but from a study of local conditions and needs. I know nothing about the absolute value of a recitation in Greek as compared with a recitation in French or English. I am convinced, however, by very concrete and quite local considerations, that when the obligations of the present year expire, we ought to purchase no more Greek instruction at the rate of 5.9 pupil recitations per dollar. The price must go down, or we shall invest in something else.[78]

In view of the pressures for economy, it would have been difficult, even under the most favorable circumstances, to resist entirely the appraisal of education in financial terms. As it was, the absence of clear-cut educational goals, the elimination of concrete criteria which had formerly been provided by traditional pedagogy, meant that there was little to stand in the way of a starkly economic approach to education. In fact, the monetary aspects of public schools were about the only ones left, so that, forced to justify and demonstrate their "efficiency" in statistical terms, school administrators had little choice but to grasp at the concrete figures provided by budgets and to defend their competence in terms of dollars and cents. Progressive education, by making evaluation of education more difficult, removed a major bulwark which might have resisted the adoption of primarily financial criteria for instructional proficiency.

A second way in which progressive education facilitated the adoption of "efficient" methods of plant management was by promoting pupils on the basis of social or chronological age rather than academic achievement. In addition to alleviating disciplinary problems, the "no failure" policy of promoting all students, regardless of their scholastic success, had economic advantages as well.

For example, in 1909 Leon Ayres published the book *Laggards in Our Schools.* Using data from school records and government agencies, Ayres reported that the schools were filled with retarded children and that most students dropped out before finishing the eighth grade. By "retarded" children Ayres meant pupils who were over-age for their grade, regardless of how well they were doing in their work. On the average, about 33 percent of all pupils in public schools were below their proper grade, but this varied from a low of only 7 percent in Medford, Massachusetts, to 75 percent of the Negro children in Memphis, Tennessee. To Ayres, the figures indicated, ". . . for every child who is making more than normally rapid progress, there are from eight to ten children making abnormally slow progress."[79]

Ayres went on to stress the economic inefficiency of such retardation. He rated fifty-eight school systems according to their "efficiency," and reported that the most efficient school system was spending $24,033 —or 6.5 percent of its annual budget—on repeaters. In contrast, the least efficient school system he found was spending $120,584—or 30.3 percent—on these retarded pupils.[80]

Challenges of this sort were taken very seriously by school administrators. A number of superintendents applied Ayres' principles to their own schools. The head of the Cleveland school system stated that between one-tenth and one-eighth of his education budget was spent on repeaters, and he added, ". . . when the school is tested for efficiency by its ability to carry children through its course on time it shows great waste." However, this condition was being remedied through the use of double promotions. By this process, ". . . the money cost of the repeater is offset by the acceleration of the stronger pupils." As a result, ". . . the school system practically checked its own losses and created a balanced sheet, the number of children who lost time being equalled by the number who gained time."[81] In a similar vein, the Johnstown, Pennsylvania, Superintendent reported that more than nine hundred pupils had been double-promoted in 1916 and 1917 with resultant savings of $16,092.[82]

In 1913 Ayres commented further on the results of translating promotion rates into financial terms:

> The importance of small changes in promotion rates may be best
> illustrated by figuring the results of a change of one percent, for

example from 80 per cent to 81 per cent, in the promotion rate in the elementary schools of a small city. Let us suppose that 1,000 children enter the elementary schools each year, the annual per capita cost for schooling is $40, and the buildings, grounds, and equipment have a value of $200 per child.

Under these conditions, the change in the promotion rate from 80 per cent to 81 per cent will have the following results: The time saved by each 1,000 children if they complete the elementary course will amount to 130 years of schooling which means a saving of $5,200 annually. The plant required to accommodate the children will be decreased by about $25,600 worth, and the salaries of four teachers will be saved. The number of failures among the 1,000 children during eight years of school life will be reduced by 70, while the number of children failing during that period will be lessened by 19. The number of overage children in the grades will be reduced by 220. These figures strikingly illustrate the importance of even the smallest changes in promotion rates.[83]

Callahan concluded that this economic motivation to promote students, along with rating the efficiency of teachers on the basis of promotions, were two potent forces which encouraged the practice of passing students regardless of educational considerations.[84] Progressive education facilitated this practice by condemning traditional policies of failure and retention on the grounds of their deleterious effects upon the pupil. Automatic promotion not only forestalled serious discipline problems, as noted in an earlier chapter, but also offered an economic incentive to cost-conscious administrators, giving them a way to demonstrate their competence in school management. Thus we have another instance in which progressive pedagogical philosophy provided a justification for procedures which were desirable for non-educational reasons.

Administrative Authority. Progressive education strengthened administrators' authority in several ways. One important area in which this occurred was that of rating teachers. Surprising as it may seem, the de-emphasizing of grades has bolstered the school administrator's position, giving him a major responsibility which might otherwise be a simple clerical task. Judging teachers by the measured academic performance of their pupils would reduce evaluation to a routine which anyone could perform merely by examining the statistics. Under such conditions, it would be more difficult to justify the principal's claim that managerial expertise, professional judgment, and graduate work in administration were necessary. As it is, teachers are rated on a number of things, and the administrator has considerable opportunity for exercising his discretion.

Blau's study of a state employment agency supports this contention. He found that supervisors did not want to evaluate their subordinates primarily on the basis of their statistical performance records:

> This would not only make the job of supervisor less interesting for him, but also undermine his authority. The fact that a civil service rating of officials depends on the judgment of their supervisor, which means that it is not directly determined by quantitative indices, is a prerequisite of supervisory authority. . . . In opposing the use of these indices for evaluation, supervisors were opposing these threats to their authority.[85]

There is a second, more fundamental way in which progressive education strengthened the school administrator's authority. By reducing the importance of subject matter and by emphasizing human relations, progressive education alleviated the problem of legitimizing authority over unfamiliar specializiations. The authority of the modern administrator depends largely on his technical competence.

> He is held to have a right to his authority because it is believed that he possesses certain expert skills or knowledge. Modern administrators are regarded as proper incumbents of office on the basis of what they know about the organization, or on the basis of their possession of technical skills.[86]

However, the administrator whose authority rests on his knowledge or on his technical skills may encounter difficulties when he tries to control subordinates whose technical specialties are different from his own. This has become a very common problem. Because modern organizations have a highly specialized division of labor, administrators may know little about the various specialties under their jurisdiction. As a result, an administrator's commands are sometimes felt by his subordinates to be illegitimate because he lacks the relevant technical skills which would justify his authority.[87]

There are two major bases for legitimating authority in modern organizations: incumbency in office, and technical skill and experience. If an administrator can establish an effective claim to both of these, there is no problem. Frequently, however, he may have only the first of these bases for legitimation. Then employees may balk at his commands because they feel that they themselves are specialists in their fields and therefore are just as competent as the administrator in deciding what the best procedures are. Gouldner concludes, "One of the deepest tensions in modern organization often derives from the divergence of these two bases of authority."[88]

The public school, like other organizations, is also confronted with this problem. In fact, the problem became more acute, through the years, as the curriculum became more diversified. Progressive education has lessened the severity of this situation in two ways. First, its emphasis upon human relations strengthened the authority of the administrator. Progressive education's advocacy of social skills helped to legitimize the establishment of the separate field of school administration. Proficiency in this new science, it was claimed, qualified its practitioners to exercise authority over school personnel. This solution to the problem of legitimacy is also being used in industry. Here, too, administration is being defined as a separate field, specializing in problems of human relations. It has led to the emergence of the new field of administrative science, drawing heavily upon the social sciences for its theoretical foundations. Colleges of business administration are requiring their students to take courses in sociology, psychology, and political science in an attempt to establish management as a specialty, distinct from the operations which are performed by the rank and file workers of the organization.[89]

Another way in which the administrator's legitimacy may be enhanced is by reducing the status of the specialists under him. The modern school administrator may not be an expert in subject matter, but neither are most of his subordinates. Progressive education's depreciation of traditional academic knowledge has meant that there are fewer teachers in a position to claim that they know more than their superiors. As scholarship became secondary to pupils' overall development, the expert in a subject area became less important and less able to challenge his superiors' authority. And, even if he did, he could be brushed aside with a comment such as: "We're not here to cram facts into kids' skulls — schools today have other things to do." Thus, to a considerable degree, the problem of authority over unfamiliar specializations was resolved by eliminating the specialist and his specialties.

Controlling Personnel. Progressive education's deemphasis of specialists, in addition to enhancing authority over teachers, was administratively helpful in other ways. For example, there is the problem of loyalty. As Barnard, Simon and others have observed, every organization requires its members to have some loyalty to it.[90] Even in the most highly regimented, strictly supervised situations, subordinates may undermine the efficiency of an organization by putting forth less than their maximum effort. Administration becomes much easier when there is some willingness of subordinates to perform according to the expectations of their supervisors. But there the specialist may pose a problem.[91]

The specialist's orientation, to a considerable degree, extends beyond his employing organization. He is concerned with developments
in his field, regardless of the particular agency or even the nation in
which they happen to occur. Furthermore, since there may be few, if
any other, experts in his field within the organization that employs him,
he must look elsewhere for professional stimulation and for competent
evaluation of his performance. This orientation toward outsiders leads
the specialist to resist pressures for "results" coming from his superiors,
and makes him less responsive to their control. To the degree that he
is linked with the outside, the specialist is less likely to be regarded as
a "company man" or "organization man," completely loyal to his employing organization.[92]

To put it another way, this is the common organizational problem
of *locals* and *cosmopolitans*. These terms have been used to differentiate
between people whose loyalties are primarily toward the organization
in which they are employed, in contrast to those who are committed
to their professions. Locals

> . . . are those who seek to fortify their organizational security by
> building up their position within it, rather than within their pro-
> fession; they are responsive to those within their employing organi-
> zation and are more highly committed to it than to their professional
> role.[93]

This problem can be observed in the schools. A high school mathematics teacher who is interested in and committed to mathematics, who
reads journals in that field and belongs to an association for mathema-
ticians, might be less inclined to accept suggestions about teaching from
the principal, perhaps a physical education or speech major, than would
another teacher whose prime concern was with pupils rather than with
subject matter.

By reducing the importance of specialists in the various subject
matter fields, progressive education facilitated the recruitment of teachers who were "locals" rather than "cosmopolitans." These teachers had
a relatively low interest in any particular subject. They tended to be
more concerned with teaching children than with teaching mathematics
or French. Their orientations were toward the particular school district
in which they were employed. Their career line lay within this district;
it was the universe within which they sought promotion, recognition,
security, or more desirable assignments. Consequently they were likely
to be receptive to the wishes of their administrators and, whether by
intent or by necessity, to demonstrate some loyalty to the district and
to its management.

A second way in which progressive education facilitated control was through human relations. Techniques comparable to those used for pacifying pupils could also be employed for manipulating teachers. Methods of democratic classroom management removed the sharp edge from administrators' commands, softening them to "requests" or "suggestions" offered by a "friend" who had his "colleagues'" interests at heart. Principals trained to approach each pupil as a worthwhile individual were in a good position to handle teachers the same way.

This made it easier for the administrator to form a direct, personal relationship with each member of his staff, thereby reducing the chances that resentful subordinates would join together in opposition against him, as they might against an aloof, impersonal superior. Progressive education made it a simple matter for school administrators to follow the advice given to business leaders by the *American Management Review:* "Treat workers as human beings. Show your interest in their personal success and welfare."[94]

Minimizing Staff Conflict. Progressive education removed a potential source of intrastaff tension. The evaluation of teachers on the basis of their pupils' numerical grades might lead to disruptive competition among teachers. This, too, was observed by Blau in the employment agency. When workers competed with each other, cordial relations and morale were disrupted. As one employee stated: "The worst thing about these records is that they create competition between interviewers to an extent that is disgusting."[95]

Cooperation is a prominent theme among public school personnel. Administrators often remind their teachers, "We are all part of the same team," and teachers themselves are inclined to feel that cooperation is important. There are a couple of reasons why this would be so. In a potentially explosive situation, where the basic work problem is control over non-voluntary clientele, teachers and administrators have a real, immediate self-interest in maintaining a united front against the students, with whom they are in close, continuous contact throughout the day. A comparable situation exists with respect to the school staff and the public, although here the potential dangers of disunity are less immediate. As we shall see in the next chapter, the school has relatively little autonomy and is probably more vulnerable than most organizations to intrusion into its affairs. Conflict within the school might attract unwanted public attention and interference. Therefore, it is in the interests of school personnel to maintain at least a modicum of cooperation with each other. This cooperation could be undermined by an excessive emphasis upon numerical indicators of pupil performance, which would pit one teacher against another in frantic efforts to present the best picture of herself.

Teachers' Versatility. Progressive education increased teachers' versatility in at least two ways. First, de-emphasis on grades reduced the possibility that teachers might concentrate on certain limited goals at the expense of other activities. The more concerned teachers are with helping their pupils to get high grades, the more they would resist other assignments which might divert them from this task, even though these other assignments might be deemed important by administrators. Public school teachers perform many tasks which, in one way or another, contribute to the operation of the school, but which have little direct bearing upon classroom teaching. In fact, an N.E.A. survey indicated that extra duties, such as watching halls, collecting bank money, patrolling the cafeteria, and participating in PTA programs, add, on the average, an extra day to the teacher's work week.[96] Teachers would be more inclined to object to such duties if they knew they would be praised or reprimanded, promoted or fired, on the basis of their pupils' academic scores.

Again Blau found a comparable situation in the employment agency. Emphasis upon performance records led employees to concentrate upon certain activities while ignoring others. In attempting to improve their records by servicing as many clients as possible, employees postponed working on a lengthy case in order to finish a large number of short ones. In other instances, to maximize their records, they might treat a client who had been laid off only temporarily as if he were seeking a new permanent job; when he returned to his original position after a few days the employment counselor would take the credit for finding him a job, even though this had not actually happened.[97] The possibility that similar situations would occur in public schools has been lessened by reducing the former emphasis upon pupils' grades.

Secondly, teachers' versatility was enhanced not simply by de-emphasizing grades but also by minimizing the importance of subject matter itself.

In reducing the differences between courses and by providing universal methods of teaching them, progressive education supplied nonspecialized teachers who were more readily interchangeable than the traditional specialist would have been. Having a generalized method of dealing with pupils rather than specific knowledge of a particular subject, teachers could be more easily shifted from football to physics, from economics to English.

This interchangeability alleviated the often perplexing problem of matching the supply of teachers to the fluctuating demand for specific classes. Because American public schools cannot restrict their enrollment, they have difficulty controlling the number of classes which will be given in any one subject from year to year. If an additional section is needed for freshman English while the enrollment in home economics or typing is below that of last year, the easiest solution, from an administrative standpoint, would be to assign the home economics instructor ✓ to teach the English class. This would eliminate the necessity of hiring another teacher just for that one class. Similarly, at the elementary level, a sixth-grade teacher could be transferred to a third grade if the need arose.

Such interchangeability is also useful during short term emergencies, where a teacher is absent for a few days. Since subject matter under progressive education is relatively undifferentiated it is easier to obtain a substitute teacher. In fact, the principal himself could handle many courses without much difficulty. By the use of generalized methods he could lead a discussion, for example, even though he might know little about the particular subject involved.

Another administrative advantage of interchangeability might be its use in controlling teachers. Even progressive teachers, in spite of their versatility, are likely to feel more at home in certain courses than in others, and most have preferences for particular grade levels. The possibility of being transferred to an undesired subject, grade or school provides some restraint upon rebellious impulses of classroom teachers. A sixth-grade teacher who has never instructed younger children is not likely to relish the idea of being shifted to a second grade. We need not think that all teachers have been on the verge of revolt, nor that many administrators have threatened teachers with unwanted assignments. Nevertheless, both teacher and administrator, subordinate and superior are aware of this possibility. The prospect of having to prepare for a variety of classes, or for courses different from those to which one is accustomed, or, at worst, being transferred to a "difficult" school in the ghetto, may encourage cooperation with the administration.

CONCLUSION

The school's responses to growth and complexity were influenced by the managerial practices of American industry, which stressed economic efficiency and human relations.[98] These responses were facilitated by progressive education. It gave the school an opportunity to redefine its goals in terms which would provide greater flexibility and security for the organization and also for its managers. In addition, it enabled administrators to cope with problems of efficiency, authority, control, conflict and versatility.

These problems and the methods of handling them are, as we have seen, by no means restricted to public schools but are also found in other kinds of complex organizations. For example, there is widespread concern over employees' loyalty to their organization. William H. Whyte's book on the *Organization Man*[99] discussed industry's efforts to strengthen the loyalty of managers to the enterprise in which they are working. As the Gouldners observe, the attempt to produce organization men is an effort to produce a new elite of loyal "locals," whose authority is legitimated in terms of deliberately cultivated human relations skills. It is a countermovement against the growth of specialized experts and technicians who may be more committed to their profession than to their corporations.[100]

Nor are these administrative problems unique to this country. Tensions between an organization's need for loyalty and its need for special expertise have been noted even in communist nations. This tension is present in the periodic Russian campaigns against "cosmopolitanism," in the conflicts between politically trustworthy army commissars and professional military men. The early Soviet purges were directed against engineers and technicians,[101] and more recent upheavals in China appear to be, at least in part, an attempt to use loyal youths to chastise "revisionist" specialists and bureaucrats in industry, education and even the Communist party.

Progressive education may be viewed, in part, as the public school's version of a more general administrative response to problems which plague many kinds of complex organizations.

REFERENCES

[1]Dahlke, *Values in Culture and Classroom,* pp. 30-31.

[2]Selznick, *Leadership in Administration,* p. 148.

[3]*Report of the Commissioner of Education . . . for the Year 1870,* p. 559.

[4]Cubberly, *Public Education,* rev. ed., p. 166.

[5]Cubberly, *Public School Administration,* rev. ed., p. 10.

[6]*Ibid.*

[7]U.S. Bureau of the Census, *Historical Statistics . . .,* p. 14.

[8]Cubberly, *Public Education,* rev. ed., p. 316.

[9]*Ibid.,* pp. 318-19; Cubberly, *Public School Administration,* rev. ed., p. 57.

[10]In 1870, only one-third to one-fourth of school-age children in major cities were actually attending school (*Report of the Commissioner of Education . . . for the Year 1870,* p. 559).

[11]Cubberly, *Public Education*, rev. ed., p. 165.

[12]The first public high school was established in Boston, in 1821. In 1850 there were fifty-five public high schools, but half of these were in Massachusetts, and many were small (Cubberly, *Public Education*, p. 259). For example, the enrollment of St. Louis's high school in its first year, 1853, was seventy-two pupils. Chicago's public high school in 1859, its fourth year, had 286 (Paul R. Pierce, *The Origin and Development of the Public School Principalship*, p. 2).

[13]Cubberly, *Public Education*, rev. ed., p. 139.

[14]Johnson, *Old Time Schools*, p. 103.

[15]*Ibid.*, p. 104.

[16]Parker, *History of Modern Elementary Education*, pp. 138-39; Pierce, *Public School Principalship*, p. 8; Butts and Cremin, *History of Education*, p. 275.

[17]Parker, *History of Modern Elementary Education*, p. 87; Pierce, *Public School Principalship*, p. 8.

[18]Pierce, *Public School Principalship*, pp. 8-9.

[19]Cubberly, *Public School Administration*, rev. ed., p. 58.

[20]According to an early account, the duties of the superintendent in Jersey City were, ". . . performed, if at all, in a perfunctory manner, and with no public expectation that thought or time would be put into the service" (Boone, *Education in the United States*, p. 111).

[21]Pierce, *Public School Principalship*, p. 1.

[22]*Report of the Commissioner of Education . . . for the Year 1870*, p. 559.

[23]*Ibid.*, pp. 432, 434, 559.

[24]*Ibid.*, p. 436.

[25]*Ibid.*, pp. 272-73, 559.

[26]Cubberly, *Public School Administration*, rev. ed., p. 59.

[27]U.S. Bureau of Education, *Biennial Survey of Education 1918-20*, pp. 126-27. This figure included smaller towns than did the earlier figures. It is doubtful, however, that this would grossly affect the comparisons, because superintendents were first hired in larger districts and eventually came to be used in much smaller systems.

[28]*Ibid.*, p. 126-27.

[29]*Ibid.*, p. 35.

[30]*Ibid.*, p. 159.

[31]*Ibid.*, p. 117.

[32]*Ibid.*

[33]Cubberly, *Public Education*, rev. ed., p. 263-64.

[34]U.S. Bureau of the Census, *Historical Statistics . . .*, p. 207.

[35]Figures on the number of school districts are elusive. The 1920 estimate is Cremin's (*Transformation of the School*, p. 275). Good reported that 187,951 districts existed in 1922 (*A History of American Education*, p. 571).

[36]Cubberly, *Public Education*, 1st. ed., p. 470.

[37]Bendix, *Work and Authority in Industry*, p. 228.

[38]*Ibid.*, p. 302.

[39]*Ibid.*, p. 267.

[40]Callahan, *Education and the Cult of Efficiency*, pp. 2-3.

[41]*Ibid.*, p. 6.

[42]*Ibid.*

[43]*Ibid.*

[44]*Ibid.*, p. 48.

[45]*Ibid.*, pp. 48-49.

[46]*Ibid.*, p. 50.

[47]*Ibid.*

[48]U.S. Bureau of the Census, *Historical Statistics . . .*, p. 98.

[49]The number of workers involved was not reported after 1905 (*Ibid.*).

[50]Bendix, *Work and Authority*, p. 265.

[51]*Ibid.*, p. 294.

[52]*Ibid.*

[53]*Ibid.*, p. 301.

[54]*Ibid.*, p. 302.

[55]*Ibid.*

[56]*Ibid.*, p. 303.

[57]*Ibid.*, p. 304.

[58]Callahan, *Education and the Cult of Efficiency*, p. 7.

[59]Lieberman, *Education as a Profession*, p. 261; Butts and Cremin, *History of Education*, p. 456.

[60]Butts and Cremin, *History of Education*, p. 289.

[61]Lieberman, *Education as a Profession*, p. 297.

[62]*Ibid.*, pp. 298-302.

[63]Spero, *Government As Employer*, pp. 314-15, quoted in Lieberman, *Education as a Profession*, pp. 301-02.

[64]Lieberman, *Education as a Profession*, p. 487. The precise moment at which this approach appeared in the schools is uncertain. On the basis of its development in industry, however, we could guess that it probably emerged during the 1920s. That it was well-established by the mid-fifties is indicated by Lieberman's observation: "Currently there is an effort to soften the impact of this hierarchical structure in education by an emphasis on human relations" (*Ibid.*, p. 486).

[65]Robert S. and Helen Merrill Lynd, *Middletown*, p. 210.

[66]Robert S. and Helen Merrill Lynd, *Middletown in Transition*, pp. 205-06.

[67]U.S. Bureau of the Census, *Historical Statistics . . .*, p. 208.

[68]*Ibid.*, p. 207.

[69]*Ibid.*, p. 208.

[70]*Ibid.*

[71]*Ibid.*; Lieberman, *Education as a Profession*, p. 302.

[72]Callahan, *Education and the Cult of Efficiency*, p. 244.

[73]*Ibid.*

[74]*Ibid.*

[75]*Ibid.*, p. 72.

[76]*Ibid.*

[77]*Ibid.*, p. 73.

[78]*Ibid.*

[79]*Ibid.*, p. 15.

[80]*Ibid.*, pp. 16-17.

[81]*Ibid.*, pp. 168-69.

[82]*Ibid.*, p. 169.

[83]*Ibid.*, p. 168.

[84]*Ibid.*

[85]Blau, *The Dynamics of Bureaucracy*, quoted in Alvin and Helen Gouldner, *Modern Sociology*, p. 370.

[86]Alvin and Helen Gouldner, *Modern Sociology*, pp. 413-14.

[87]*Ibid.*, p. 414.

[88]*Ibid.*, pp. 414-15.

[89]*Ibid.*, p. 415.

[90]*Ibid.*, p. 416.

[91]*Ibid.*

[92]*Ibid.*

[93]*Ibid.*

[94]Bendix, *Work and Authority,* p. 265.

[95]Blau, in Alvin and Helen Gouldner, *Modern Sociology*, p. 372.

[96]National Education Association, Research Division, *The American Public School Teacher 1960-1961*, Research Monograph 1963-M2, p. 56.

[97]Blau, in Alvin and Helen Gouldner, *Modern Sociology*, p. 372. Dalton's *Men Who Manage* describes some unanticipated consequences of emphasis on costs in a manufacturing plant.

[98]An even more basic question regarding the rapid rise of school administration between 1870 and 1920 merits further study: Were full-time non-teaching administrators solely an inevitable consequence of the schools' increasing size and complexity, or were they also partially a response to the example set by American business, where increasing proportions of personnel were neither owners nor production workers, but rather salaried managers?

[99]Whyte, *The Organization Man.*

[100]Alvin and Helen Gouldner, *Modern Sociology*, p. 417.

[101]*Ibid.*

five

THE PROBLEM OF
AUTONOMY

LOCAL CONTROL OF PUBLIC SCHOOLS IS A FAMILIAR FEATURE OF AMER-
ican education. Along with its advantages, however, local control poses
a serious problem for the actual operation of a school system. Because
public schools are largely governed and financed by the community in
which they are located, they have less autonomy than many other types
of organizations. At the same time, they have problems with which laymen are unable or unwilling to cope.

The school must rely upon local sources for most of its financial
support. Until very recently, the federal government has contributed little money to the actual operation of the public schools. In the 1949-50
school year, less than three percent of the total revenue of American
public schools came from the federal level. Contributions from the
county level were also very low, with only six percent coming from this
source. The states contributed forty percent, leaving the local school
districts to raise fifty-one percent of their income within their own
community.[1]

But, the fact that the school needs money does not by any means
guarantee that the community will supply it. Many requests for funds
are rejected at the polls, whether the proposals involve the sale of bonds
or increases in the tax rate. The latter is particularly apt to be a sensitive
issue, posing a conflict of interests between the school and the more
influential segments of the community. School taxes are generally levied
in the form of property taxes. People who own property are more likely
than other citizens to vote; among other things they have a direct

financial stake in the outcome of these elections. Furthermore, along with their greater inclination to go to the polls, property owners are more likely to have political and economic power in the community, and therefore are in a position to put pressure upon the school and its personnel. Whether they actually do so in a given instance is not as important as the fact that they have the capacity to make things easier or more difficult if they should so desire. Consequently, the school is likely to be especially concerned with maintaining good relations with property owners and therefore tries not to antagonize them.

Even when there is little active opposition to a particular proposal for revenue, general apathy may result in failure to vote for increased taxes or bond elections. Therefore the school must persuade the voters that it is necessary to take additional money out of their pockets, and to do this it must create an atmosphere in which such a process will be more favorably received.[2]

In a similar way, local citizens influence many aspects of policy and decision making. Full formal control of the school is invested in the board of education, which is chosen by the local electorate. The board members are laymen who exercise the practically complete power delegated to them by the state department of education. The local board usually appoints the superintendent and he is responsible to it. He in turn directs the daily decisions regarding personnel, curriculum, expenditures, etc., all of which are at least theoretically dependent upon the board's approval. Although the state department of education has some power over the schools, it usually does not take an active part in the operation of each local district. However, it may regulate the ultimate legal limits of the board's actions. The county superintendent has very little voice in local affairs. He acts primarily in an advisory capacity, and may also assist the districts in record-keeping, consultation on curriculum, maintaining a library of audio-visual materials, and so forth. In general, then, the actual operation of the schools is left to the local districts.

At first glance, this might appear to give the schools a great deal of freedom. However, the situation is not this simple. If we think of the public school as a formal organization consisting of paid employees and the buildings in which they work, we realize that it has relatively little insulation against community pressures. The most obvious rein upon it is the publicly selected board which governs it. Although usually delegating specific aspects of curriculum or personnel to school employees, the board does have the power to intervene in any issue it chooses. This power may seldom be exercised, but school personnel are concerned about the possibility that it might be, and therefore they try to avoid action which might be questioned by board members. This general desire of most employees to avoid scrutiny by suspicious superiors is based partly on the fact that work seems to proceed more comfortably when no one is looking over their shoulders. Added to this, however, is the spectre of job insecurity. While increasing numbers of classroom teachers are protected by tenure, especially in larger districts, this is not true of administrators. Superintendents and principals lack the protection of tenure, and retain their administrative posts only by the sufferance of the governing board. Firing or demotion may not be an everyday occurrence but it happens often enough to discourage administrators from antagonizing influential members of the community who might put pressure on the board to have them removed or, less dramatically, might withhold their cooperation in some venture.

Another factor limiting the school's autonomy is its visibility. Few other organizations are as completely open to public scrutiny. The school's basic worker, the teacher, performs in full view of several dozen members of the community who, although immature themselves, observe her hour after hour, week after week, month after month, and may report even the most trivial aspects of her appearance and behavior to their parents. Proximity is another factor; schools are conveniently located, so that they are more accessible than most other community agencies. It may be miles to the city hall but there is usually a school within walking distance of every home.

Finally, the school's autonomy is restricted still further by the tradition that public schools belong to the people. Although few laymen keep a close watch over the schools or participate actively in their affairs, many nevertheless feel they have the right to do so if they wish. This tradition has created a large public which is usually inert but which might be mobilized for action at any time either for or against the school and its personnel.

For reasons such as these the school's relationship to the community has become a major concern of school administrators. This chapter examines the emergence of this problem in the latter part of the nineteenth century, the school's response to the problem, and the ways in which these responses were facilitated by progressive education.

THE TRADITIONAL ERA

Once again we start with the fact that public schools in their present form were practically unknown during the traditional period. Consequently, the issue of autonomy did not really emerge until public schools financed largely by local taxation appeared around the time of the Civil War. Before that time there was no uniform system of public control and support; limited suffrage and practical realities minimized public participation in school elections, and the financial stake in the school was very, very small.

As previous chapters have indicated, most school districts in the traditional era consisted of one teacher in a single small building. There was no large staff of employees who would have a personal interest in the continued smooth operation of the school. There was little money invested in large buildings, grounds, supplies and equipment. Thus, the consequences of losing public support were minute. At the very worst, if the community became incensed at the teacher, he would be the only person harassed or in danger of being fired. If the district ran out of money, the small schoolhouse could easily be locked up for weeks, months or even years, with little cause for concern over major economic loss.

The present form of school financing is a relatively recent development, going back barely a century. Before that time a variety of methods had been tried. These included public and private sources, and ranged from endowments, donations and taxation to lotteries, fines and license fees. As the inadequacies of one method led to its replacement by another, school financing evolved slowly toward its present form. This evolution followed a typical pattern in thousands of independent districts. First, education was almost completely supported by churches, philanthropic associations and benevolent individuals. Next, the state assisted these private efforts with public revenues. Then the state permitted local communities to levy taxes for schools, often starting only with schools for the poor and later broadening this support to provide schools for everyone. Then this permissive legislation was followed by compulsory laws requiring minimum rates for partial taxation. The final step made the schools entirely free.[3]

These changing methods of finance were brought about by the difficulties encountered in attempting to support education by former means. For example, private endowments, which had traditionally been sources of money for education in Europe, were scarce and unreliable in the colonies. Another method favored for a time consisted of granting to private individuals the exclusive rights to develop and operate such public utilities as ferries and mills. In return for the franchise, a certain percentage of the profit was to be turned over to the community for education. This method also failed. In many instances the grantees gave up their privileges and the utility was taken over by the town government, which then had the burden not only of operating these community services but also of producing the revenues needed for maintaining other services, including schools.[4]

Another early source of money for education was the sale of federal land. The Northwest Ordinance, passed by Congress in 1787, reserved the sixteenth lot in each township to provide income for a local school, and two entire townships were set aside for the endowment of a university. Although much of the revenue received from these sales never reached the schools, this method did, at least, establish the policy of providing land grants for the support of educational institutions.[5]

In some areas, such as New York and New England, an intermediate step between private and completely public support was the rate bill of the early-nineteenth century. Under this system a teacher was employed by civil officials who were responsible for his salary. Part of the expenses were paid from public funds derived, for example, from the sale of public lands or levied as a local tax. The remainder was obtained by assessing parents according to the number of days their children attended school. This assessment was added to the parents' tax bill and was collected by the civil government just like other taxes.[6]

Although the rate bill system substantially lowered the direct costs of instruction born by parents, it did not completely eliminate them. Consequently there were many children still unable to afford schooling. Various plans were suggested to help them. One of these was the New York Law of 1812, which provided that all indigent children should be admitted to schools without charge, and the cost of their instruction was to be apportioned among the remaining parents who could pay. This attempted solution was resisted by two groups. Parents who had money objected to paying for the education of poor children. The poor did not want to be stigmatized as recipients of charity, and many kept their children out of school rather than having them labeled as paupers.[7]

For reasons such as these, most schools relied upon a blend of several sources of support. Many schools continued to seek private donations even after they were largely financed by public resources. Moreover, it often happened that public funds were managed by private individuals, acting as trustees for the original gifts that had started the school, rather than as government officials.[8]

In sum, during the traditional period there was a gradual shift, away from several sources of revenue towards a single source, away from dependence on individual support and philanthropy toward joint community financing.

Much that has just been said about revenue also applies to control. The present form of local non-sectarian control by a popularly elected board of laymen has become prevalent only within the last century or so. Prior to that time there was almost as much variation in the forms of control as in the methods of support. There were public schools under civil control, private schools operating on an endowment or supported by a religious organization, small private-venture schools in which one teacher tutored individuals or small groups of pupils—for example, the *dame school* conducted by women in their own homes for instruction in the three Rs—incorporated schools controlled by self-perpetuating boards of governors, and other types.[9]

Originally, American education operated under the authority of the king of England. This authority was subsequently delegated to stock companies, governors, proprietors, or colonial legislators. As colonial legislatures gradually became more powerful, they claimed the right to control education. After the Revolutionary War the various states retained this authority.

The beginnings of decentralization had been apparent in the seventeenth century when colonial legislatures had delegated the authority to conduct schools to the towns. In the eighteenth century the trend was continued as states began to permit towns to divide into smaller districts for the direct operation of their schools. This reflected conditions of life on the frontier, the expansion away from towns, and the conflict between urbanized commercial interests and the rural parts of the community. The latter group saw little need for the Latin education prevalent at that time and believed that, if schooling were necessary at all, the three Rs would be quite adequate. Moreover, it was difficult for the children of farmers and backwoodsmen to travel into town to attend school. Considerations such as these led to demands by rural people for more voice in the control of the schools.

In response to these demands various arrangements were tried. One proposed solution was the *moving school*. Under this system the teacher traveled from one part of town to another, giving instruction to children in the outlying districts for a short time each year. The teacher continued to be hired and supported by the town's selectmen. After a while, however, two problems of the moving school became apparent. In the first place, the moving teacher could spend very little time in any one district. Furthermore, the residents of these outlying districts had little control over the teacher. Consequently, a further innovation emerged in the form of the *divided school*. Under this arrangement a teacher was assigned to conduct a school in each of the several districts of the town, but these teachers remained under the control of the town authorities. However, not even these divided schools were considered satisfactory by the people living out in the country, and by the end of the eighteenth century a still further development had emerged: the *district school*.

Under this system each local district was delegated full control over its school, with the power to set up the school, build the schoolhouse, hire a teacher, choose the curriculum, set the length of the school year, and provide for its support. Thus evolved the extreme of decentralization which occurred during the second and third quarters of the nineteenth century.

Freedom from religious control also developed slowly during the traditional period. American schools were, to a considerable degree, religious in origin, and only gradually changed into non-sectarian institutions. In places where the civil government was primarily religious, the government would authorize schools, requiring them to be of a specific denomination. Where dissident religious groups arose, however, they claimed the right to conduct their own religious schools. Often this right was obtained only after persistent struggles against the opposition of established churches and ruling political groups. But these dissenting movements had three important effects. They led to the establishment of private education instead of, or in addition to, the religious public schools. Second, they weakened the public education which was controlled by civil government. Third, they contributed to the decline of those state educational systems which were devoted to specific denominations. Thus, religious diversity resulted in new patterns of control over education in the eighteenth century.

Still another factor which delayed the appearance of the present pattern of public control was a vestige of the European stratification system. Separate, distinct types of training were considered to be suitable for young people from the different social classes, with the result that a dual educational structure was almost universal in the American colonies. Elementary schools and apprenticeships were provided for the lower classes, while Latin grammar schools and colleges were designed for the upper strata. This dual-track system eventually began to weaken about the time of the Revolutionary War, as an emerging middle class demanded more practical training.

The response to this demand was the *academy*, a private school giving instruction in utilitarian subjects. Academies received charters from the civil government, became very popular, and provided a model after which public high schools of later years were patterned. Still further division of state control arose when, as noted earlier, farmers and other backwoods residents rejected both the Latin grammar school and the academies as unnecessary, believing that the three Rs were enough for their spartan needs. They resisted payment of taxes for schools which they thought would only benefit the children of coastal merchants and other town dwellers, and they wanted schools which would help them maintain their own national cultures and religions, or would otherwise satisfy their rustic requirements.

While these transitions from earlier forms of control to those more familiar to us today were fairly well under way by the beginning of the nineteenth century, this did not necessarily mean that the process in any given community was complete until after the Civil War. In many places the emergence of the present structure of control did not occur until the end of the traditional period. The schools of New York City provide an example of the relative recency of this development. In 1800 the population of the city was sixty thousand but it had no school facilities for the masses other than those provided by churches,[10] and even these charity schools were meagre. Until 1806 there were only five charity schools in the entire city and these were small enterprises reserved for the benefit of members of the religious sects which supported the schools.[11]

In 1806 a group of public-spirited citizens received a charter from the legislature to establish a Free School Society. After a fund-raising campaign, enough subscriptions were obtained to erect a two-story school building. In 1809 the Society opened a school for all poor children who were not provided for by any religious society.[12] For these and subsequent operations the society obtained money from various sources, including subscriptions, collections in the wards, special grants from the state legislature, grants from the New York City Council, membership fees in the Society, and the General Act of 1813, which granted the society a share of the public school fund.[13]

The Free School Society thus played a major part in establishing free public education in the city. It raised money, built schools, hired and trained teachers, and aroused the public to the point where free popular education came to be accepted as a general community obligation. During the next decades other school societies merged with the Free School Society. In 1842 the city established a public school department; to its elected board of education was delegated the responsibility for supervising these schools and others partially supported by public funds. Finally, in 1853, the Society turned its buildings and equipment over to the city's public school department. Thus, it was not until the middle of the century that the school system of the nation's largest city attained its present form, completely controlled by the public. Prior to that time, more than 600,000 children had been educated and 1,200 teachers trained by philanthropic associations.[14]

In sum, the present structure of control was not firmly established until the time of the Civil War. The two previous centuries had witnessed a shift from control by colonial or state legislatures to that exercised by the local community, from religious or private control to that which was non-sectarian and public.

Another factor which minimized problems of autonomy during the traditional period was restricted suffrage. The proportion of the population eligible to vote in those days was far smaller than it is now. Barriers of race, sex and economic status prevented large segments of the adult population from participating in elections. At the time of the American Revolution the franchise was so severely limited by various qualifications that only one-seventh of the free males were eligible to vote when Washington took office.[15]

In New York, for example, to vote for members of the assembly one had to be a freeholder of land or tenements valued at forty pounds free from all encumbrances.[16] In Pennsylvania the franchise was limited to those who owned at least fifty acres of land "well seated" with twelve acres "cleared," or other property worth at least fifty pounds. Virginia law required the voter to own at least fifty acres of land if there was no house on it, or twenty-five acres with a house at least twelve feet square; a town dweller had to own a plot of ground with a house at least twelve feet square.[17]

As a result of such limitations, relatively few people were entitled to vote, and many more who were qualified did not bother to do so. At times in Connecticut and Massachusetts, where about 16 percent of the population were eligible, only two percent took the trouble to go to the polls. Similar conditions existed elsewhere. Consequently it was only a small proportion, even of the freemen, who actually took part in this aspect of government.[18]

During the next decades economic qualifications for voting were liberalized, and had virtually disappeared by the middle of the nineteenth century. Nevertheless, the right to vote was still denied to large sections of the adult population, especially to women and Negroes. In 1824 only three percent of the American population voted in the presidential election. By 1860 the proportion had risen to thirteen percent and, in 1868, fifteen percent of the population voted for president.[19]

Of course, elections were not the whole story. Many if not most decisions in the day-to-day operation of the school did not come to a public vote. Moreover, there may have been individuals who were important in the local power structure who were not eligible to cast a ballot. Nevertheless, voting patterns give at least some indication of the power structure during traditional times, and suggest that the democratization of educational control is a relatively recent development.

For reasons such as these, autonomy did not become a problem during the traditional era. The financial stake in the school was small, there was no single uniform pattern of public control and support, and restricted suffrage and other practical realities of a predominantly pre-industrial society minimized public participation in school affairs.

THE TRANSITIONAL ERA

Most of the changes which affected the schools' autonomy after the Civil War are by now familiar to us and therefore require only passing mention here: the establishment of a free public school in every community in the nation; the tremendous growth of these schools from crude, small, simple structures to large permanent edifices representing, with their books, equipment, grounds and supplies, a sizeable financial investment; the emergence of full-time administrators—these have been covered in previous sections of this study. One new ingredient, the nature of public participation in school affairs, remains to be considered.

A larger percentage of the population was voting than in the early days of the nation. Fifteen percent of the American population cast ballots in the presidential election of 1872. The proportion climbed almost imperceptibly until the end of World War I, when the ratification of the Nineteenth Amendment in 1919 enfranchised women, doubling the possibility that laymen might be involved in school affairs. Immediately, the proportion of the population voting jumped from eighteen percent in the 1916 presidential election to twenty-five percent in 1920.[20] Certainly, then as now, not all of those eligible to vote actually did so, but other developments in the larger society increased the possibility of such participation.

As the bulk of the population climbed above the level of mere subsistence, more people were free to direct their attention and their energy to issues beyond the basic struggles of earning a living or raising a family. A higher level of job security and shorter working hours for men, and labor saving devices for women left more time for other, less urgent matters. The energies mobilized in the fight for female suffrage could, after the passage of the Nineteenth Amendment, be redirected to such issues as local schools and the education of their children. Rising literacy rates and technological advances in communication facilitated greater awareness of school affairs, while urbanization and improved transportation reduced the physical distance between the school and the public. It was no longer necessary to travel over dirt roads for an hour or more; now most people lived within a few blocks of a school.

Another factor which increased the possibility of public participation in school affairs was a consequence of the growing size of the nation: the shift of decision-making power away from the neighborhood, from the city and even from the state, to the national level. Many aspects of the individual's life were beyond his control. He had no voice in decisions about income taxes and utility rates, about war or peace. These matters were decided without consulting him. Whether or not these factors objectively outweighed the trends mentioned in the previous paragraph, they may have raised his expectations so that he felt increasingly frustrated by his lack of power.

However, there remained one area in which he could have a voice and that was the school. In most districts questions of school taxes and bonds are approved or rejected by the voters. While all citizens are eligible to participate in these elections, relatively few people usually do so. Consequently, questions of school taxes and bonds are approved or defeated, board members are selected or rejected, by the votes of only a few thousand people and often less. Thus, an aroused layman, if he desires, still can influence a public institution, not merely by casting his own ballot but also by organizing others for concerted action. The typically low rate of voter turnout gives him some chance of success. There is the possibility that usually apathetic citizens may be persuaded to vote, and a relatively small number may be sufficient to shift the balance in the direction he desires. Thus the public school was the one institution over which the average citizen could still hope to exert some influence. It became the most convenient target for people who, frustrated by any of the innumerable aspects of modern life, might express their resentment by voting against the school's requests.

THE PROGRESSIVE ERA

By 1920 the stage was set for the struggle for autonomy. Four ingredients were present: the schools had more at stake; there was a potential threat to their autonomy; there were employees free to concentrate upon the problem; and there was a method available for coping with the problem. The first point needs little elaboration. School districts had thousands, even millions, of dollars invested in buildings, grounds, equipment and supplies. Furthermore, staffs consisting of hundreds or even thousands of persons had been acquired. It would not be easy to discharge them all, if funds ran out, and then rebuild the staff when money was again available. Ample, continuous funding had become extremely important.

Secondly, there was a greater potential threat from the public than there had been before. More people were eligible to vote and were in a position to exert informal pressure on the school through personal contacts with board members, the superintendent, other administrators and teachers. This did not mean that all of those eligible would actually vote or that increased public participation in school affairs was necessarily on the negative side, going against the school's plans of action, but even the possibility that such opposition could occur was threatening enough to encourage precautionary measures.

Third, there were staff members available who could take such precautions. This was the result of the emergence of school administration as a full-time job, distinct from teaching. Freed from classroom duties, these principals, supervisors, superintendents and other personnel were able to concentrate directly upon the problem of community relations.

Fourth, there was a method available for doing this. The increasing importance of human relations and its widespread acceptance in the business world provided school administrators with a body of techniques which were applicable to this problem. The human relations principles which administrators were already beginning to use for controlling teachers were potentially of even greater value in dealing with the public. Teachers were legally recognized as subordinate to administrators' authority, but the school, in contrast, was supposed to be the servant of the public and was therefore expected to conform to its wishes.

To gain support for policies and financial needs and to minimize public interference, schools attempted to shape public opinion, placing considerable emphasis upon public relations. Techniques similar to those used in the business world were employed in attempting to create a favorable climate of opinion toward the school. The importance of public relations was suggested by the comments of California's former State Superintendent of Public Instruction. He declared:

> Creating good public relations is education's greatest problem in California. . . . If that can be solved, the other two main problems, the quality and quantity of education, will solve themselves.
>
> Without public support, public schools couldn't exist. With mediocre support, our programs will be strictly limited. With full public support, we can overcome the pressing problems of exploding student population and maintaining high educational standards.[21]

In Massachusetts a board member commented:

> It does not matter how good a job a superintendent is doing in other areas or how far the education his school system provides excels that of other systems, if he keeps it a secret from the public. . . . It seems to us that public relations is the one area of school administration in which the school superintendent cannot be less

than excellent and hope to provide his community with an educational system with which it will be satisfied.[22]

A textbook for administrators, in a section entitled "Community Planning a Must," observed:

> In many school systems, the growing interest in developing an effective public relations program is evolving from the administrator's experiences in unsuccessfully seeking the community support needed for new building programs or centralizations.[23]

As a result of these failures, the authors concluded:

> Planning the new school plant cannot be accomplished without the active cooperation of the entire community. The awareness of this need for cooperation has grown through first-hand experience rather than through tradition.[24]

Functions of Progressive Education

Progressive education facilitated the adoption of a public relations program in at least three ways. The new definition of the school's objectives stressed the necessity for close contact with the community. In addition, the everyday activities of the progressive school were easier to publicize than the austere traditional educational process would have been. Finally, the new role of school personnel emphasized skill in human relations rather than knowledge of subject matter. Thus progressive education legitimated the school's efforts to inform the public of its needs, the new curriculum supplied material better suited for publicity, and the personal qualities of modern teachers and administrators were more likely to make a favorable impression upon the public than would the dour schoolmaster or the prim old schoolmarm of the past.

Community Contact. Progressive education encouraged the use of public relations through a general belief that education involves *all* of youth's activities, and a more specific belief that these activities must be related to the local community. As Dewey put it, "The role of the community in making the schools vital is just as important as the role of the school itself."[25] Several aspects of progressive doctrine pointed to a closer relationship between the school and the community: the child's interests and needs should shape the curriculum; children learn by doing; children should learn to solve the same kinds of problems they will meet after their school days are over. All of these, progressives claimed, could best be achieved by working more closely with the local community.

Dewey wrote in 1915, "Schools all over the country are finding that the most direct way of vitalizing their work is through closer relations with local interests and occupations."[26] He noted that traditional education, which strived for uniformity, neglected "everything characteristic of the local environment," with the unfortunate consequence that children were not "really deeply touched." "In contrast, progressive efforts to bring the work into vital connection with pupils' experience began to vary school materials to meet the special needs and definite features of local life."[27]

Consequently Dewey observed: "A great many schools . . . are using the activities of the community as a means of enriching the curriculum, and using the school plant for a neighborhood center."[28]

More recent statements were offered by Anderson and Davies. In attempting to reach the desired ". . . stage of perfection in which all avenues of the entire school program are permeated by co-operative school-community action [the administrator] uses every opportunity to increase community involvement and to draw the school and the community into closer working relationships."[29] Another statement explicitly links education with public relations:

> The development of an educational program which merges the interests and efforts of the school and the community means enriched experiences for youth and adults and represents the "action" method of creating a community-centered school and an expanding program of public relations.[30]

The deep concern expressed by progressive educators for community relations is illustrated by the following passages from *Principles of Elementary Education,* an introductory textbook for college undergraduates:

> As a rule good schools exist only in communities in which the people are aware of their presence, have an interest in them, have frequent personal contacts with the schools, have reasonable familiarity with their program and policies, feel that their children are getting good schooling, and know the needs of the schools. These conditions can prevail only if the school and its teachers have many and varied contacts with the community and its adults.[31]

Warning against a one-way relationship, in which either the school personnel or the public dictates to the other, Otto explains that it:

> . . . should be a mutually cooperative, interacting relationship in which parents and teachers manifest a frank but friendly concern for the welfare of children and the development of a school program which serves children adequately in present day society. In such a friendly working relationship teachers and administrative

and supervisory officers will be able to give professional leadership to the lay groups.[32]

A successful relationship between school and community, according to Otto, requires the efforts of the superintendent and all the principals and supervisors, but the classroom teacher's role is so significant that administrators' efforts will be of little value unless the teacher also performs her part well. "The teacher is the key person, for she fills several strategic positions in community relations."[33] Her role in "Good day-by-day classroom teaching which includes skillful and sympathetic living and working with children is the most important element in community relations." In addition, teachers have ". . . other active roles in community relations."[34] To illustrate this point, Otto lists the following: teacher conferences with individual parents; visits by the teacher to children's homes; parents' visits to the classroom and observation of the activities there; programs produced by the pupils for their parents; unit-culminating activities; periodic reports to parents of children's progress in school; pupil participation in school and community improvement projects; utilization of adults and community agencies in the school program; and participation by teachers in the P.T.A.[35] Summing up, Otto remarks:

> It is essential that teachers recognize these as important expressions of school and community relations and that they should assume responsibility for making these contacts effective and constructive influences in building a wholesome relationship between the school and the community.[36]

The combination of concern for creating a favorable climate of opinion toward the school, along with progressive encouragement of close school-community ties, has resulted in extensive public relations programs. As an illustration we may examine a program proposed in Anderson and Davies' text for school administrators. They list "ten basic characteristics of operation on which a functional public relations program can be built."[37]

1. A community-wide educational program
2. "Open door" policy for use of school buildings
3. Relations with the press
4. Educational radio and television
5. House organ for professional staff
6. Reports to the community
7. School-parent relations

  8. Meetings for the community
  9. Lay advisory committees
 10. The staff

Because this program exemplifies current practices and objectives in the public schools, practices facilitated by progressive education's community-centered orientation, it will be worth examining in some detail.

The first channel is "A community-wide educational program" in which the school functions as a community center, offering an educational program for adults as well as children. "The administrator and his staff should create a feeling of warm, friendly hospitality that establishes the school as the educational, social and recreational center of the community." The school's role as a training institution for the young ". . . should be operationally secondary to its impact on the community as a vital 'nerve-center' for an extensive program of practical, diversified education."[38]

In addition, local individuals and groups "can serve as valuable community resources to the education program."[39] For example, the Philadelphia schools send their high school students to large business and industrial plants for occupational previews of job responsibilities and placement opportunities. Other schools maintain a file of names of local residents who are available to talk with interested pupils about their occupations and hobbies. Many communities provide school-work programs in which pupils gain actual experience in sales, industrial and office jobs. Thus, in progressive terminology, "Using the community as a giant laboratory for the school program and the school as an experimental center for community education enhances the total program of educational opportunity for children, youth, and adults."[40]

The second channel for building a functional public relations program is dedicating the school building to maximum use by the community. Anderson and Davies point out that many new schools provide special wings which can be used by the public for community activities during regular school hours without interfering with the pupils' regular program. "The gymnasium, the library, the auditorium, the home economics center, the classrooms, the shops, the laboratories, and the school grounds offer an appropriate environment along with the facilities and equipment that are needed by the total community for a comprehensive program of year-round education."[41] The authors describe a high school whose swimming pool is used throughout the year by almost every age group in the community. During the summer, the school bus carries residents of the district to and from the pool.[42]

A third channel for "interpreting the schools to the public" is the press. Newspapers can be very influential in ". . . clarifying school programs and policies and in developing public interest and support for local school needs." Anderson and Davies note that best results are achieved through an organized program. The school employee responsible for public relations should be in close contact with newspaper people. "Personal knowledge of the special interests of individual feature writers and direct contacts with these writers can lead to excellent feature coverage."[43] Particularly worth noting, in view of a point which will be taken up subsequently, is the following statement:

> Human interest stories that present achievements of individual pupils and accounts of unusual programs in the schools provide worthwhile copy for the press and are effective in attracting public interest and attention.

Also advocated are press conferences,[44] with prepared news releases and statistical information available for distribution at the conferences. "Professional personnel who are close to the operation of the project should be present to answer reporters' questions."[45]

Educational radio and television constitute a fourth channel. Student activities in fields such as ". . . the fine or industrial arts, demonstrations of good manners, and exploration of local resources can be brought to life for the community."[46]

The fifth channel is a house organ for professional staff. Although designed primarily for use within the school, copies of the house organ may also be distributed to influential people and organizations outside the schools.[47]

Reports to the community constitute a sixth channel of communication. A number of districts issue attractive booklets describing unusual school activities. In other instances, ". . . a small printed folder describing methods of teaching and learning used by the schools can be inserted into the envelope containing the pupil progress record." Even the superintendent's annual report ". . . offers an excellent opportunity to review progress and present needs based on the year's program."[48]

A seventh channel involves school-parent relations. The authors note that the Parent-Teacher Association is ". . . one of the most popular and widespread existing channels of the organized educational public relations program." Through P.T.A.s and parent study groups the administrator "creates increased understanding of children and of the aims, the operation and the needs of the school program." These groups offer opportunities for ". . . the development of friendly cooperation and interaction between teachers, administrators, and parents. . . ."[49]

Further recommendations involved specially planned informational meetings for the community when support is needed for reorganization or financing new buildings; lay advisory committees including influential citizens who will lend their support to improving the school program; and a carefully selected public relations staff led by a specialist in this field.[50]

Along with its positive aspects, there are other facets of public relations which, though not usually emphasized in textbooks, are nevertheless important. For example, the public relations officer can also be helpful in covering up the "seamier side" of school affairs. The creation of a favorable public image entails not only emphasis upon admirable accomplishments, but also the suppression of unfavorable matters which might bring discredit to the school. This is suggested by a newspaper report of a school board meeting:

> Fred Breen, a member of the Richmond Union High School board of trustees, says he knows of "three major scandals" kept out of the press by the district's coordinator of publications. Breen made the comment last night at a meeting of the trustees in justifying supervisory positions such as that of coordinator. "[The coordinator] handles many delicate functions which we don't always like to talk about . . ."
>
> He added:
>
> "It is necessary in such a large school district to have a person to handle public relations, to squelch rumors with facts, to represent teachers and the superintendent to the public and to help reporters correct errors that may occur."
>
> [The coordinator explained] "We've had several problems during the past 10 years I have been coordinator of publications." In one case involving bad checks, Blumenson said, he persuaded the merchants not to prosecute and the newspapers not to use the story if there was no prosecution. "One or two morals cases not involving children . . . were handled in somewhat the same manner," he said.[51]

These varied attempts to influence public attitudes were facilitated by the progressive definition of education as *a process involving the community as well as the school*. From a peripheral activity of questionable legitimacy, public relations became a vital adjunct to the instructional program.

Easily Publicized Activities. A second major contribution of progressive education involved the actual process of instruction itself. Progressive methods added action and concreteness to the curriculum, making school more interesting for the public as well as for the pupils. A traditional classroom, with students studying quietly at their desks, would not be very interesting to most people and would not provide much material for newspaper photographs or feature stories. Progressive education, however, with its emphasis upon learning by doing, upon shaping the curriculum in terms of the child's interests and needs, provided more tangible,

often spectacular, products. Ranging from science experiments and colorful bulletin boards to dramas and models of frontier villages, these
products lend themselves more readily to publicity releases. They are
more appealing to many people, and enable the school to keep itself in
the public eye to a degree which would not have been possible under the
austere methods of more traditional styles of education. Anderson and
Davies observed, "Sometimes a striking news item will result in a captioned picture in the press. And educational news of fundamental significance may lead to coverage in editorial form."[52] Progressive education
has increased the likelihood that this will occur.

An early example was provided in Dewey's *Schools of Tomorrow*.
Discussing "Education Through Industry," he wrote: "The problem of
general public-school education is not to train workers for a trade, but
to make use of the whole environment of the child in order to supply
motive and meaning to the work."[53]

He went on to describe a successful attempt to achieve this goal:

> In Gary this has been done more completely than in any other single
> place. Superintendent Wirt believes firmly in the value of muscular
> and sense training for children; and instead of arranging artificial
> exercises for the purpose, he gives children the same sort of things
> to do that occupy their parents and call for muscular skill and fine
> coordination in the business of everyday life. Every child in Gary,
> boy and girl, has before his eyes in school finely equipped work-
> shops, where he may, as soon as he is old enough, do his share of
> the actual work of running and keeping in order the school build-
> ings. All of the schools, except one small one where there are no
> high school pupils, have a lunchroom where the girls learn to cook
> and a sewing room where they learn to make their own clothes; a
> printing shop, and carpenter, electrical, machine, pattern, forging,
> and molding shops, where boys, and girls if they wish, can learn
> how most of the things they see about them every day are made.
> There are painting departments, and a metal working room, and
> also bookkeeping and stenography classes. The science laboratories
> help give the child some understanding of the principles and pro-
> cesses at work in the world in which he lives.[54]

Dewey's chapter on the Gary schools is illustrated by four photographs of student activities. Two of these photographs show boys working
in the shop, the third portrays boys and girls at the counter of a model
grocery store, complete with actual canned and packaged goods on the
shelves, and the fourth picture depicts girls "making their own clothes
in sewing class." The first three pictures were captioned "Learning mold-
ing and manufacturing school equipment," "Real work in a real shop

begins in the fifth grade," and, "Children are interested in the things they need to know about."[55]

Few aspects of the modern curriculum illustrate the potential publicity value of progressive education more than the annual Christmas pageant produced in so many American schools. Although commemorations of Christmas are not necessarily recent additions to the school's program, they attained more impressive dimensions during the progressive era. A great deal of time is devoted to their preparation, much if not all of which is done during regular school hours. Plans for the pageants are made weeks in advance, perhaps even before Thanksgiving. Scripts are drawn up, parts assigned, songs selected, costumes prepared, sets painted, chorus rehearsed, and so forth. These preparations are made not only in the rather obvious and traditional subjects like art and music, but costume-making is seen as training in dressmaking, script writing may be an exercise in English, and the "research" or theme for pageants entitled "Christmas in Europe" or "Our Latin American Neighbors Celebrate Christmas" can be subsumed under the heading of social studies. The pageant can be—and is—justified pedagogically as a "culminating activity," summarizing various "units" or "projects" engaged in during the previous months.

The Christmas pageant attracts many people who rarely, if ever, visit the school on other occasions. In fact, it rivals the drawing power of Open House Night during Public Schools Week and, in some ways, has even more public relations value. By commemorating Christmas, the school connects itself with one of the more firmly established traditions in our culture. Moreover, it is not just any tradition but a joyous tradition at that, and the halo of warmth and goodwill which accompanies it may, hopefully, also color the public's feelings toward the school. Furthermore, it is a group observance. In contrast to Open House, during which parents are dispersed throughout the entire school visiting their child's classrooms, the Christmas play brings everyone together into the same room. In addition to any beneficial results which might accrue through such expressions of community solidarity, it avoids the unpleasant feelings which sometimes arise when parents examine their child's regular work or talk with his teachers. The Christmas pageant allows even the most backward or mischievous pupils to appear, if only for one evening, as angels.

Progressive education, then, facilitated public relations by encouraging activities which were more tangible, colorful and dramatic than the drab, predominantly mental exercises of traditional times.

A further point is worth noting here. Schools were not merely trying to attract attention; they were also attempting to convey the idea that they were providing services to the community. As Callahan observed, the "service" idea was used to create favorable attitudes toward schools and especially toward their administrators. It was understandable that administrators, faced by a public which was often critical and almost always concerned with economy, would utilize the concept of a service station.[56] In 1925, for example, Superintendent McAndrew of the Chicago schools reported that 291 principals had displayed in their schools, where they were "likely to meet the eye of visitors," 2,024 "attractive placards" emphasizing the service theme. Among the slogans were statements like these:

> We are here for service.
>
> America's service station, a public school.
>
> We want to please the public. Help us.
>
> To the public: This school desires to serve you. The principal will be glad to receive your comments.
>
> Our motto is service. The principal desires your comments.[57]

Superintendent McAndrew reported that, under his leadership, the number of "services" performed by students during *Clean Up Week* increased from 363,672 in 1923 (the year before his appointment) to 3,242,462 in 1926. In addition, he worked out a system whereby students received recognition for such "Civic Service" as building bird houses, cleaning empty lots, and so forth.[58]

This principle of service, adopted as a means of increasing the public's support of the schools, was bolstered by progressive methods and curricula. In learning by doing, in letting pupils' interests shape the curriculum, in learning to solve the same kinds of problems students would meet after their school days were over, progressive education simplified the task of demonstrating the school's usefulness to the local community. Anderson and Davies' textbook on public relations, in a section entitled "Improving Community Relations Through Curriculum," describes a variety of ways in which specific schools have performed public services. The examples range from soil conservation to race relations, from recreation for adults to training for positions in the economic life of the community.

In one school, biology students tested the acidity of soil samples referred to them by friends, parents and neighbors. The soil owner was given a report of the findings and a list of plants which would grow best in that particular soil, together with suggestions about fertilizers, etc. The students also inspected trees, alerting householders to suspected cases of Dutch Elm disease.[59]

Another example described a *Brotherhood of Youth* program at Longfellow Junior High School in Yonkers. Besides year-round classroom instruction, the project involved pupil "task forces" which presented findings on intercultural relations to school and community groups; "Fairs of Nations" with student exhibitions and panel discussions; teas for parents, social workers, editors, clergymen, educators, and state and local officials; and pupil participation in a televised film based on a report by the National Committee on Civil Rights.[60]

This program brought recognition from the National Education Association, commendations from the New York State Commission Against Discrimination, and praise from other state and national intercultural groups. According to the authors of the text, "The results of this project have been evident in terms of improved human relations in the school and its neighboring community."[61]

Other examples of "community service through curriculum" include Levittown's art workshop in which adults as well as children were welcome. Age levels from three to seventy engaged in music, drama, poetry, and dance. They explored various techniques of painting, studied the folklore of many nations through stories and classical music, viewed films on mobiles, and tape-recorded their poetry readings. Group exhibitions were prepared for display in local buildings, and parents and pupils received a bi-weekly newsletter concerning plans for forthcoming workshops. These activities helped to ". . . transform the school into a studio devoted to the community's 'art of Living.' "[62]

In still another example, a seventh-grade class at Croton-on-Hudson organized a week-long workshop in "practical civic education." Sessions were held at a nearby camp equipped with cabins, arts and crafts facilities, and a large area for hiking and outdoor study. This "real school-community enterprise" included an overnight session at which the mayor and the town clerk discussed government, a board of education member supervised the work program, a local scientist led a study of geology and a nature census, and the village historian conducted a tour of historic locations. The supervising principal described the workshop as ". . . the fruitful results of a school and community working and planning together."[63]

Another area in which progressive education facilitated public relations was that of extra-curricular activity. Incorporated into the established program of the school, these activities supplemented the regular, more traditional subjects of classroom instruction. In fact, the assimilation has been so complete that it is often difficult to distinguish these activities from the basic curriculum itself. The degree of this assimilation, as well as the justification for it, is suggested by the preferred term *co-curricular,* rather than *extra-curricular,* activities.

Whatever they are called, they have been encouraged by progressive education's emphasis upon learning through activity which is meaningful to the pupil and which develops his physical and psychological well-being, rather than merely his intellectual capacities. A recent progressive statement, by which the prominent place of these activities in the curriculum could be justified, appeared in Anderson and Davies' text on public relations:

> Curriculum today is viewed as extending far beyond the confines of a comprehensive body of subject matter. Curriculum involves all of youth's activities within the school and in the community as well.[64]

Commenting on the emphasis given to extra-curricular and out-of-school activities in American schools, a British specialist in comparative education noted:

> Games and athletics loom large in such programmes, of course, but they form in reality only one small part of the whole ... there is a wide variety of activities ranging from pupil government of the school and student councils to movie clubs, school bands, rodeos (in the far West), broadcasting stations, running their own cafeteria, organizing their own bus services, down to the more humdrum European idea of out-of-school activities such as dramatic societies, dance clubs, language clubs, debating societies, producing the school magazine, and so on.[65]

At the end of World War II, a survey of 532 schools in the United States counted forty-two different activities classified by the school as co-curricular. The most common ones were assemblies, clubs, safety patrols and safety councils, school papers, and a variety of music groups, including choral singing, glee club, marching band, and orchestras. Only two of the more than five hundred schools did not offer any co-curricular activities.[66]

Much that was said about progressive curriculum also applies here. These activities are more likely to be of general public interest; they lend themselves more readily to news releases, to feature articles, and to photographs than did the drab, predominantly intellectual processes of traditional schooling. The public relations potential of these contemporary activities is relatively obvious, so we will look briefly at two familiar examples, athletics and music.

Athletics attracts the attention of many who would otherwise find little of interest in the school. This is true not only for students but also for a large and strategically important section of the public. Success in football, basketball or baseball, and even in some of the "minor" sports, is a source of civic pride to local businessmen and politicians, who may compliment the school on its outstanding performance. As a board member of a small California elementary school district exclaimed, upon hearing of a victory by the track team, "This really puts San Pablo on the map!"[67]

Certain music, such as that produced by choruses, glee clubs, and bands—especially marching bands—may serve similar functions. There is little place in American public schools for the sedate stringed instruments and their "high brow" music, but spirited vocalists and brassy marching bands have more public appeal and are consequently in constant demand. The following situation in Elmtown was typical of thousands of other districts as well:

> Music is stressed heavily in the extracurricular program as a part of the school's public relations program. Local organizations rely on the high school for free entertainment on special occasions. . . . In 1941-42, the school furnished 131 programs out of the 140 requests received.[68]

These extra-curricular activities, in addition to their educational and entertainment value, also provide a tangible reminder of the "service" that the school provides for the community. This public relations function is quite probably one of the factors contributing to the growth of extra-curricular activities in recent decades.[69]

Human Relations. The human relations orientation of school personnel was a third major area in which progressive education bolstered the struggle for autonomy. Progressive emphasis upon the pupil, rather than upon what he is taught, encouraged the use of human relations in the school and facilitated the recruitment of teachers and administrators who were sensitive to people and knew how to get along well with them. While these qualities were considered primarily with regard to children, they were also helpful in relations with the public. Personnel who had such qualities were valuable assets in the school's efforts to gain support from important individuals and groups in the community. Influential organizations, like the Chamber of Commerce, and the Elks and Rotary clubs, must be brought into the circle of the school's friends. Therefore, administrators often belong to such groups, either by choice or as a requirement of their positions. A typical example was provided by a study of a California school system:

> The . . . Superintendent uses the extent of community participation of a member of the school system as one of the major criteria in promotional policy. According to the Superintendent, the rationale behind the emphasis on community participation is his conception of key educational persons as public relations officers.

The principal is encouraged by the superintendent to devote time to achieving an understanding of the children, their parents and the neighborhood groups. All male principals are members of at least one of the local social organizations and many have held or are holding positions of leadership.[70]

The superintendent himself made frequent appearances as a speaker, giving an average of two talks a week.

He also holds active memberships in diverse local organizations, including the Elks and the Eagles; Chamber of Commerce and American Legion; Congregational Church; Native Sons and Daughters of California; and Boys' Clubs of America. As he expressed it to the research worker, "My only prejudice is liking people."[71]

In short, the same psychological principles advocated in progressive methods courses as ways of handling children also enabled teachers and administrators to make a more favorable impression upon parents, board members, and the general public.

CONCLUSION

In order to gain support for its policies and financial needs, while at the same time minimizing interruption of its day-to-day operations, the American public school has tried to maintain a delicate balance between too little and too much public interest, between apathy and interference. To do this, the school has adopted some of the same public relations techniques used in business, and progressive education has provided a rationale for their adoption.

While the basic concept of local public control suggested that the school should keep its nominal masters—the public—informed, the progressive doctrine of community-centered education provided further justification for communication between the school and the community. Consequently, public relations did not have to remain a marginal activity, operating in the shadows, but instead became a legitimate and even mandatory aspect of the school's program. From informing the public, it was only a minor step to propagandizing on behalf of the school; the same mechanisms established for the former could also be used effectively for the latter.

REFERENCES

[1]U.S. Office of Education, *Statistical Summary of Education,* 1951-52, p. 24. Of course, these national averages obscured wide variations between individual districts. For example, in 1951, New Hampshire's public schools obtained ninety-one

percent of their revenue from local sources, while public schools in Louisiana received only five percent of their income from the local district. Nevertheless, most American school systems have to rely upon the local community for financial support (Dahlke, *Values in Culture and Classroom*, p. 33).

[2]For a study of school bond defeats in two communities, see Horton and Thompson, "Powerlessness and Political Negativism: A Study of Defeated Local Referendums," *A.J.S.* (March, 1962), pp. 485-93.

[3]Cubberly, in Butts and Cremin, *History of Education*, p. 244.

[4]Bailyn, *Forming of American Society*, pp. 111-12.

[5]Eby and Arrowood, *Development of Modern Education*, p. 548.

[6]Butts and Cremin, *History of Education*, pp. 247-48.

[7]*Ibid.*

[8]Bailyn, *Forming of American Society*, p. 109.

[9]This discussion of control during traditional times, unless otherwise indicated, is based upon Butts and Cremin, *History of Education*, pp. 97-115.

[10]Cubberly, *Public Education*, rev. ed., p. 125.

[11]*Ibid.*, pp. 124-25.

[12]Cubberly, *Readings in Public Education in the United States*, p. 132.

[13]*Ibid.*, p. 134.

[14]Cubberly, *Public Education*, rev. ed., pp. 125-26.

[15]Cremin, *American Common School*, p. 2; Muzzey, *The United States of America*, p. 348.

[16]Charles A. and Mary Beard, *A Basic History of the United States*, p. 73. Exceptions were New York and Albany, where all men formally admitted to civic right as "freemen" could vote.

[17]*Ibid.*

[18]*Ibid.*

[19]Cremin, *American Common School*, p. 3; U.S. Bureau of the Census, *Historical Statistics . . .*, pp. 7, 682.

[20]U.S. Bureau of the Census, *Historical Statistics . . .*, pp. 7, 682; and *Statistical Abstract of the United States 1966*, p. 368.

[21]*San Francisco Chronicle*, December 1, 1959.

[22]Neal Gross, *Who Runs Our Schools?*, p. 104.

[23]Anderson and Davies, *Patterns of Educational Leadership*, p. 66.

[24]*Ibid.*, p. 67.

[25]John and Mary Dewey, *Schools of Tomorrow*, p. 128.

[26]*Ibid.*, p. 150.

[27]*Ibid.*

[28]*Ibid.*, p. 165.

[29]Anderson and Davies, *Patterns of Educational Leadership*, p. 69.

[30]*Ibid.*, p. 78.

[31]Otto, *Principles of Elementary Education*, pp. 373-74.

[32]*Ibid.*, p. 374.

[33]*Ibid.*

[34]*Ibid.*

[35]*Ibid.*

[36]*Ibid.*

[37]Anderson and Davies, *Patterns of Educational Leadership*, p. 100.

[38]*Ibid.*

[39]*Ibid.*, p. 101.

[40]*Ibid.*, p. 102.

[41]*Ibid.*

[42]*Ibid.*, pp. 102-03.

[43]*Ibid.*, p. 103.

[44]*Ibid.*

[45]*Ibid.*, p. 104.

[46]*Ibid.*, p. 103.

[47]*Ibid.*

[48]*Ibid.*, pp. 106-07.

[49]*Ibid.*, p. 108.

[50]*Ibid.*, pp. 108-10.

[51]*Oakland Tribune*, June 1, 1960.

[52]Anderson and Davies, *Patterns of Educational Leadership*, p. 104. Progressive education would make it easier to illustrate news about school projects. The bleak traditional curriculum would have offered few suitable subjects for the "action photography" recommended by Anderson and Davies (p. 106). The most active aspect of old-time education was probably the schoolmaster's whip.

[53]John and Mary Dewey, *Schools of Tomorrow*, p. 181.

[54]*Ibid.*, p. 182.

[55]*Ibid.*, pp. 184, 194, 205.

[56]Callahan, *Education and the Cult of Efficiency*, p. 230.

[57]*Ibid.*, p. 226.

[58]*Ibid.*

[59]Anderson and Davies, *Patterns of Educational Leadership*, pp. 70-71.

[60]*Ibid.*, pp. 73-74.

[61]*Ibid.*, p. 74.

[62]*Ibid.*, p. 71.

[63]*Ibid.*, pp. 72-73.

[64]*Ibid.*, p. 38.

[65]Mallinson, *Comparative Education*, pp. 182-83.

[66]Otto, *Principles of Elementary Education*, pp. 229-30.

[67]Heard by the author at a school board meeting.

[68]Hollingshead, *Elmtown's Youth*, p. 199.

[69]"The development of school athletic events, musical productions, and speech and dramatic shows has expanded rapidly during the last 25 to 50 years. Coaches and administrators are frequently hired and fired largely on the record of the school's athletic team. It is now common for a number of contracts in every school to provide for a major share of the teacher's time to be given to the direction of activities that entertain" (Jensen, "The Teacher as Director of the Learning Process," in Stiles, ed., *The Teacher's Role in American Society*, p. 97).

[70]Conrad, *The Administrative Role: A Sociological Study of Leadership in a Public School System*, p. 69.

[71]*Ibid.*, p. 58.

six

PUBLIC SCHOOL
PERSONNEL

So FAR, WE HAVE BEEN DISCUSSING PROBLEMS FACING THE SCHOOL AS an organization. However, organizations consist of people and it is the characteristics and capabilities of these people which largely determine what the organization is able to do. For school employees there was a direct connection between their own interests and those of the organization. Teaching has been, in several respects, a relatively unrewarding occupation. Its salary, working conditions and job security have not compared favorably with other professions, nor even with some manual trades, and its prestige has left much to be desired. The ease of entry into teaching, the oversupply of prospective teachers, the many women, the weakness of occupational associations—all contributed to a popular image of teaching as a refuge for misfits who could not succeed in other, more prestigious types of work.

This image has some basis in fact. The more capable people generally choose jobs offering higher pay and more prestige. This situation existed in the traditional era and it has continued with little change down to the present.

It is not surprising, therefore, that public school teachers would be receptive to an educational doctrine which gave them some hope of raising their status. The same progressivism which contributed to the solution of organizational problems also offered teachers and administrators a way of improving their occupational image, from the inept scholar to the trained professional educator.[1]

THE TRADITIONAL ERA

The picture of the traditional teacher was not a happy one. Most old-time schoolmasters were inexperienced, inadequately trained, and transient. Of course, there were exceptions, especially in towns and cities, where a number of pupils were fortunate enough to receive instruction from the well-prepared graduates of private academies.

Generally, however, many kinds of people taught in the district schools up through the first decades of the nineteenth century. In summer, when only younger children attended, women were often employed. During the winter term, when grown boys came in from the fields, it was the practice to hire men. As we have seen, "The supreme test of a teacher's competence lay in his ability to keep order," and only men were thought capable of controlling older boys. A small percentage of the men were career schoolmasters who had proven themselves to be competent in this "rough and ready system of elimination and survival." However, there apparently were never enough of these hardy professionals to satisfy more than a fraction of the demand of the rapidly expanding nation.[2]

The deficit was made up with vast numbers of casual teachers. Some of them taught during lulls in other occupations. Others spent a few years teaching as a stop-gap while preparing for other careers in law, business or the ministry. Many teachers were young college students trying to earn just enough to enable them to continue with their advanced education. Others found that a short stint of teaching in a common school gave them enough general background to enable them to enter one of the professions without further specialized training. Another large group of common school teachers were farmers; after learning all the district school could offer them, they tried to imitate what they had seen, as pupils, a short time previously. Thus, most teachers were inexperienced, poorly trained, stayed only a short time at any given school, and, after a few years, dropped out of teaching entirely.[3]

The quality of instruction remained at a low level after the 1820s, when increasing numbers of women began to enter teaching. Most of them were young and unskilled. Few qualifications were considered necessary for the job. Often the teacher was merely the daughter or some other unmarried female relative of a school board member. She had finished the common school and in a few instances had gone to a local academy for a short time. Her job was primarily to keep order, and she was expected to be of good moral character. This was the limit of the formal requirements for the position.[4] Of course, the difficulties involved in maintaining order should not be underestimated. Other than this, however, her educational duties were relatively simple. Instruction was on an individual basis. The teacher remained at her desk most of the day, calling up pupils one at a time to examine their slates, hear them recite their lessons from memory, or give assistance where needed. Even when a group of pupils came forward, the teacher usually took them one-by-one for questioning.[5]

Two factors seemed largely responsible for this shift away from male teachers. The first was a feeling, derived from the Jacksonian concept of democracy, that any citizen of the community could qualify for any public office; in the case of teaching this meant that no special qualifications were believed necessary. The second factor was that women could be paid less than men for the same amount of work. This appealed to the school district's concern for economy. Figures of average salaries for teachers during 1841 show that men in rural schools received $4.15 weekly compared to $2.51 for women. In city schools the difference was even larger, with male teachers averaging $11.93 per week, in contrast to a mere $4.44 for women.[6]

Although absolute figures mean little by themselves, comparisons with other pre-Civil War wages and costs of living indicate that teachers were barely making a marginal living. Their salaries, while slightly above those of blue-collar workers, were far below what the reformers of that day considered to be adequate professional payment.[7]

Several justifications were given for the low salaries of teachers. One often-heard argument maintained that teachers were inept individuals who could not succeed in business or a profession and, therefore, did not deserve any more money.[8] For example, a Virginia newspaper in 1843 stated that many teachers were "invalid, some were slaves to drunkenness, some too lazy to work, most of them ignorant of the art of teaching, and a terror to their pupils."[9] Their "chief recommendation was their cheapness."[10] An Ohio teacher in the 1820s reported that his salary was ". . . $10 per month. As the trustees were looking for a *cheap* teacher for the summer school, I had a call, though I had just passed my 16th year."[11]

Teacher training institutions, as such, did not appear until late in the traditional period, when concern over the low quality of public school education eventually led to increasing demands for better-prepared teachers. American travelers in the early-nineteenth century had been impressed by the methods used in France and Prussia, where teacher training facilities were a central element in the state educational systems. The enthusiastic reports of Horace Mann, Henry Barnard and others provided a major stimulus for the establishment of similar facilities in the United States.[12]

In 1818 a Lancastrian model school was established to give quick preparation to teachers and monitors in the Lancastrian system. However, the first real teacher training schools in this country were private institutions which began in 1823 in Concord, Vermont, and in 1827 at Lancaster, Massachusetts. These *normal schools* offered a basic program similar to that of the English curriculum in the academies, and added other courses in discipline, teaching methods and the management of children. While relatively few teachers attended private institutions such as these, they nevertheless were important because, until 1865, they trained most of the common school teachers who received any specialized training at all.[13]

The first public normal schools in the United States were founded in the face of considerable opposition in Massachusetts in 1839. They were attacked by people who feared they would "Prussianize" the schools. Schoolmasters considered them to be derogatory, the academies saw them as competitors, and many taxpayers believed that public normal schools were an unnecessary expense because the private academies were already performing very well. Nevertheless, a third public normal school opened in Massachusetts the following year and, by the time of the Civil War, twelve of these schools had been established in eight states.[14]

The established colleges and universities offered little in the way of teacher training. Washington College in Pennsylvania started lectures on the "art of teaching" in 1831, Brown in 1850, and the University of Michigan in 1860. Although New York University announced plans to establish a chair in education for instructing public school teachers, there is no evidence that the lectures were actually given.[15]

In sum, teaching was a lowly occupation during the traditional period, and there was little machinery for improvement. Formal training of teachers, though a beginning had been made, left much to be desired. The few institutions which did exist were small, had few students, and usually operated for only a few months of the year. Most of the normal schools were concentrated in a few northern and eastern states; the first state normal schools away from the Atlantic coast opened in Illinois in 1857 and in Minnesota in 1860.[16]

While there were some teachers' organizations before the Civil War, no vigorous, unified group developed which might have worked effectively for tenure, better salaries and high teaching standards. An occupational consciousness or *esprit de corps* was virtually non-existent.[17]

THE TRANSITIONAL ERA

The general status of teaching improved little, if any, during the transitional era. Although changes occurred there were also changes in other occupations and in other areas of society which largely neutralized the absolute gains teachers had made. The most important trends during this period involved teacher training and certification. While teacher training institutions began late in the traditional era, their real development occurred between 1870 and 1920, and subsequently enabled them to become the principal disseminators of progressive education.

Although a number of normal schools had been established by 1860, they were inadequate in several respects. There were few entrance requirements and few applicants were denied admission. Most entrants had only the rudiments of common school education. Instruction was mainly at the secondary level, semesters were short, and the entire course of study required only one or two years. Even then, most students took only part of the course, and many attended for only a few weeks.[18]

By 1900, however, a number of changes had occurred. All of the forty-five states then in the union had some sort of public normal schools. In Massachusetts, for example, students were required to have a high school education or its equivalent. The two-year course for future elementary teachers included three areas: first, background in history and principles of education, psychology, general methods of instruction and school law; second, methods of teaching the various subjects; and, third, observation of actual teaching in public schools. One normal school also offered a four-year course intended primarily for secondary teachers and administrators. Although Massachusetts' standards were high, the situation there indicated the direction toward which other states were beginning to move.[19]

Another development during the transitional period was the *teachers' college*. Its growth was encouraged by several factors, including greater concern for the quality as well as quantity of education, the pressing demand for college graduates as high school teachers, a vast extension of the courses offered in teacher training institutions, the attention given to education in university programs, and the use of accrediting associations.[20]

In 1890 the state normal school at Albany, New York, was reorganized as a teachers' college offering some advanced instruction, but the first normal school actually to become a regular college was authorized in Michigan in 1897, and its first B.A. degree was awarded in

1905. By 1913 there were nine of these colleges, and by 1920 the number had increased to forty-six.[21]

A third major development after the Civil War was the *university department of education.* The first permanent chair of education at the university level was established in 1873 at the University of Iowa, and its school of education was founded in 1907. The University of Michigan established a permanent position in "The Science and Art of Teaching" in 1879. The number of such positions increased rapidly after 1890, jumping from half a dozen to almost 250 by 1900. Liberal arts colleges also began to offer education courses and, by the end of the century, over a fourth of these colleges had regular instruction in teacher training.[22]

Unfortunately, the emergence of these opportunities for teacher education did not necessarily mean that all teachers would utilize them. The proliferation of public schools after the Civil War continued at such a pace, decade after decade, that many, perhaps the majority of American teachers, were still inadequately prepared. For example, in Massachusetts during 1897-1898, only 38.5 percent of the public school teachers had received any normal school instruction, and only 33.5 percent had graduated from a normal school course. Massachusetts was in an unusually advantageous position since it had the third-highest number of normal schools in the nation. The situation in other states was considerably worse. Butts and Cremin, in reviewing the inadequate training of most teachers during this time, stated that, "It seems safe to assume that the overwhelming majority were appointed to teaching with little regard for their academic or professional training."[23]

However, interest in certification supported the increasing emphasis upon teaching methods and encouraged the growth of teacher training institutions. At the same time it helped to eliminate examinations based on knowledge of subject matter. Teacher certification underwent considerable improvement after 1870. The major development here was the tendency toward centralizing of certification, placing it in the hands of larger administrative units. In the last part of the century this trend began to offset local autonomy. By 1911 certification laws had been enacted by a majority of the states. By 1920 twenty-six states issued certificates, seven states had arrangements by which county authorities could issue some certificates to individuals who complied with rules and examinations prescribed by the states, and ten more made the county the administrative agent and certifying authority for carrying out regulations issued by the state.[24]

Along with the extension of certification, the requirements for it were tightened. After the Civil War increasing proportions of teachers were given certificates on the basis of normal school diplomas rather than examinations. By the early years of this century a number of states began to require high school graduation for an elementary teaching certificate. By 1921 four states required a high school education and some professional training for certification. Fourteen states stipulated four years of high school but did not require professional training. The remaining thirty states had set no definite academic requirements.[25]

Teachers' pay is another factor to be considered. While some progress in salaries was made between 1865 and 1920, there was still some room for improvement. A study by W. R. Burgess indicated that there had been a general increase in teachers' actual wages during this period. Women's pay tended to increase more rapidly than men's, reducing the traditional distance between male and female remuneration. Nevertheless, the differences between rural and urban salaries persisted.[26]

A comparison of teachers' wages with living costs indicates that these pay increases were really meaningful. While teachers' pay increased two or three times during the period between 1865 and 1915, the cost of living grew less than 30 percent. After 1915, however, the situation reversed as the sharp inflation, touched off by the war, sent costs rising far more rapidly than salaries.[27]

A similar pattern was revealed by comparing teachers' wages with those of artisans and laborers. Burgess found that teachers' pay increased more rapidly between 1865 and 1915 than did the blue-collar workers', but this trend also reversed during the war, as workers' salaries shot upward while teachers' pay remained fairly constant.[28]

If we consider salaries in light of the preparation required for the two vocations, it appears that here, too, teachers did not fare well. Burgess noted that training requirements for artisans had not changed much since 1865, while the qualifications expected of teachers, especially those in cities, increased considerably. In short, although teachers' salaries rose during the transitional period, it is questionable, when other factors are taken into account, whether they were really much better off financially than their predecessors had been.[29]

This period also saw the beginnings of provisions for pensions and retirement. Before the Civil War, most people, including teachers, thought that these were individual matters, to be solved by each teacher as best he could. During 1869, however, it became necessary on several occasions to solicit donations for the burial of New York City teachers who had died without leaving any assets. The collections led to the establishment of an informal agency, the New York City Teachers' Mutual Life Assurance Association, to provide for death benefits through voluntary contributions. Other districts soon established similar associations, to cover illness a well as death, and some even set up retirement systems. Eventually, arrangements were made for public funding of these benefits. Between 1905 and 1914 public retirement plans were established in sixty-five cities. There was also some progress toward statewide retirement schemes but, by 1910, only four states had accomplished this. Most progress was being made at the local district level.[30]

Tenure protection remained weak throughout this transitional period. The most significant aspect of the few laws that were passed in this area was their educative value. They brought the concept of tenure to the attention of many people who had been unfamiliar with it, but they provided little actual protection for most teachers. By 1918 only seven states and the District of Columbia had enacted tenure legislation, and even these scanty laws were full of loopholes, providing tenure as long as "good service and behavior" were offered. Generally, however, good service and behavior were so vaguely defined that the local school districts had considerable independence in their interpretation of these concepts. The freedom of local boards to hire and fire teachers was virtually unlimited during the traditional period, and it was tempered only slightly in the period before the First World War. Job security, for most teachers, still depended on remaining in the good graces of the administration and the school board.[31]

Femininization was still another factor hindering any marked improvement in teachers' status. The transitional period witnessed the continuation of the shift from an occupation that was predominantly male to one overwhelmingly female. Trends which began in the 1820s accelerated during the Civil War, when many men left teaching to enter military service or to take better-paying jobs in business. When the war was over they did not return. Thus, by 1870, only thirty-nine percent of American school teachers were men, and by 1920, men constituted only fourteen percent of the teaching force.[32] This femininization made it more likely that teaching would be considered a second-class occupation, stigmatized as "women's work" which few capable, self-respecting men would enter. This unfavorable image may well have offset improvements in such areas as salary, certification, and retirement benefits gained during the transitional period. The status of teaching continued to be marginal, located in the lower levels of the middle class.

THE PROGRESSIVE ERA

Although teaching conditions following the First World War were different from those of traditional times, we cannot conclude that the contemporary teacher is really much better off than his predecessors were. In comparison with other occupations today, the rewards of public school teaching are still moderate.

Many manual workers, for instance, made more money, and had shorter hours and stronger protection against arbitrary management actions than did teachers. By 1950 teachers' salaries had reached an all-time high of $3,300 for the country as a whole. Nevertheless, this was still far below the average for physicians of $12,500, for lawyers of $9,400, and for dentists of $7,800. The members of other professions averaged two to four times as much as teachers. In the 1950 Census listing of eighteen occupations requiring at least a B.A. degree, the salaries of teachers ranked fifteenth. From the beginning of the century, teachers' incomes have either actually decreased, or increased more slowly than those of other occupations. Since 1929, at least, the average annual salaries for public school teachers have been very close to the national average for all employed persons.[33]

Lower salaries for teachers are sometimes justified on the basis of teachers' short work year, but here too, past advantages of this work year are disappearing. As Lieberman observes, "The number of days worked per year has declined in every major occupation except education, where it increased from 147 in 1904 to 182 in 1953. Furthermore the number of hours worked per day has increased in education but has decreased in practically all other occupations."[34]

A further indication that teachers' salaries were low is given by outside work. Many teachers held other jobs along with their teaching positions. A study by the Bureau of Labor statistics found that the percentage of men teachers holding two or more jobs during December, 1960, was four times as large as the average for all male workers. In the N.E.A.'s 1960 survey, 72.5 percent of male teachers had extra jobs. Other employment during summer vacation might be expected, but 55 percent of all the men teaching held extra jobs during the months that school was in session. These extra jobs were not very lucrative. Those working extra jobs within their own school systems averaged a little over $400 per year, while those working on an outside job made slightly more than $700 from their added effort.[35]

Tenure protection for teachers, even at mid-century, was far from complete. One summary observed that ". . . in more than ¾ s of the states there are tenure provisions applicable to at least some of the teachers of the state."[36] While this was better than nothing it still left room for improvement. For example, it meant that about a dozen states had no such protection at all. Furthermore, even in the three-fourths of the states where some of the teachers were protected, there were many other teachers who were not. Only fifty-six percent of the city systems in the 1951 N.E.A. survey had tenure or protective continuing contracts.[37] In other words, almost half of the cities reporting lacked this protection. And, since such conditions are usually better in cities than in smaller districts, it is likely that considerably more than half the teachers in towns and rural areas were without tenure or other similar protection.

Still another factor depressing the status of teaching is the frequency of breaks in the career. Recalling the intermittent character of teaching before the Civil War, it is significant to find this pattern persisting a century later. Forty-four percent of the teachers surveyed in the 1960 N.E.A. study reported an interruption in their teaching career. This gap was often a long one, with the average absence from teaching being 8.3 years. The figures were considerably higher for married women, who often stopped teaching in order to raise a family. Perhaps more surprising was the fact that men, too, did not stay continuously in teaching: one-fourth of all males had been out of teaching for a while. For them, the average absence was four years. Thus, teaching continued to be a relatively casual occupation which practitioners could enter, leave and re-enter without too much difficulty.[38] This casual character suggests a relatively low commitment to the occupation, and a low degree of technical competence.

In his study of occupations, Gross has pointed out that one criterion of a profession is a high degree of involvement in the job.[39] Many professions have became so technical and deal with such abstract commodities that competence is difficult for laymen to judge. At the same time, the client expects the professional to take a serious interest in his, the client's, problem, treating it as intently as if it were the professional's own personal concern. Therefore, since professional proficiency is difficult to evaluate yet is important to the client, professionals are also judged in part by factors other than technical competence. Among these other criteria is the degree of involvement in one's work: how seriously is the practitioner committed to his profession? Thus, the casual, intermittent character of many public school teachers' careers has not enhanced the prestige of their occupation.

Low entry requirements also undermined the image of teaching. Lagging certification practices did little to counter the popular belief that almost anyone could teach. As late as 1952, only one-third of the states required college degrees for elementary teachers; five states required two-and-a-half to three years of college, eighteen states required only one-and-a-half or two years of college, and requirements in the remaining eight states ranged from one year of college to none at all. Certification for secondary teachers was more strict. In 1950, over three-fourths of the states required four years of college and only six states required less. The other four states required more than four years.[40]

Even these college requirements, mild as they were, principally affected only new entrants into the profession. They did not really touch people who had been teaching for some time, nor did they do much good in the many communities which were unable to hire enough fully prepared teachers to fill all the vacancies. Consequently, half of the nation's 600,000 elementary teachers were not college graduates.[41]

Certification requirements are also mild with respect to examinations. Since large numbers of teachers have not even finished four years of college, one might expect that, as an alternate way of demonstrating their competence, they would be required to pass an examination. This is not the case. Around 1900 certification by written examination was a common practice, but it has almost completely disappeared today. By 1955 only five states still certified teachers on the basis of examinations.[42]

This is very different from the situation existing in most other professions, where examinations on a statewide basis are still a requirement for entry. In some cases the professional association developed an examination used in several states. In dentistry, medicine and nursing, the state licensing boards typically use tests prepared, given and graded by the national professional association. The trend in most professions is toward introducing examinations in the few states which do not already require them, and using standardized tests prepared by the national professional association.[43]

And yet, while state board examinations are very common in other professions, proposals to bring them back into teaching have met with vigorous opposition, particularly from teacher training institutions. Critics observe that people who do well on examinations do not necessarily make good teachers, and that some fine teachers would do badly on examinations.[44] Whatever the validity of these arguments, the result is that this is still another area in which teaching differs from the more prestigious professions.

Related to the issue of certification is the matter of professional autonomy. For the most part, regulation of professions in the United States has been left to the individual states. Consequently, professional control over entry and expulsion usually has been achieved through control of the state boards which license the practitioners. In most professions, the state licensing board is composed of practitioners of the occupation itself. Thus, in every state of the union, the licensing boards which regulate the practice of medicine are staffed by doctors; those regulating the practice of law are composed of lawyers; and those regulating the licensing in dentistry are made up of dentists. This, however, is not true of public school teachers.[45]

In 1952, there were only five states in which teachers comprised all or most of the membership of the board certifying them. Barbers, beauticians, chiropractors, and chiropodists held more control over entry into and expulsion from their occupations, for each group controlled its own licensing board in at least two-thirds of the states.[46]

This situation, serious enough as it is, is growing worse rather than better. In an increasing number of states, teachers are excluded by law from the boards which control entry into their profession.[47] By 1951, ten states expressly excluded professional educators from their state boards of education. In many other states, professional educators were excluded indirectly, by mandatory inclusion of representatives from other groups on a board of limited size. Oregon's state board of education, for example, has seven members among whom, according to state law, there must be an employer, an employee, a homemaker and an agriculturist.[48]

One reason why this mandatory exclusion of educators from their licensing boards has increased is that educators themselves, instead of opposing this trend, have approved and encouraged it. Since 1921 the National Education Association has advocated non-professional control over state boards licensing teachers.[49] Whatever the reasons for doing so, this lack of teachers' control over their certification has not enhanced the prestige or the power of the profession.

As this might suggest, teachers' organizations, too, lacked vigor until recent times. Before 1960, they seldom had the strength or the will to engage in direct confrontations over issues involving many aspects of teachers' status and well-being. The N.E.A., largest of the associations, with over 600,000 members, continued to direct most of its attention to research, to problems of salary and curriculum, and to "professional" behavior on the part of its members. When it did take an interest in more controversial issues, it relied upon informal attempts at persuasion. Even the A.F.T., though more militant, remained unable to do much. At mid-century its members comprised less than five percent of all teachers in the United States.[50]

The attractiveness of teaching continued to be undermined by sensitivity to community mores which insisted that teachers observe the time-honored taboos against smoking, drinking, dancing, dating and card-playing, even though adults generally, and parents in particular, no longer abided by them.[51]

In light of these factors it would not be surprising to find that other professions and the public generally would regard teachers as having only mediocre ability. More significant, however, is that educators themselves also held this belief. It has often been claimed in educational circles that superior intelligence is not a requisite to successful teaching. Instead, other qualities, such as adaptability and sympathy for the child's point of view, were believed to be more important. Lieberman observed:

> ... much educational literature, especially the literature devoted to recruiting high school or college students to teaching, actually encourages young men and women to enter teaching by advancing the claim that only average or slightly above average intelligence is required for successful teaching.[52]

As an example he quotes the statement that a teacher:

> ... need not be graduated *cum laude*, nor does his intelligence have to rank in the very top levels.
>
> Actually, there is a good deal of evidence to support the theory that the most successful teachers are found frequently among people who possess only a little better than average mentality. This is always supplemented, however, by qualities of adaptability and a wide range of interests that provide consistent stimulation.[53]

Such a statement, regardless of the qualifications which might be added to it, would not do much to improve the status of any occupation. Yet some educators go even further than denying the necessity of superior intelligence for teachers. They claim that intelligence is not only unessential; it may actually be a detriment to good teaching:

> Just what the optimum IQ is for successful teaching nobody knows. Certainly there is a lower limit, also there are cases on record of teachers who are so intellectually inclined and so expert in their areas that they succeed only in confusing and discouraging their pupils. Too, there are teachers who have no more than average intelligence and who have had great difficulty with a particular subject area, but who are highly successful, especially with slower pupils, because they have more sympathetic understanding for the kind of problems such youngsters usually meet.[54]

Whatever their objective validity, these beliefs are important because they influence behavior. This is especially true of two groups: those selecting a career, and those occupying strategic positions in the educational system. With respect to the first, the belief that superior ability is not important probably attracts some people into teaching who might not otherwise consider it. For example, a common sentiment among education majors was reported by Stiles: "Soon I learned that engineering required too much theory so I switched to education."[55]

Secondly, the attitudes held by education professors and public school administrators are also important. Because these men occupy strategic positions—it is they who train, certificate, hire, and fire teachers—they play a major part in determining what types of people will become a part of the school system. If they believe that superior intelligence is unimportant or even undesirable, their evaluations and decisions are likely to reflect this view. It tends to become a self-fulfilling prophecy.[56]

As a result of these factors, the overall prestige of public school teaching during the second quarter of this century was about the same as it had been during traditional times. If the image of Ichabod Crane no longer prevailed, its demise was due as much to the disappearance of men from teaching as it was to any marked improvement in the public's conception of the occupation. There was some variation within education in that administrators and high school teachers were rated above the rank and file elementary teachers. All in all, however, teaching continued to be viewed as an occupation not much above the average of all types of work.

One of the first studies of occupational prestige using a rating scale was conducted by George Counts in 1925. He asked various groups of high school and college students and teachers to rate forty-five occupations in terms of their prestige. Bankers received the highest rating, locomotive engineers were twenty-third, at the midpoint of the scale, and ditch-diggers were placed at the bottom. High school teachers were ranked tenth, elementary teachers appeared thirteenth, and rural school teachers (who at that time still comprised the bulk of the nation's teachers) were ranked nineteenth, just a little above the average and in the company of skilled tradesmen, clerks and small businessmen.[57]

The relative prestige of teaching generally, as well as the variations between the subdivisions within education, have been subsequently confirmed by other studies. It is interesting to note, a generation later, that "public school teacher" was still only a short distance above "railroad engineer." One of the most extensive studies of occupational prestige found that public school teaching was ranked only a little above the average of ninety representative occupations. In 1947 the National Opinion Research Center interviewed a national cross section of Americans in order to explore some basic public attitudes regarding occupations. "Public school teacher" was ranked thirty-fifth, somewhat below priests, artists, accountants and musicians, and considerably below physicians, bankers, lawyers and architects. It was about equal to building contractors and county agricultural agents.[58]

Perhaps the status of teaching can be summed up by a *Woman's Home Companion* poll, which listed teaching as the second best job or career that a girl could ". . . follow today for her best future opportunity and satisfaction."[59]

Characteristics of Teachers. Associated with this long history has been the recruitment of personnel who possessed certain distinctive characteristics. Of course, individuals in any group may differ tremendously from the average; we must be wary of attributing to particular individuals the traits of the groups of which they are members. Nevertheless, our understanding of progressive education can be deepened by considering overall characteristics of American public school teachers as a group. Their social origins, academic ability, professional preparation, experience and teaching assignments have inclined teachers toward certain directions and away from others; have made them more capable, more comfortable in some areas and less so in others.

Their social status, at least in terms of their fathers' occupations, is apparently no higher than it was a generation or two ago. This was most recently indicated by the N.E.A.'s 1960 survey. That year 43.6 percent of American public school teachers came from white-collar families, about 30 percent were the children of manual workers, and 26.5 percent came from farmers' families.[60] When the oldest teachers, those who were fifty-six or older at the time of the survey, were compared with the youngest, those under twenty-six, the increase among those coming from white-collar families was only four percent. However, the proportion from working-class homes almost doubled, rising from 16.3 percent among the oldest teachers to 31.2 percent among the youngest. There was a corresponding drop in the percentage of teachers from farmers' families.[61]

Even the four percent increase in teachers from white-collar families has actually been offset by changes in the larger occupational structure. In 1900, for example, white-collar workers comprised 17.6 percent of the male labor force. By 1940, however, about the time that the youngest teachers were born, the proportion of white-collar workers had increased to 26.7 percent, a nine percent rise. Thus, the proportion of teachers recruited from higher-status families did not keep up with the expansion of these categories in the labor force. The proportion of blue-collar workers in the labor force grew from 40.7 percent to 51.6 percent, a rise of about eleven percent. During this same period the proportion of teachers from blue-collar homes rose approximately fifteen percent.[62]

In his analysis of teacher education in the United States, James D. Koerner observed: "By about any academic standard that can be applied, students in teacher training programs are among the least able on the campus. . . . All major studies that have been made of the subject have arrived at the same conclusion."[63] One of the first such studies examined the intelligence and scholastic achievement of over 45,000 Pennsylvania high school and college students in 1928, 1930 and 1932. Standardized tests scores of students in education were lower than those of any other major. Other findings indicated that the median IQ score for 26,000 unselected high school seniors was higher than the median for seniors in education at one college, higher than the education graduates of another college, and the graduates of two-year certificate programs at two other teachers' colleges. Furthermore, the median intelligence scores of a large group in the teachers' colleges studying for two-year certificates was only slightly higher than the median of the unselected high school seniors.[64]

The study also contained many comparisons of the scholastic attainments of unselected high school seniors with college seniors preparing to teach. These comparisons indicated that substantial numbers of high school seniors were scholastically better qualified than large numbers of college seniors in education. This was often true even in the very subject the prospective teachers were preparing to teach.[65]

Discussing the minimum level of knowledge which a public school teacher should have, the Pennsylvania researchers continued:

> While a theoretical minimum may be difficult to fix, a practical minimum becomes extremely easy when we find pupils at a level where these teachers will work surpassing them on their own territory. A superior fund of matured general knowledge, though perceptible in the average, is evidently not an indispensable qualification for the individual teacher as prepared in these Pennsylvania institutions, nor is it necessary that he command even the verbal tools of education to an extent equal to that of many whom he will seek to instruct.[66]

The authors pointed out that there was no reason to consider the findings restricted to the state surveyed. "One tends to conclude, upon putting together all the findings, that they [teachers] have inferior minds."[67]

Recent studies have been more comprehensive but have come to the same conclusion. For instance, in 1951-53, the *Selective Service College Qualification Test,* an intelligence test with both "verbal" and "quantitative" items, was given to nearly half-a-million college men in order to determine their draft status. Data from the tests given during these three years were analyzed by the Educational Testing Service, and indicated that students majoring in Education scored lowest in every grade each year the test was given. Subsumed under *Education* in the tabulation of the data were twenty *Central* and *Related* specialties, such as "Secondary Education," "School Administration" and "Guidance." In reviewing the findings Koerner concluded:

> This is some of the most comprehensive information available. Putting the best possible light on the matter, one must obviously conclude that Education attracts very large numbers of men . . . who consistently exhibit the lowest academic ability of any major group in higher education, far below that of students in the basic academic areas.[68]

Similar trends were observed in a third major study, reported by Wolfle in 1954. The study tabulated scores on standardized intelligence tests (AGCT) for a sample of 10,000 college graduates and 4,500 graduate students at more than forty American colleges and universities. As a group, education majors graduating with bachelor's degrees were very low, ranking seventeenth among twenty major fields.[69] The same situation occurred at the graduate level, where education majors ranked sixteenth among nineteen different fields.[70] In fact, there is some reason to believe that the position of students in education may be even lower than these statistics indicate. Although special efforts were made to place students in the most appropriate category, the lowest two groups, home economics and physical education, contained a large but undetermined number of education students, since majors in these fields commonly take the usual sequence of education courses and are considered in many schools to be bona fide education students.[71]

The conclusions of these three studies are reinforced by many other less extensive ones. No matter how the subject is approached, whether we look at state-supported institutions or prestigious private universities, at one school or at several, the pattern remains the same. At Harvard, for instance, a 1957 survey of the student body (including Radcliffe students) indicated that very few intended to go into public school teaching; those who did came from lower academic ranks.[72] At the University of California in Berkeley, a report indicated that academically capable students received lower grades in student teaching than did the less able students. Students who got As in student teaching in January, 1955, made poorer scores on the *Ohio State University Psychological Test, Form 21*, "a measure of the general verbal intelligence or academic aptitude," than did students who received Bs in student teaching.[73] This study suggests that the less capable students receive the best grades in education courses and presumably more encouragement to continue their preparation for a teaching career than do the gifted students. Similarly, upon completing their training, they would be more likely to receive the best recommendations for teaching positions. In contrast, the more academically gifted students, in receiving lower grades in practice teaching, would be less apt to be encouraged by the education department to go on with their preparation, and would be less likely to receive a high recommendation from the faculty if they did apply for a teaching job.

What is the significance of IQ test scores? Although there is considerable doubt concerning their validity as indicators of a broad intelligence encompassing all the complex abilities of the human mind, "intelligence tests" are still recognized as being, if nothing else, indicators of probable academic success. The consistently low scores of education majors suggest that they would have difficulty in a traditionally oriented curriculum.[74]

There is evidence that teachers themselves are aware of this. For example, a survey of beginning teachers conducted by the Office of Education during the 1950s reported ". . . a feeling of greater adequacy in the human relations than in the subject matter aspects of teaching. This pattern appears generally and in each of the four sex and teaching level groups."[75]

A large proportion of American public school teachers did not have an academic major in college. Instead they majored in "education," which consists mainly of courses in methods, educational philosophy, school administration, guidance, etc. Although they may have had some work in other fields, they generally lacked depth in them. During his study of teacher education in the United States, Koerner examined transcripts of the college work done by many prospective teachers. He found certain patterns appearing over and over again, and he commented on several transcripts he felt were typical. For example:

> This kind of case occurs with great frequency, in both state colleges and university schools of education. Note that English, the major subject, counting the course in "Effective Speaking" as part of it, is far from strong: it shows no advanced composition, no grammar, no work in any literary figure except Shakespeare, no classical literature in translation, no non-English literature of any kind, and no work in any literary period . . . . There is, of course, no work whatever in mathematics, philosophy, economics, physical sciences, or in many other subjects.[76]

And,

> This is a fairly representative transcript for a teacher in that most protean of fields, social studies, though this individual has had the advantage of more semester hours than is normal. Because the scope of this field is without any practical limit, the custom is for students to sample a bit of everything in history (in this case confined to a year's survey of American history!), economics, sociology, political science, and perhaps geography. Note the plethora of 3-hour intro-

ductory courses, meaning that the student becomes, not a specialist in anything, but a shallow generalist in half a dozen things. He necessarily suffers in knowledge and discipline from this pervasive superficiality. Even so, it is a better education than that received by a great many secondary teachers.[77]

The amount of teaching experience and the type of subjects taught are also important. The N.E.A.'s 1960-61 survey, involving teachers in districts of all sizes throughout the United States, indicated that many teachers were relatively inexperienced and were further handicapped by assignments to classes or grades other than those in which they were best prepared.

Although the median length of teaching experience was 11.0 years, more than one-fourth (27.5 percent) of all teachers had four years or less of teaching experience.[78] The figure was considerably higher for men as almost half (46.9 percent) had taught four years or less.[79]

Lack of classroom experience was not the only problem. One-third of all teachers (31.4 percent) were teaching in grades or fields other than that of their major preparation. Among new teachers, those in their first or second year, the proportion was even higher, rising to 40.9 percent. While trying to teach outside of one's specialty would be hard even for a seasoned instructor, it would be especially difficult for someone just beginning his teaching career. Even the N.E.A. report, usually restrained, was moved to comment: "To the inexperienced teacher, such assignment could be a serious disadvantage."[80]

The N.E.A.'s survey also found that 40.3 percent of all secondary teachers were teaching non-academic, *skill centered* courses. These courses consist of all curricular fields other than the *book centered* subjects (science, mathematics, English, social studies, foreign languages and general education or "core" subjects). Among the skill centered courses are such fields as agriculture, physical education, industrial arts, music and driver education.[81]

Functions of Progressive Education

Progressive education, at least as it was popularly understood, offered American teachers three major advantages. First, it reduced academic demands to the point where many teachers and other personnel could satisfy the minimal requirements of their jobs. Second, it aided in pupil control, a crucial problem for individual teachers as well as for the school. Third, it supported teachers' claims to professional status.

Job Requirements. Progressive education suited the modest scholastic abilities of many public school employees. It helped them to qualify for positions, not by raising their level of competence, but rather by changing the requirements for the job. As we have seen, many teachers and administrators lacked the requisites for successful teaching in a traditional subject-oriented curriculum. Progressive education assisted them in several ways. It reduced academic demands by de-emphasizing subject matter and by substituting the development of the whole child as the goal of education. It substituted an easily acquired, generalized method for extensive teaching experience and thorough knowledge of subject matter, and it increased the number of non-academic positions within the school system: driver-training, "senior problems," home economics, and similar courses provided jobs for many teachers who would not have had a place in a more traditional school.

De-emphasis upon subject matter was a boon to teachers who lacked ability, training, and experience in academic fields. Traditional curriculum, being centered on subject matter, relied more heavily on comprehension of a body of facts and theory. It would, therefore, be less compatible to the talents of school personnel who lacked preparation in a traditional academic area such as English, history, mathematics, or biology. On the other hand, progressive education minimized reliance on knowledge of such subjects, and was more suited to teachers and administrators whose background in an academic field was inadequate.

This does not imply that teachers in the legendary "good old days" were capable or well-trained. Far from it. As we have seen, large numbers of them were little more than "live bodies" striving, often desperately, to keep their energetic pupils under control. Today's teachers, with all their shortcomings, probably have just as much scholastic ability as their predecessors and the vast majority of them are better educated than the schoolmasters of old. Teachers' colleges and university education programs, in spite of their faults, are better than no college at all. Even if future teachers learn as little as some critics claim, they at least are several years older and more sophisticated than were many traditional teachers.

In short, traditional teachers were probably no more capable than teachers today. What have changed are the demands of the teacher's role. Education has become a more complex task, so that what would have been adequate performance a century ago would not suffice today. The traditional teacher did not have to know much beyond the fundamentals of reading, writing and arithmetic. On the rare occasions when students progressed beyond this level, the limited knowledge called for was relatively easy for the teacher to acquire and relay to her pupils. Today, however, knowledge in all fields is far more extensive; the rote learning of state capitals or the birthdates of great men is no longer sufficient. Textbooks and reference materials are widely available and contain much information formerly provided by the teacher. As a result, the teacher's mastery of the material, made more complex today by the vast fund of available knowledge, is no longer as necessary. The older subjects have deepened and new fields have been added to the curriculum. As teachers' mastery of subject matter became more difficult and less necessary, a new role emerged, that of directing the learning process. The teacher can stimulate pupils; she can tell them where to look; she can help them to present material they have already acquired.

This new role required less competence in specific subjects and more ability in guiding learning in several areas. In this respect, the methods of progressive education suited not merely instructional exigencies but also the capacities of the teachers themselves. In place of mastery of a particular subject, a specific body of theory and fact, progressive education provided a generalized method useful in a variety of situations. For people of modest social origins, low scholastic capacity, and inadequate academic preparation, this method (at least as it is commonly presented) is faster and easier to acquire than subject-matter mastery could be. The method is transferable; it can be applied to social studies or physics, to language arts or mathematics. A teacher can start a discussion, show movies, have pupils do research for reports, make scrapbooks, paint murals, or build models in a number of courses. He does not necessarily have to know much about the particular subject. General methods for stimulating interest can be used with some effectiveness without much knowledge of the specified area involved. This was recognized, for example, by the General Elementary Supervisor in an urban California system who explained, ". . . although elementary teachers do not have too much special training in science they are not afraid to teach it."[82]

Another related function is that it increases the number of non-academic positions within the school. This, too, fits the particular personal characteristics of many public school teachers. Many areas in the curriculum today are somewhat removed from the traditional discipline, but are justified because of their benefit to the pupil's overall development. In addition to these benefits, they also provide jobs for the many teachers who would not feel at home in academic subjects. The N.E.A. 1960 survey found that one-third of all secondary teachers were spending the majority of their time teaching non-academic courses. Possibly some of these teachers would rather have been teaching academic courses. Nevertheless, the low academic ability and preparation typical of many American teachers suggest that many teachers of non-academic subjects would prefer to remain where they are.

Thus, progressive education provided new areas in which, given their personal characteristics, school personnel could succeed. Today, many non-academic courses provide areas in which neither teachers nor pupils will be handicapped by their social origin, scholastic shortcomings, or lack of adequate preparation or experience. A man who grew up on the wrong side of the tracks and was deprived of the cultural background which facilitates scholastic achievement could still find a niche in the school as a P.E. coach or shop instructor. In fact, his humble background may well be an advantage, in that he will better understand the home conditions of his students and the problems of the community.

Classroom Control. A second major area in which progressive education was helpful to school personnel was the perennial problem of discipline. Progressive education enabled teachers to keep better control over their pupils, thereby contributing to the solution of what is probably the teachers' most fundamental task. Although this is no longer stated as bluntly as it was in former days, keeping pupils in hand continues to be the teachers' most basic work problem. This goes beyond being only an organizational concern. It is far more than a formal requirement which she, as a teacher paid by the district, is expected to fulfill but which, like many official duties, can often be ignored by individual employees. It is even more than an altruistic desire to help children develop or to prevent them from dropping out of school. Instead, each teacher, whether she likes it or not, has an immediate, personal stake in maintaining discipline. At best, keeping the pupils under control makes her work much easier; it is more enjoyable and requires less energy on her part. At worst, if she cannot keep control, her job is jeopardized. Two or three "incidents" in her classroom will come rather quickly to the attention of the principal and her "inability to establish rapport with the children" will be considered a just cause for dismissal.

Thus, knowledge by itself is not enough. Regardless of a teacher's proficiency in mathematics, no matter how well-versed he might be in English literature, such knowledge will mean little unless he can keep his pupils under control. In this respect, there may be some truth in the educational theorists' contention that a teacher's scholastic capacity is unimportant. In fact, an academic orientation may even handicap a teacher if it leads him to neglect or underestimate the harsh realities existing in elementary and secondary classrooms today. The problem of supervision is not a passive one; the mere presence of an adult in the classroom is not, in itself, enough to maintain order for long. Since many pupils are not interested in studying and only attend school because they must, classroom control requires active effort on the part of the teacher. His knowledge of subject matter will not be of much assistance in this situation. A Doctor of Philosophy concerned primarily

with developing the intellectual powers of his pupils would have difficulty coping with problems he would meet in many public schools. In
order to maintain sufficient control to last the entire school year, something else would be necessary.

Thus, progressive education, in solving problems for the school,
also facilitated the teacher's job. By orienting pupils' learning around
their own experiences, progressive education was at least partially successful in arousing their interest in school to the point where they were
willing to go along with the teacher's wishes on most of the basic aspects of discipline. Instructional methods employing movies, games,
models, television, committees and murals were more enjoyable to many
pupils than traditional techniques, and were therefore less likely to stir
up rebellion against the teacher. In addition, extra-curricular activities,
ranging from hobby clubs to athletics, provided further incentive to conform to at least the minimum standards of discipline. Moreover, the
shift in emphasis from subject matter to the pupils themselves reduced
the intellectual demands which would frustrate many students who were
not academically inclined. Finally, human relation skills enabled teachers
to win at least a modicum of cooperation from the majority of pupils.
While these functions were helpful for the school as an organization, they
also aided teachers with an immediate, very real problem of their own.

Professional Status. A third major function of progressive education
was its support of the teachers' claim to professional status, bolstering
their prestige and offering them some protection against attack. This
drive toward professionalism is a common phenomenon in Western society. Professionalization is, in part, forced upon various occupations by
the inexorable processes of an increasingly complex society. In addition,
it is sought voluntarily by practitioners themselves. Members of a wide
range of occupations — not merely nurses, social workers, librarians,
etc., who are on the lower fringe of professionalism, but also many of the
working class — are concerned with improving their public image and
their pay by professionalization. They attempt to move away from the
idea that their work is just a job which almost anyone could perform, to
the idea that they are rendering an essential, highly skilled service which
they alone have the training and experience to perform. Progressive education supported the claim that teaching is a profession in at least two
ways.

The first involves knowledge of specialized techniques. "The professional," explains Gross, "is the man who knows."[83] He has power
because he is a repository of special techniques and knowledge which
his client does not have. Traditional pedagogical methods were so simple

that they supported the belief that anyone could be a teacher and that people unable to succeed in other occupations could nevertheless do a passable job in teaching. This belief may have actually increased toward the end of the traditional era. With the disappearance of classic studies, which at one time formed the backbone of the curriculum, teachers were left with no specialized knowledge on the basis of which they might claim some distinction. In those earlier times, even though teachers were not highly regarded, it was apparent that they knew something which most people did not. But, by the late nineteenth century, demand for this esoteric knowledge was fading, leaving teachers with little except the three Rs.

Progressive education mended this weakness in teachers' occupational image by pointing to a new body of specialized knowledge in teaching methods, growth and development, and child psychology. This knowledge provided educators with a new field of competence in which they alone could claim to know what was best for the pupil. Even the physician, with his concern for the immediate physical health of the child, was concerned primarily with the special needs of sick children and was therefore not as qualified as the public school teacher in guiding the pupil's overall social, psychological and educational development. In sum, progressive education provided teachers with an area of unique, distinctive competence.

It is interesting to note, in this connection, that the introduction of infant or *primary* schools in the first half of the nineteenth century, usually conducted along the lines of Pestallozian principles, ". . . tended to give a new dignity to teaching and school work by revealing something of a psychological basis for the instruction of little children."[84]

Another feature of a profession is its concern with an unstandardized product. According to Gross, "A professional activity is one in which general knowledge is applied to solve particular problems, each of which is different from all other such problems."[85] The physician, ideally at least, approaches each patient as unique; if not in symptoms, at least in the patient's attitudes, the degree to which he will follow instructions, the support provided by the patient's family, and the chances of successful treatment. This individuality of approach was absent from traditional teaching. All that the old-time teacher was expected to do, beyond keeping order and leading a moral life, was to give assignments, hear pupils recite their lessons, and grade the pupils' work. Even when students recited separately, the same techniques and procedures were followed for all. A student's failure was considered to be his own misfortune. Undoubtedly, some teachers attempted to help individuals who were having trouble, but these teachers were considered to be exceptions; attention to individuals was not expected.

Progressive education, in emphasizing the importance of treating each child as a unique individual, eliminated the bogey of standardized, relatively undemanding services, suggestive of manual labor or factory work rather than of a profession requiring careful consideration for each case. In theory, at least, repetition of the same simple service for every student was replaced by a fund of special knowledge necessary for tailoring education to fit the unique configuration of needs of each individual pupil.

Professionalization aided teachers in at least two ways. First, it increased their occupational prestige. Little need be said about the advantages of prestige. It provides psychic reward, in the form of self-esteem and the admiration of others. It also supports requests for higher pay. To the extent, therefore, that teaching can climb away from the multitude of mere *jobs* into the ranks of the *professions*, it will bring to its practitioners more personal satisfactions and more economic remuneration.

In addition to supporting teachers' claims to higher status, professionalization through progressive education also served a protective function. It deterred attacks upon the competence of the public school and its personnel by shifting the school's emphasis from subject matter to pupils themselves. While obscuring standards by which others might evaluate the school's effectiveness, it established a special field over which the school asserted exclusive jurisdiction. Although parents, college professors or businessmen might claim to be judges of scholastic achievement, and might criticize the school for inadequate intellectual training of pupils, they would be less able to disprove the school's contention that it was successfully developing the whole child, and that it alone had competence in this field.

This new position was easier to defend than the older one had been. Formerly, teachers would have found it more difficult to protect themselves against charges that they had failed to teach a particular pupil to read. About all they could do would be to retort defensively that the pupil was a "blockhead," incapable of learning — a counter attack which would have left the pupil and his parents upset and resentful toward the teacher. With the support of progressive education, however, the teacher could sidestep the charge, claiming that her goals were broader than mere reading or any other specific skill; she was concerned instead with the development of the whole child. His present difficulty was perhaps only a temporary one which would disappear with increasing maturation. At any rate, the child had other assets which were developing him, with the school's expert assistance, into a likeable individual and a good citizen. The teacher could claim that she alone had the necessary specialized training required for this important task, and that laymen or members of other professions were outside of their field of competence here.

Sometimes this argument is stated more forcefully, as the following newspaper report indicates:

LET SCHOOL PROFESSIONALS RUN SCHOOLS
Sacramento (AP)

A state school official struck out today at "the fearful, the disgruntled and the disillusioned" who, she said, criticize public education in areas best left to the professional.

Helen Hefferman, chief of the elementary education bureau, said in effect that the public should provide support for schools and let educators alone determine school programs.

"The educational leaders of our state and nation know now the changes in education which would vastly improve its quality," she contended in a prepared statement.

"Putting these changes into operation is actually being delayed by the cacaphony of the critics.

"We will have to forsake our basic democratic values if we take seriously the hysterical demands of these critics of American education that we pattern our program on the outmoded patterns of European societies."[86]

A final point is worth noting. Contradictions in an ideology are not necessarily serious handicaps. They can be, and often are, glossed over or ignored altogether to suit the purpose of those who support them. For example, one might raise the question of juvenile delinquency: "If the schools are concerned with the 'whole child', why don't they do something about youthful lawbreakers?"

The progressive educator can reply that schools can't do everything: "We're doing a good job, the best possible, but we can't work miracles." The blame for delinquency can be shifted to bad home conditions, over which the schools have no control. The educator's denial of responsibility is supported by a mass of sociological and psychological writing which emphasizes the importance of a child's early experiences within his family. The pupil's personal record, which follows him throughout his public school career, contains background information about his home life. This file serves a double function: it helps the teacher to understand the pupil and it gathers evidence to provide the school with an alibi for the pupil's shortcomings.

In sum, ideologies, like political platforms, do not have to be logically consistent in order to be effective. Progressive education offered the educator the best of two worlds, allowing him to claim credit for students' successes while avoiding the blame for their failures.

CONCLUSION

While the salary, status, and working conditions of public school teaching remained about the same, relative to other occupations, progressive education offered, if not higher prestige, at least a more realistic yet favorable image of those in public education. Aside from increased femininization, patterns of recruitment into teaching have not changed appreciably since traditional times. Teachers still have only modest academic ability. However, the expectations regarding teaching have been fundamentally altered. Teachers are no longer perceived as storehouses of knowledge — a wealth of learning materials now serves this function. Instead, they have become directors of learning. Progressive education was very useful in this transformation because it focused on methods of teaching rather than on subject matter. It made acceptable the moderate capabilities of the personnel already recruited into the public schools. It legitimized the change from the impossibly high ideal of the scholar to the more realistic level of the educator, a professional whose competence is certified by his special training in teaching methods and child development.

REFERENCES

[1]"Teachers" are not a homogenous group. Discussion of "teachers'" status may obscure the sizeable differences which often exist between subgroups within the occupation, particularly between administrators and classroom teachers. These differences were mentioned briefly in Chapter 4 and will be examined in detail in Chapter 7.

[2]Reisner, *The Evolution of the Common School,* pp. 312-13.

[3]*Ibid.*

[4]Butts and Cremin, *History of Education,* p. 286.

[5]Cubberly, *Public Education,* rev. ed., p. 327.

[6]Butts and Cremin, *History of Education,* p. 284.

[7]*Ibid.,* p. 285.

[8]*Ibid.*

[9]Quoted in Cubberly, *Public Education,* rev. ed., p. 326.

[10]*Ibid.*

[11]Quoted in Cubberly, *Readings,* p. 295.

[12]Butts and Cremin, *History of Education,* p. 286.

[13]*Ibid.*

[14]*Ibid.,* p. 287; Cubberly, *Public Education,* rev. ed., p. 380.

[15]Butts and Cremin, *History of Education,* p. 287.

[16]*Ibid.,* p. 449; Cubberly, *Public Education,* rev. ed., pp. 380-83.

[17]Butts and Cremin, *History of Education,* p. 288.

[18]*Ibid.,* p. 449.

[19]*Ibid.,* pp. 449-50.

[20]*Ibid.,* p. 451.

[21]*Ibid.*

[22]*Ibid.,* pp. 451-52.

[23]*Ibid.,* p. 450.

[24]*Ibid.,* p. 453.

[25]*Ibid.* By 1910, three-fourths of the states required some education courses for certification.

[26]*Ibid.,* p. 454.

[27]*Ibid.*

[28]*Ibid.* In 1920, the average annual earnings of public school teachers ($936) were still considerably below the $1,407 average for the thirteen industries and occupations presented in *Historical Statistics* . . . . Only farm laborers were paid less ($810). For example, ministers were paid, on the average, an annual salary of $1,428; postal employees $1,844; coal miners $1,386; and wage earners in manufacturing $1,358 (U.S. Bureau of the Census, *Historical Statistics* . . . , p. 91).

[29]Butts and Cremin, *History of Education,* pp. 454-55.

[30]*Ibid.,* p. 455.

[31]*Ibid.,* pp. 455-56.

[32]*Ibid.,* p. 285; NEA figures cited in Lieberman, *Education as a Profession,* p. 242.

[33]Lieberman, *The Future of Public Education,* pp. 187-88; Butts and Cremin, *History of Education,* pp. 601-02.

[34]Lieberman, *Future of Public Education,* p. 188.

[35]N.E.A., *The American Public School Teacher 1960-1961,* pp. 22-23.

[36]N.E.A., "The Teachers' Role in American Society," from *N.E.A. Research Bulletin* (February, 1952), pp. 22-23.

[37]*Ibid.*

[38]N.E.A., *The American Public School Teacher 1960-1961,* p. 40.

[39]Edward Gross, *Work and Society,* p. 78.

[40]Butts and Cremin, *History of Education,* p. 606.

[41]*Ibid.*

[42]Lieberman, *Education as a Profession,* p. 148.

[43]*Ibid.,* p. 149.

[44]*Ibid.*

[45]*Ibid.,* pp. 92-95.

[46]*Ibid.,* p. 95.

[47]Lieberman, *Future of Public Education,* p. 185.

[48]Lieberman, *Education as a Profession,* p. 97.

[49]Lieberman, *Future of Public Education,* pp. 184-85.

[50]*Ibid.,* p. 179.

[51]Butts and Cremin, *History of Education,* p. 603.

[52]Lieberman, *Education as a Profession,* p. 232.

[53]*Ibid.*

[54]Richey, *Planning for Teaching,* pp. 218-19.

[55]Stiles, *The Teacher's Role in American Society,* p. 18.

[56]For example, a University of California study found that more intelligent students received lower grades in student teaching than did less intelligent ones (From figures presented in Linn, *A Comparison of the Mean Test Scores and Standard Deviations on the Department of Education Test Battery and Student Teaching Grades*).

[57]Lieberman, *Education as a Profession,* p. 458n.

[58]National Opinion Research Center, "Jobs and Occupations: A Popular Evaluation," in Bendix and Lipset, ed., *Class, Status and Power,* pp. 411-14.

[59]By a two-to-one margin, nursing was the first choice of this reader poll. The poll did not claim to represent a typical cross-section of the United States public opinion (*Ibid.,* pp. 420, 695).

[60]N.E.A., *The American Public School Teacher 1960-1961,* p. 16.

[61]*Ibid.*

[62]*Ibid.*

[63]Koerner, *The Miseducation of American Teachers,* p. 39.

[64]Learned and Wood, *The Student and His Knowledge; a Report to the Carnegie Foundation on the Results of the High School and College Examinations of 1928, 1930, and 1932,* pp. 39, 43, 64, 351, in Koerner, *Miseducation,* pp. 39-40.

[65]Koerner, *Miseducation,* p. 39.

[66]Learned and Wood, in Koerner, *Miseducation,* pp. 39-40.

[67]*Ibid.*

[68]Koerner, *Miseducation,* p. 41.

[69]Wolfle, *America's Resources of Specialized Talent,* p. 199.

[70]*Ibid.,* p. 200.

[71]Koerner, *Miseducation,* pp. 42-43.

[72]*Ibid.,* p. 45.

[73]Linn, *Comparison of Mean Test Scores.*

[74]Intelligence scores obtained from students majoring in different fields were actually representative of people working in these fields (Wolfle, *America's Resources,* p. 199).

[75]Mason, *The Beginning Teacher,* p. 90.

[76]Koerner, *Miseducation,* p. 141.

[77]*Ibid.,* pp. 141-42.

[78]N.E.A., *The American Public School Teacher 1960-1961,* p. 92.

[79]*Ibid.*

[80]*Ibid.,* p. 41.

[81]*Ibid.,* p. 49.

[82]Richmond (California) School District, *Board Bulletin 6-B,* 1961.

[83]Gross, *Work and Society,* p. 78.

[84]Cubberly, *Public Education,* rev. ed., p. 142.

[85]Gross, *Work and Society,* p. 77.

[86]*The Richmond Independent,* October 26, 1960, p. 30.

seven

DIFFERENTIAL SUPPORT
FOR PROGRESSIVE
EDUCATION

WE HAVE BEEN DISCUSSING PROBLEMS FACING THE SCHOOL AND ITS PER-
sonnel as a whole. However, organizations are far from monolithic,
homogeneous entities. On the contrary, they consist of diverse subgroups
which are apt to differ from one another in many ways, including the
degree to which they support and benefit from the official ideology of
the organization. In American public schools, support for progressive
education varies considerably between different groups of school employees. It is more likely to be supported by younger, inexperienced
teachers than by those who have taught many years. It is more likely
to be favored by teachers in the lower grades than by secondary teachers, more by teachers of non-academic courses than by those of academic courses, and more by administrators than by teachers.

Summarizing these trends, a traditional approach would most likely
be found among older, experienced high school teachers of academic
subjects, while the progressive approach would be associated with lack
of teaching experience, non-academic orientation, and administration.
This, in fact, is the argument which will be presented in this chapter.
The previous chapter offered some reasons why school employees generally might benefit from progressive education. It is suggested here
that seasoned secondary teachers of academic subjects had little to gain
from it, while administrators, especially principals, profited more.

The next section reviews evidence concerning differential support
for progressive education. Subsequent sections deal first with high school

academic teachers and then with other instructors. The remainder of the chapter discusses administrators, particularly principals, and their stake in progressive education.

EVIDENCE OF DIFFERENTIAL SUPPORT

One of the most extensive studies comparing the attitudes of various groups of public school teachers was conducted by David Ryans. Although primarily interested in other things, he looked into teachers' pedagogical orientations. He found:

> ... from the standpoint of age, teachers under 30 years of age, in both the elementary and secondary schools, appeared to be more liberal in their educational beliefs, and teachers over 45 years of age, at all levels, seemed to be the most traditional.[1]

He also observed that progressive methods were more likely to be found among less-experienced teachers, in high schools as well as elementary schools:

> Elementary teachers with smaller amounts of teaching experience (up to four or five years) tended to express more permissive educational viewpoints, and those with ten years or more of teaching experience more traditional. On the secondary level there was a definite tendency for teachers with experience beyond 15 years to be more traditional in educational viewpoints.[2]

These patterns appeared regardless of the grade level or subject taught. Within each subject and level:

> ... there was a significant trend ... for teachers with less experience to be significantly, and substantially, more inclined toward child-centered, permissive educational viewpoints, and teachers with greater amounts of experience, favoring viewpoints reflecting a learning-centered, traditional emphasis.[3]

With respect to age, "There is a consistent tendency here for older teachers to emphasize learning-centered educational viewpoints, and younger teachers more permissive, child-centered viewpoints."[4]

Another important finding concerned teaching level. "Secondary teachers as a group tended to express educational viewpoints more toward the traditional, academic end of the scale and elementary teachers toward the child-centered, progressive pole." Furthermore, "This trend toward greater academic emphasis in the higher grades was observable even within the elementary school."[5] Teachers in the seventh and eighth grades had the most traditional viewpoints, while those down in the primary grades had the most permissive point of view.

A third pattern involved the type of course being taught: "In the secondary school, business education, mathematics and science teachers tended to be more traditional in educational beliefs and values, while English and social studies teachers leaned toward liberal, permissive viewpoints."[6] Additional evidence on this point is provided by Ward Mason's survey of beginning teachers. Mason found ". . . teachers of non-academic subjects were most likely to feel that education courses had been helpful, and teachers of academic subjects least likely."[7]

The most important difference of all is between teachers and administrators. Administrators are more likely than teachers to favor progressive, pupil-centered education. This difference is suggested, for example, by a survey which reported that ". . . teachers held a significantly dimmer view of methods courses than did administrators and board members." When asked if teacher training institutions should increase methods courses, fifty-one percent of the administrators said "yes" compared to only thirty-three percent of the teachers.[8]

The difference also appears during educational controversies such as the one which developed in San Francisco in 1960. A committee of university professors, in criticizing the public schools, expressed the belief that ". . . the purpose of education is to inform the mind and develop the intelligence." Instead, they complained, "Recent pedagogical theory . . . has tended to make 'education for life in a democracy' the primary purpose of the public schools, interpreting and applying that phrase in a sense profoundly hostile to excellence in education."[9]

Many teachers agreed with these criticisms, while the strongest opposition to the professors' report came from principals. For instance, a newspaper reported:

> Bertram Callen, president of the Teachers Association of San Francisco, also said his organization had been "pounding away for three or four years at many of the things the report says."
> But an elementary school principal said he would challenge the report's statement that it is wrong to emphasize that schools are preparing students for life in a democracy. "We are doing that, and we should do it," he said.[10]

Further indications of administrators' propensity to support progressive education are offered by the types of situations which are considered to be "typical." The kinds of incidents selected and the types of people assigned to the various roles suggest the feelings which others have toward these situations and the people involved in them.

A textbook for school administrators presented case studies ". . . illustrating typical human relations problems . . . directly related to a major operational phase of the administrator's daily work."[11] A number of these problem cases suggest that the existence of traditionally oriented teachers is one of the major problems confronting administrators. Thus, the very first incident in the book, entitled "A Troublemaker Joins the Staff," deals with a traditional instructor in an elementary school:

> She believed that stricter discipline should be enforced among the student body in classes, study halls and club activities. She maintained that the fifteen-minute daily assemblies should be cut to five minutes so that assemblies would be "educational" rather than for "pure enjoyment," and that the pupils in the cafeteria should be silent during the lunch session.[12]

The faculty had been ". . . amiable and satisfied until this new teacher quietly, but relentlessly, engaged in her campaign of stirring up dissatisfaction."[13] Teachers could be heard complaining to one another about the advantages which students took of the "sincere, hardworking" teachers. Teacher-pupil relationships in several classes began to deteriorate, discipline problems arose where they had not previously existed, and the beginnings of antagonism were apparent within pupil groups. "Several teachers in the school became alarmed at the unwholesome influence" she was exerting upon their co-workers and upon the actual functioning of the school.[14]

The manner in which this incident is reported does not make clear whether the trouble arose because the teacher was generally a disruptive person, who would have upset any group by her backbiting, gossip, and so forth, or whether it was specifically her traditionalistic educational orientation which created the disturbance. Actually, however, this confusion, this tendency to equate a troublesome person with one who holds a traditional perspective, is itself significant because it suggests the general attitude of administrators toward subject-centered teachers.

A second "typical" incident described a similar situation in which a beginning high school principal encountered problems when he tried to "improve" the curriculum. His faculty, however, prided itself on its high academic standards.[15] They believed that the principal's progressive ideas were "an attack on their methods of teaching and on the traditional standards they wanted to uphold."[16] After the principal introduced his views, he received a communication, signed by every member of the faculty, stating the belief that ". . . the proper education of youth depends upon students' gaining the knowledge that can be absorbed only in the specialized study of subject matter."[17]

A third incident involved the same basic problem. In this case, a principals' association was attempting to "modernize" the curriculum. However:

A major difficulty in revising the curriculum lay in the unwillingness of large numbers of faculty members to emerge from their specialized subject-matter fields. Many of these teachers maintained that school administrators were lowering educational standards by introducing programs of general education. They claimed that students could not read or write adequately because of "growing laxity of the educational program."[18]

Finally, the contrasting attitudes of principals and teachers are suggested by the following comments.

A seventh-grade English teacher reported:

The principal came in while I was explaining the difference between the nominative and objective forms of pronouns; when to use "I" and "me" in sentences. He called me aside after the class and told me: "Don't try to teach them all that grammar and stuff— just entertain them."[19]

And an elementary principal in another district explained his attempts to "modernize" instructional methods:

I assist a teacher by showing her how to get her youngsters more interested in their studies. You don't do this by having them answer questions at the end of the chapter. . . . You have to make their work more meaningful for them . . . have them work on murals, dioramas, models, committees and other learning activities.[20]

How can we account for these differences? Why should support for progressive education be higher among younger, inexperienced teachers, those in the lowest grades, and those teaching non-academic subjects? And why should administrators be more favorably inclined toward it than teachers were? To answer such questions we may look at the various positions and findings in light of the three general functions of progressive education discussed in the previous chapters.

High School Academic Teachers. Progressive education, it was said, enabled personnel to qualify for the job, helped them with the basic work problem of pupil control, and bolstered their marginal security and prestige. These contributions would be least helpful to experienced, well-prepared high school instructors of academic subjects. Such teachers would be the ones most likely to feel at home in a traditionally oriented school. For many of them, interest in teaching was subordinate to their interest in the subject matter itself. Their primary concern was with French or physics of mathematics; their decision to enter public school teaching came later, when they turned to teaching as a way of earning a living through their academic interests. As undergraduates they majored in an academic field rather than in education or its common companions, home economics or physical education. In 1960, over one-third (thirty-six percent) of United States' high school teachers held advanced degrees; [21] while many of these were in education, there were a fair number whose graduate work was in an academic field.

Of all school personnel, the high school academic instructor comes closest to the traditional image of the teacher as scholar. His training and background in subject matter, and the fact that he teaches in an established field, leave little doubt about the nature of his work. The subject itself provides the focus for his activities and the justification for his position. No further defense for his existence is needed. The subject mtater is there, it is cut and dried — if he wants to treat it that way — and it is his acknowledged job to convey it to his pupils.

The high school teacher of traditional academic subjects was least likely to be bothered by discipline problems. His classes were more likely to be selective, drawing more ambitious students from white-collar families. The really troublesome pupils were diverted into other, less demanding courses. Consequently, academic teachers had less need for progressive education's assistance in controlling obstreperous pupils.

Elementary and Non-Academic Secondary Teachers. Progressive education could be more helpful to people in the broad middle-ground between high school academic instruction and administration; that is, to high school teachers in non-academic areas, to junior high school instructors and elementary teachers. In addition, there were inadequately prepared people teaching academic classes. It often happens that one or two classes are left without teachers after the regular staff members have been assigned a full schedule. Someone must fill the gap, yet it is usually not practical to hire another specialist for just one or two classes. In such a situation, a teacher from another field, who happens to have a light teaching load, may be assigned to teach the courses.

Sometimes the additional courses will be relatively close to the teacher's field of competence: for example, an algebra teacher may be assigned to business math, or a chemistry instructor to physics. Often, however, the extra courses are not related to those which the teacher usually conducts, so that physics may be taught by the athletic coach and European history by the typing instructor. Incongruous assignments like these may not be welcomed by the teachers, but there is little they can do about them and they have to get along as best they can. Those who have taught for a long time can draw upon their own experience. The subject matter may be new to them but, at least, they know generally what to expect from pupils, they know how to organize the material, and how to teach the course.

This is not true, however, for younger teachers who lack experience in the classroom. For them, progressive education may be helpful and reassuring. By relaxing the traditional authoritarian structure, and by encouraging a more permissive climate in the classroom, the progressive teacher shifts responsibility to the pupils and reduces academic pressure on himself. He is not burdened with being the source of knowledge, the final authority on the subject. Instead, he directs his efforts toward motivating his pupils, using his human relations training to stimulate their general willingness to try, using audio-visual methods and materials for presenting some basic information prepared by supervisors or commercial firms, and by suggesting ways in which pupils might present their findings — through oral and written reports, displays, working models, and so forth. The students themselves find and learn the relevant material.

There is much to be said for such a process from a pedagogical perspective. The point here, however, is that it also serves a function for the teacher who lacks background in teaching academic subjects. It changes the method of teaching to one better suited to his personal qualifications.

Progressive education might also be helpful to the forty percent of all secondary instructors who are teaching non-academic subjects.[22] Home economics, industrial arts, physical education and the like did not exist in the high school curriculum of 1900, but they are taught by thousands of teachers today.[23] A large number of these teachers, lacking an academic background, would be unable to teach in high school if the curriculum had remained as it was a half-century ago. As it is, these teachers are now an integral part of the school's staff.

This is important for many of these non-academic instructors because teaching, especially in high school, is an avenue of social mobility. Many of them came from working class or rural homes. The N.E.A.'s 1960 survey found that more than half of all high school teachers were the children of blue-collar workers or farmers.[24] Although some farmers were well-off, many were not, and therefore teaching would be a decided step upward for their children. The relative lack of opportunity and, in particular, the low level of intellectual stimulation often characteristic of such a background is a handicap to the achievement of competence in academic areas. These people have a better chance to succeed when success does not depend upon academic factors. Thus the progressive school, offering non-academic courses and emphasizing personal relations and easily acquired teaching methods rather than scholastic achievement as qualifications for employment, provided an avenue of social mobility for its personnel, as well as for its pupils.

A second major function of progressive education useful to many teachers is class control. Support for progressive education is highest where selectivity is lowest. Problems of control depend, to a considerable degree, on selectivity. In selective classes such as calculus or advanced foreign languages, which enroll only the most capable and highly motivated pupils, there is relatively little trouble with discipline. In contrast, where there is little selectivity, as in the elementary grades, control will be more difficult. In general, selectivity increases with each grade of school. The highest percentages of school-age children actually attending school are in the lower grades. In 1920, over ninety percent of the population between the ages of nine and thirteen were enrolled in school. Among older children, however, there was a sharp drop in the proportion enrolled, so that only half of the sixteen-year olds and a third of the seventeen-year olds were in school. During the next twenty years the proportion in these older groups increased tremendously. By 1940, the percentage of sixteen-year olds enrolled in school had risen from 51 to 76 percent, and the proportion of seventeen-year olds climbed from 35 to 61 percent. The trend continued even further. By 1960, over three-fourths of the nation's seventeen-year olds were in school.[25]

Thus, the problems posed by an unselected clientele have confronted elementary teachers for some time. Since World War I they have had to accommodate pupils representing practically the entire spectrum of human capacity. Until more recent times, teachers in secondary schools have escaped many of the problems posed by pupils of extremely low ability and motivation. Consequently, control over pupils is least likely to be a problem for the high school teacher of solid, elective subjects. Within the comprehensive school, which theoretically offers all pupils the same or "equivalent" educational fare, academic courses can continue to be very selective, drawing those students with the highest motivation and the most ability relative to the student body as a whole. The exceptions to this are English and social studies, the courses most likely to be required of all students, regardless of ability or vocational goals.

In 1910, English was taken by fifty-seven percent of high school pupils, making it, even then, the most "popular" subject, closely followed by algebra and United States history. By 1928 English had become by far the most common subject, enrolling ninety-three percent of all public high school pupils.[26] In 1949 the percentage was still the same, but the proportion of the school-age population actually attending school had steadily increased.[27] As a result, high school English teachers, by the second quarter of this century, had to contend with practically the entire range of pupils. Since English was required of all students, these teachers faced the same problem of an unselected and often involuntary and uncooperative student clientele that confronted teachers in the lower grades. In some respects, these problems were even more acute at the higher level. Although some potential troublemakers dropped out before they reached secondary school, those who remained often compensated for their absent cohorts by their greater size, strength and cynicism regarding school rules or the necessity for getting an education.

As a result, high school English teachers were more likely than other academic instructors to encounter serious problems in maintaining control. In compulsory English classes there was pressure to "just keep 'em quiet." Here, if anywhere in the modern high school, the ancient game of "turning out the teacher" could still be played with a vengeance —and the teacher did not always win. While statistics are unavailable, it is probably the academically oriented teachers who lost out in such struggles. Those who succeed in staying often owe their survival to progressive teaching methods: reducing academic pressures upon pupils, using audio-visual aids partly for education but also for entertainment, concentrating on pupils as individuals rather than as mere receptacles into which knowledge was to be poured, and so forth.

Consequently, Ryan's finding that English teachers were more likely than math or science teachers to favor progressive education is understandable. To a lesser degree, the same holds true of social studies. Although a lower proportion of pupils across the nation are enrolled in them, social studies courses are more likely than other academic subjects to be required of all students. Consequently, they also are difficult courses to handle. When problems similar to those confronting English teachers are encountered, the custodial controls offered by progressive methods will be helpful.

The more intensive support for progressive education in the lower grades is illustrated by another "typical" incident presented by Anderson and Davies. They noted the willingness of junior high teachers (greater than that of senior high teachers) to accept a new promotion policy which would consider the pupil's chronological age, physical growth and social adaptability rather than merely his mastery of subject matter.

The junior high school studied had seventeen pupils between fourteen and sixteen-and-a-half years of age, and a number of them were:

... physically, mentally, or socially ill-adjusted. Under the new junior high policy, pupils who had reached the age of 14 "were considered ready, in most cases, for the experiences of the senior high school." ... the junior high school teachers and their principal agreed that the placement of over-age pupils with others of their physical and social maturity was beneficial to the over-age student, as well as to younger junior high school pupils. However the staff of the senior high school objected that the new policy "pampered the pupil." They wanted to retain "the Weapon of competitive grading and high-percentage failure." They wished to retain a traditional curriculum that would attract to the senior high school only the most highly selected students.[28]

Although the discipline problem is not mentioned, this is usually what is meant by *older pupils who are "physically, mentally or socially maladjusted."* Progressive education offered junior high personnel a justification for passing on some of their problem pupils to the high school. High school teachers, in contrast, had nothing to gain from such "social promotions." Their work would become more difficult because of the progressive concept which burdened them with pupils who, under a traditional system, would not have gone beyond elementary school.

The elementary school is the least selective of all. Teachers at this level are most likely to be confronted by pupils who are mentally retarded, physically handicapped, or culturally deprived. Although this was already a problem by the end of World War I, the lack of selectivity has become even more prominent, particularly in the primary grades. The proportion of the population attending school has increased to 98 percent for children aged ten through twelve, and among younger children the rise has been more pronounced. In 1920, for example, 83 percent of the seven-year olds were in school, compared to 97 percent in 1960.[29]

Although elementary teachers may possibly have one advantage over their secondary colleagues in that smaller children are, in some respects, easier to control, the advantage is largely negated by other factors. Elementary schools continue to be less selective. While differences in proportions of the enrolled population are small, even a few percentage points near the extreme ends of the distribution can make a big difference in the types of pupils enrolled. Let us think in terms of the bell-shaped normal curve. We can see that, while a relatively small number of cases lie more than two or three standard deviations away from the mean, these extreme cases are further removed from the average than are the bulk of the cases. It is these atypical pupils, especially those below the average, who are likely to cause trouble in the school, and it takes only one or two such individuals to disrupt an entire classroom.

A second factor, perhaps more relevant than selectivity, is inflexibility of the elementary school. There are fewer possibilities in the elementary grades for removing problem pupils from the regular classroom. The diversified curricula of junior and senior high schools is not present at the grammar school level, so there is less possibility for separating the troublemakers from the usually tractable majority. Without special classes in shop, home economics, art and the like, all pupils, fast and slow, quiet or belligerent, are placed together in the same room.

One approach to this problem is *homogeneous grouping,* which puts all the fast pupils in one room and all the slow ones in another. This system, however, also has drawbacks and is not universally accepted by teachers and administrators. Among its disadvantages, it puts a severe burden on the teacher who gets the slow class. She is likely to have a half-dozen explosive pupils along with twenty or thirty others who would present pedagogical problems even if disciplinary difficulties were entirely absent. In heterogeneous classes there are usually at least a few bright pupils whose presence can be helpful in correcting papers, assisting slower classmates, and so on.

A third contribution of progressive education involves its support of a favorable occupational image which would bolster the teachers' status and security. Instructors are engaged in a variety of activities, many of which have little apparent connection with education in the traditional sense. Along with their regular instructional duties, teachers of most subjects perform a number of non-educational tasks, such as keeping attendance registers, collecting milk money, or patrolling yards and hallways. The N.E.A.'s survey reported, "Miscellaneous assignments beyond class instruction and related duties add the equivalent of an additional day to the average teacher's weekly schedule."[30] Among the more distasteful duties, "Monitorial or managerial functions, such as hall duty, luncheon duty, playground duty, traffic duty, bus duty" were reported by 91 percent of the elementary teachers and 65 percent of secondary teachers.[31] "Handling money—banking, milk, collections, tickets . . ." was listed by 62 percent of the elementary teachers and 36 percent of the secondary teachers.[32] "Official records other than for one's own class" were kept by 47 percent of the elementary and 44 percent of the secondary teachers.[33]

Although such tasks do not add to the luster of the occupation, teachers must handle them. Because some of the more degrading tasks are more likely to be demanded of elementary teachers than of secondary teachers, it is not surprising to find the former are especially concerned with establishing their claim to professionalism. Since their lack of command of a particular subject matter prevents their basing this claim on traditional academic grounds, progressive education provides them with an alternative means of claiming professional status. Knowledge of specialized techniques and the ability to apply such knowledge to the solution of the unique, individual problems of every student are thus more helpful to the elementary teacher than to her secondary colleagues.

A similar situation exists with reference to teachers of non-academic subjects. These teachers are rather vulnerable to demands to "cut out the frills," to eliminate, for example, driver-training, home economics and senior problems. Such courses are less vulnerable if they can be defended as contributing to pupils' development.

Administrators. This chapter has suggested some reasons for the greater support given progressive education by younger, inexperienced non-academic teachers in the lower grades than by their more experienced, academically oriented colleagues in high school. Turning now to administrators, we may ask why they would be more likely than other school personnel to support progressive education. To answer this question we must first look at administrators' backgrounds and abilities, the type of work they are doing and the expectations confronting them.

The conditions which led to the recruitment of administrators differed from those affecting the majority of teachers, although they did have one point in common: knowledge of subject matter was not crucial for either. In fact, it was even less important for administrators than for most teachers. General success in teaching was not a consideration in their selection. In contemporary school systems, principals and other administrators are more likely to be chosen for their ability to cope with pupil control, public relations and plant management.

This is indicated by time-allotment studies in which administrators have kept records of how their time was spent. A survey of secondary school principals, for example, found that they did little or no teaching themselves and spent only a small fraction of their time on matters related to classroom instruction. Instead, most of their time went into "administrative routine," "co-curricular activities" and "attendance and discipline."[34] A similar situation exists at the elementary level where, on the average, only three percent of the principals' time was spent in "classroom teaching" while 62 percent of their time was taken up by "community work," "organization and management of the school," and "clerical work."[35]

In addition to principals' own accounts of their work, there is considerable evidence that superintendents do not consider teaching ability to be an important factor in administrative success. The National Association of Secondary School Principals' *Bulletin* mentioned:

> A high school principal may have an excellent academic and professional training, and still be an ineffective school leader through an unfortunate lack of certain personal qualities so necessary to success.[36]

So rare is the practice of selecting administrators on the basis of superior teaching ability that its existence at all was considered worthy of notice in an educational journal. A news item stated:

> Whether or not it is true, the Lindenhurst, N.Y. school district bases its administrator recruitment plan on the belief that the best classroom teachers make the best administrators. . . .[37]

The skeptical tone of the initial clause suggests that the wisdom of this practice is dubious.

Further support for the contention that teaching success is not a factor in promotion is provided by evaluation forms used by school systems for rating principals and other administrators. A typical example is the form used by the San Francisco Unified School District. It evaluates its administrators according to the following twelve points:

> Personal characteristics
> Enthusiasm shown in work
> Imagination in problem solving
> Qualities in leadership
> Ability to build morale
> Professional understanding
> Success in supervision
> Success in administration
> Relations with colleagues
> Relations with students
> Relations with community
> Attention to details and routine

Again, such factors as teaching ability or knowledge of curriculum are not even mentioned.

Finally, a survey by the National Education Association asked 350 school superintendents to list the qualities which they believed principals should have. The attributes mentioned most often were, in order of frequency:

> Ability to get along with people
> Personality
> Leadership
> Organizing and executive ability
> Tact and diplomacy

"Ability to teach" ranked ninth on the list, being mentioned by less than ten percent of the superintendents.[38]

The superintendent's image of his subordinates is important because it is, to a considerable extent, a self-fulfilling prophecy; he has the power to make his ideas come true. It is he who plays the largest part in the selection of principals. In addition to being the formally designated head of the school, to whom responsibility for selection of personnel has been officially delegated, he occupies a strategic point in the control and communications structure. He can withhold information or otherwise manipulate the opinions of the board members if they initially disagree with his choices. Therefore, a major determinant of the principal's characteristics is the *superintendent's idea of what he should be*. Teaching skill does not appear to be of much importance in the selection of principals. Superintendents and the principals themselves considered other attributes to have higher priority.

These expectations of superintendents, and the actual job requirements, have resulted in the recruitment of school administrators who are likely to possess certain characteristics. They are apt to be proficient in social relations while having relatively little background in the teaching of academic courses. This is indicated, for example, by a comparative study of men in different occupations. During the Second World War, seventeen thousand men were given extensive aptitude tests in order to assess their fitness for flight training. In 1955 and 1956, further information was obtained concerning the subsequent histories of more than ten thousand of the original group. Included in the follow-up group were the sixty-eight principals described as follows:

> The high school principals tended to come from small town or rural backgrounds . . . they were . . . likely . . . to have majored in education, social sciences, or biological sciences. They tended not to have majored in physical sciences and mathematics. In school they had frequently done well in history and in public speaking but not in physics. Associated with the academic success in public speaking was free-time experience in speech-making and dramatics. They had seldom worked at skilled manual work, but relatively frequently at unskilled manual work, retail or door-to-door selling, and instructing or working with groups. In general, they appeared to be verbally fluent and socially competent, but not technically or mechanically oriented.[39]

Many school administrators had little or no experience in teaching academic subjects and therefore lacked first-hand knowledge of the troublesome situations which can arise in these classes. The former physical education instructor, for example, did not face the same problems of discipline or of encouraging pupils to study as did the English teacher. The national median teaching experience for male elementary principals—and most principals are men—is only 5.2 years.[40] In fact, many administrators have not had any teaching experience at all. An N.E.A. survey, for instance, revealed that over one-third of the superintendents in cities of a half-million or more did not have teaching experience of any kind.[41] The same condition apparently exists elsewhere in less cosmopolitan communities. In Texas, for example, Stiles found ". . . only about half of the principals and administrators . . . have been classroom teachers."[42]

An analysis of the Berkeley, California, schools indicated that many school administrators lacked an academic major and did not have extensive experience teaching academic courses in the classroom. Two of the four secondary principals majored in physical education and the third had some other non-academic major. The fourth principal was the only one who had chosen a traditional field, political science. Only four of Berkeley's fourteen elementary principals majored in academic subjects. Six others majored in education, one in social welfare and one in commercial studies. One had a combined major in education with other subjects. The last did not indicate his major.[43]

The average teaching experience of the four secondary principals was 12.2 years. At first glance this seems quite impressive. However, three of the four had not taught regular academic subjects at all; their experience was limited to physical education or manual training. Two of the principals, including the principal of the only high school in town, had been physical education instructors, one for eighteen years and the other for eight. The third principal had fourteen years of teaching experience but all of this was in manual training. Thus, only one of the four had taught regular classroom subjects: along with social studies, English, business training and arithmetic, he, too, had conducted physical education classes and had coached extra-curricular athletic activities. Therefore, the actual average for regular classroom teaching experience was not 12.2 but only 2.2 years, and even this figure is misleadingly high because it includes instruction in physical education and business.[44]

If this is the situation in a city renowned for its university, there is little reason to believe that academic qualifications would receive more emphasis elsewhere, in an ordinary community.

The absence of an academic background and the frequent lack of extensive teaching experience of any kind is understandable in view of the magnitude and complexity of present-day school systems. To handle the many urgent non-educational problems, specialists in other areas have been recruited, and many of these men have had relatively little experience in classroom teaching, the basic activity of the organization.[45] In spite of this, however, school administration has not been fully recognized as a field of its own, and administrators are still expected to be experts on education. For example, the president of the Chicago School Board stated:

> Certainly, the school or college functionary must be a learned man over and beyond his other necessary qualifications. [He] must be a student and a philosopher, rather than an executive or factotum. [He] must maintain himself as the scholar-statesman of the school system.[46]

Continuing in this vein, he added:

> School leaders should be educators first, administrators second. [They must be] experts in scholarly and educational matters ... [should have] some time to think, some leisure to prepare classes, some time to develop special interests among their pupils, some moments in which to read the scholarly literature in their field, some opportunity, or perhaps the requirement, of producing their own scholarly works.[47]

The principal, too, sees himself as providing leadership for the instructional program[48] and claims that he is basically still a teacher.[49]

This image of school administrators as teachers and scholars has an historical basis. The principal, for example, was originally the *principal teacher* who, in addition to his fulltime schedule of classroom teaching, was responsible for supervising the other teachers and maintaining the physical necessities of the school.[50] The high intellectual qualifications of early principals were suggested by Pierce:

> Two examinations designed to test the academic knowledge of the candidates were introduced at an early stage by many city school boards. Cincinnati in 1838 had two grades or certificates, the "first principal's certificate" and the "second principal's certificate." The branches in which candidates for these certificates were examined were English grammar, reading, spelling, handwriting, geography and arithmetic. Ten years later the certificates were known as the "Male Principal's Certificates" and the "Female Principal's Certificate."[51] Candidates for the Male Principal's Certificate were examined in all of the common branches, and in addition, in natural history, elements of natural philosophy, algebra, constitution of the United States, astronomy, geometry, trigonometry, mensuration and surveying. ... Failure in one subject by a candidate meant failure in the entire examination.[52]

In subsequent decades, however, the pressures on public schools, discussed in earlier chapters, led to a radical transformation of the principal's job. While his original obligations, emphasizing the scholarly aspects of his role, have continued to the present, these have been over-shadowed by the pressures of pupil control, plant management and public relations.

Why, then, does this inaccurate image of the principal persist? Why do principals support this mythical view of themselves as experienced teachers when so much of their work has little to do with teaching? Although the laymen's misconception of the principal's role may be attributed to lack of information, this does not explain the continued insistence by school personnel themselves that differences between teachers and administrators, if they exist at all, are really of no consequence. Instead of distinguishing superiors from subordinates, principals insist that they themselves are teachers.

There are several reasons for supporting this fiction. One major incentive is job security. In some respects public school administrators have less job security than do teachers. Superintendents may have contracts but these usually must be renewed. Lesser administrators, such as principals and supervisors, generally lack formal guarantees against dismissal or demotion; if they have tenure at all, it is only as teachers. This merely entitles them to teaching jobs in the district. However, because of the great differences between administration and teaching, differences in prestige, income and working conditions, the possibility of a big reduction in pay and of returning to a classroom full of lively children or surly adolescents provides little cause for rejoicing.[53] Furthermore, competition for the numerous teaching positions, paying low-to-moderate salaries, is negligible compared to that which exists for the relatively few administrative openings.

The principal's security is strengthened if he can claim his position by virtue of being a teacher as well as an administrator. For the general public, the legitimacy of teaching is more apparent than is that of managing schools. Hughes' distinction between "historic" and "less historic" occupations may clarify this:

> An historic occupation is historic, not because its chief activity
> is an old one but because it has long had a name, a license, and a
> mandate, a recognized place in the scheme of things.[54]

Teaching has long been known in many cultures throughout the world, whereas the concept of *administration* is fairly recent.[55] To most people in the community, the need for teachers is probably more obvious than the need for administrators. The concept of *teacher* is more familiar. Laymen have some idea, regardless of its accuracy, of what a teacher is and ought to be. Teachers are obviously necessary, but the need for administrators, especially if they receive high salaries, is not so well established.

The myth which claims that the principal is an expert teacher is also functional financially. It enables principals to obscure the sizeable differences between their own salaries and those of teachers. If, for example, principals were clearly defined as separate entities within the educational structure, their relatively high pay would be more likely to come to public attention and consequently would attract criticism. However, by blending themselves in with teachers, principals protect their salaries with the popular belief that teachers are underpaid. Furthermore, by linking themselves to the teachers' pay schedule, principals decrease the possibility of being refused a raise. One teacher, the salary committee chairman for the local teachers' association, made the following comment after a successful attempt to win a wage increase:

> ... and all the time, the principals didn't have to lift a finger. In fact, one of them said to me the other day, "You do the work and we get the gravy." They're tied into the teacher salary schedule and automatically get a raise whenever we do. For instance, on a straight percentage increase alone, a teacher making $5,000 gets a $200 raise while a principal at $10,000 gets $400. He's earning twice as much to begin with and still he gets double the raise we do. Yet the public blames the high cost on teachers. It's even listed in the budget that way.[56]

Newspapers usually report the raises granted to teachers, but they are less likely to mention that principals and superintendents received increases also. As a result, some people become resentful toward teachers because "they're getting another raise." The public doesn't realize that administrators receive much larger increases than do teachers.[57]

Even the standard form on which schools arrange their budgets is misleading. In California, for example, there are ten major categories: *Administration, Instruction, Auxiliary Services, Operation, Maintenance,* etc. Principals' salaries are not listed under *Administration* but under *Instruction.* Only the immediate members of the superintendent's staff are listed under the former category, while teachers and principals are placed under the heading of *Instruction,* along with curriculum supervisors, district librarians, and others.[58]

Another factor behind the claim that the principal is a teacher concerns the authority relationship between the principal and his subordinates. The norms of the school system and of modern organizations generally specify that technical competence shall be the criterion for assigning an individual to a position. Whatever the actual reasons might be, the principal supposedly holds his office by virtue of his ability to perform the duties attached. Underlying many of these duties is the assumption that he is proficient in teaching. If this assumption were to be challenged, much of his authority over teachers would be jeopardized. Thus, the precarious position of a manager over professionals who have more knowledge and experience than he may lead to his attempts to bolster his authority by claiming to be a teacher.

This image of administrators as teachers facilitates control in another way. By being accepted as "one of us," administrators can and do take an active part in teachers' professional associations and hold offices at all levels. The situation in California illustrates a pattern common throughout the nation. Twelve of the fourteen presidents of the California Teachers Association from 1911 to 1961 had been superintendents or assistant-superintendents, one was a college instructor and one was a high school teacher who was married to a county superintendent of schools. The executive secretary of the C.T.A. is also an influential position. Two of the four executive secretaries who have held office during this same period were formerly superintendents, another had been a principal and the fourth was a college president.[59]

In addition to influencing decisions at various levels within the state school system, administrators have used the C.T.A. to block legislation which would have benefited classroom teachers, but which might have been hindrances to principals and superintendents.

The myth that principals are experienced teachers may also serve a psychological function for the administrator, quite apart from his relationships with other people. Lacking a realistic definition of his duties, the principal may have feelings of insecurity and futility. He cannot evaluate his own performance if he is uncertain as to what it is that he is trying to accomplish. If many of his daily tasks seem to have little connection with education, he may seek reassurance in the belief that, regardless of what he does, he is nevertheless a teacher contributing to the welfare of the pupils. On one hand, many of his duties presuppose a knowledge of teaching—planning curriculum, hiring and evaluating teachers, and suggesting methods of teaching specific topics. On the other hand, a number of his activities appear to be far removed from his supposed job of "providing vigorous leadership for the instructional program." Taking tickets at football games, chaperoning dances, and ordering supplies for lavatories have little apparent relation to education. An elementary principal remarked:

I get the feeling that I'm just an odd-job man. I blow up balls, answer the phone, take sick children home, and run errands for teachers. I know somebody has to do these things, and the teachers don't have time to, but sometimes I wonder what I'm doing around here.[60]

In the absence of other indications that his work is constructive, he may welcome the idea that at least he is a teacher, thus connecting himself with an endeavor which is widely accepted as worthwhile.

Thus the principal has something to gain from this double role of teacher-administrator. It bolsters his authority, giving him a more legitimate role in education together with the higher pay and prestige of an administrative position.

Yet, it also aggravates the serious strains in the principal's role. He has to perform duties for which he lacks adequate preparation. Although primarily recruited for his ability to handle problems of pupil control, plant management and public relations, he is also required to make crucial decisions regarding classroom instruction and, in fact, is presumed by the public to be an expert in educational affairs. To make matters worse, his claim to the position is uncomfortably tenuous. He has no legal or procedural safeguards for his job, and may be demoted or transferred on a moment's notice.

Functions of Progressive Education

Most of the benefits which progressive education offered teachers were also helpful to administrators. In fact, administrators on the whole gained more from it than did teachers, because it permitted them to maintain the functional myth that they were authorities on education. It enabled them to qualify for their positions, it helped them with control, and it bolstered their marginal security and prestige.

Job Requirements. The reduction of emphasis upon academic preparation or even on teaching experience of any sort enabled many men to qualify for administrative positions who would not have been able to do so if traditional scholastic requirements[61] were still in force. The former physical education coach or shop teacher is not penalized for his lack of an academic major, nor does his relatively brief experience in teaching offer an unsurmountable handicap.

Instead, progressive education enables him in several ways to support his claim that he is basically a teacher. When confronted with a situation in which he is called upon to exercise his knowledge of teaching, the generalized, pupil-centered method of progressive education provides a workable substitute for academic knowledge or for experience in the classroom. His acquaintance with psychology enables him to play the role of an authority on education by giving advice about teaching. When pedagogical problems come his way, he can at least say *something* about them. If, for instance, a teacher asks him for advice because her pupils are having trouble in their studies, progressively oriented administrators, regardless of what the subject is, may suggest that the teacher give more attention to motivation: making the lessons more interesting through games, reports, committees, attractive room environment, etc. This allows the administrator to fulfill the formal requirements of his position while shifting the actual responsibility back to the teacher. The administrator has diagnosed the trouble and has offered specific suggestions, and it is then up to the teacher to carry out those suggestions effectively. For example, at one time this writer was teaching a sixth-grade class in which many of the pupils were unable to read more than a few words. This problem was brought to the attention of three administrators, in response to their general offers of assistance, but none of them made suggestions pertaining specifically to reading. Instead, each offered a variant of "motivation." The principal suggested the use of games to make reading more exciting; the vice-principal advised changing the colored paper mats on the bulletin boards from orange to green, so as not to distract the pupils from their studies; and the supervisor suggested that the teacher could inspire his class to greater efforts by keeping his shoes shined.

These suggestions were given in all seriousness. They were not to be taken lightly, because public school teachers are formally evaluated on just such grounds as these. A teacher may lose his job if he falls down in "motivation of his pupils," "knowledge of teaching methods," "attractive learning environment" and "personal appearance."

In short, progressive pedagogy strengthens the administrator's authority. Defining almost anything as *education* permits administrators to claim some connection with the educational process, and this is important. In contrast to teachers, who average eight hours a week on duties not directly related to classroom teaching, the administrator spends *most* of his time on non-educational activities. Therefore, to support his claim of being a competent educator, it is even more necessary for him to legitimate his activities by tying them to education. The progressive approach helps him to do this by broadening the school's aims to such a degree that many kinds of work can be interpreted as contributing to education. In fact, as we have seen, it can be difficult to rule out any activity as not being connected, in some way, with the "development and welfare of the whole child."

Discipline. An additional area in which progressive education may be helpful to principals is that of discipline. Their concern with pupil control and the divergent views held by teachers and administrators toward progressive education were the subjects of another "typical" situation described by Anderson and Davies. This one concerned a high school whose student body had changed during the previous decade from middle-class to lower-class. A third of the pupils were Negroes and many of them came from broken homes. Racial tensions were increasingly evident in the school.

> The majority of faculty members had served the teaching profession for a number of years. They were convinced that students should master the subject matter prescribed in traditional courses of study as a necessary part of their education. In attempting to impose this subject matter, teachers created a serious disciplinary problem which resulted in tension both among students and between students and faculty members.
> The principal and his new assistant were in complete accord in considering curriculum revision a basic need of the school. The principal's previous attempts at revision had met with concerted faculty resistance. His present policy was one that combined efforts toward staff-principal compatibility with the institution of as much gradual change as possible.[62]

Administrators have a personal stake in the control of students. Although they are not in as close continuous contact with pupils as are teachers, they bear the brunt of the responsibility for maintaining order in the school. Yet, they cannot "solve" discipline problems in the same way that teachers can—by passing them on to someone else. For the teacher, the logical solution to problems raised by particularly obstreperous pupils is removing them from her class: by suspending them, by transferring them to another room on the basis of "personality conflict" or, if all else fails, by promoting them out of the room at the end of the semester. Such solutions are practical for individual teachers; a few pupils can be sent to the office and perhaps spanked by the principal and sent home for a few days.

But, while teachers may be able to get rid of troublemakers this way, the principal cannot; he is at the end of the road. For practical reasons, one of which is the protection of his reputation as a capable administrator, he cannot pass undesirables on to someone else. There is no place outside of his own school to which he can send problem pupils. Transferring them to another school requires the approval of that school, and calls the attention of his fellow principals to his inability to handle the problem. It also may require the superintendent's approval, and in many districts, such transfers require approval by the board of education as well. Outright expulsion or assignment to juvenile authorities may encounter even greater obstacles. Consequently discipline, for practical purposes, must be handled within each school. The problem was aptly described to the writer by an elementary school principal:

> Tuesday a child was sent in here because he called the teacher a "liar." You can't let that kind of thing go by. I talked to him to find out why he did it. I didn't get anywhere. I called in his parents. Many times you can't find them, but his mother came in. She told me "Take down his pants and beat him with an electric cord; that's what I do."
>
> What can I do? The teachers don't know what to do. I don't know what to do. I have kids in here sometimes with lash marks all down their legs. . . . I can't use my "persuader" and yet they're wrecking the classroom. . . . Sometimes I send them home, but there's no one there. They roam the streets and get into more trouble. Sometimes the police pick them up and bring them back here and ask why they aren't in school. What do you do then?
>
> I talk and talk and talk with them and that doesn't help. They're not impressed by my talking; they don't even hear me. Their parents scream at them all the time. I've got to back up the teachers, but how? The teachers can't help me. The central office can't help me. The parents are at their wits' end already. What do you do? . . .[63]

Since neither corporal punishment nor expulsion is practical, principals are inclined to minimize academic pressures in order to forestall the eruption of disciplinary problems. This minimizing is facilitated by progressive education.

Human Relations. Another area in which progressive education is especially helpful to administrators is human relations. The same skills, activities, and personal qualities which aid in understanding pupils and in gaining community support for the school also help its employees to strengthen their own security through direct personal contact with the public, as well as indirectly through the reputation of the school and the school system.

This is particularly important for administrators. Unlike teachers, they usually lack the security of tenure. If they happen to have it, tenure generally provides no protection against demotion, but merely assures them of menial positions as classroom teachers. In effect, the school administrator's hold on his job depends largely upon his popularity with the public and with his superiors; if strong sentiment builds up against him, he can be transferred, demoted, or fired, regardless of his educational or administrative ability.

It is to his advantage, therefore, to gain the backing of influential groups in the community. Large, active PTAs and Dad's Clubs could be reservoirs of reinforcement in case his job were threatened. Similar protection may be secured from the local Chamber of Commerce, fraternal orders and civic organizations. The shortcomings of a principal who is supported by key figures in the local power structure would have to be grave before his superiors would seriously consider firing him or transferring him to a less desirable post. Realizing this, administrators may devote a great deal of effort to making themselves seem irreplaceable. In the process of making friends for the school, they are also gaining valuable allies for themselves.

Human relations is useful to administrators in legitimizing their authority over their subordinates. This is not only a concern of the organization but is also important for the individual administrator. If he cannot maintain sufficient control over his subordinates, he is in danger of being replaced by someone who can. This problem becomes especially serious when the administrator attempts to exercise authority over specializations in which he is not highly qualified. High school teachers of academic subjects, for example, may be reluctant to acknowledge the authority of a former physical education instructor who is now their principal.

To avoid such resistance, school administrators have attempted to enhance their authority on the basis of specialized knowledge in human relations. They have engaged in graduate study to attain advanced degrees and special administrative credentials certifying their right to command. While much of this work involves areas such as school finance, there is also considerable attention devoted to personnel management, psychology, and the like, topics which, through progressive education, have become the legitimate interest of public school personnel.

CONCLUSION

In many ways, the modern school administrator's position is similar to that of managers in business. Both have positions which are considerably more desirable—in power, prestige, and working conditions—than those lower down in the organization. Yet, their positions are somewhat precarious because they lack the security of tenure laws or of strong unions giving ordinary workers and teachers some protection against demotion or dismissal. In addition, administrators in industry and in education may be appointed on the basis of their abilities in human relations rather than in skills more directly related to the basic activities performed by the organization.[64]

This raises the common problem of establishing authority over unfamiliar specializations. One solution to this problem, as Gouldner pointed out, is to claim authority on the basis of specialized knowledge in human relations. Business executives, like school administrators, attempt to legitimate their occupancy of managerial positions by university study in the social sciences, through special knowledge of personnel management, industrial psychology and related fields.[65] Thus, human relations, quite apart from its benefits to the organization, enables individual administrators to strengthen their hold on their jobs and to move upward into even more desirable positions. Bendix's observations indicate that this is not limited to school administrators; in business, too, ". . . an adroit man can use the symbols of personal adjustment and teamwork for his own advance as well as for human relations . . . " in the company's behalf.[66]

In business as well as in public education, human relations is more useful for administrators than for their subordinates. In industry Bendix noticed that, while the human relations approach was helpful to managers, it was of little use to the rank and file worker. As for the schools, human relations is of some help to teachers, especially the less experienced ones, in controlling their students. Principals and other supervisors, however, receive more benefit from it and would be more likely to support an ideology which justifies its use. Here again, commenting on the support of human relations techniques by business executives, Bendix observed, "They have a strong interest in advocating a view of management which maximizes their importance in the scheme of things."[67]

The school administrator, who is "verbally fluent and socially competent" rather than technically or mechanically oriented, is the pedagogical counterpart of industry's "organization man," who uses human relations for his own benefit as well as for the company's. Historically, the emphasis on personality and psychology was a consequence of changing conditions of employment, from working alone to being employed by a large organization, in which effort is rewarded by a career consisting of promotions from lower to higher positions.[68] The traditional schoolmaster resembled the independent entrepreneur, an isolated individual in a small school or shop. And, like the businessman of a bygone age who succeeded through aggressiveness and technical competence, the old-time schoolmaster has been replaced by a new type of administrator whose success depends, to a considerable degree, upon winning friends and influencing people.

REFERENCES

[1]Ryans, *Characteristics of Teachers,* p. 152.

[2]*Ibid.*

[3]*Ibid.,* p. 295.

[4]*Ibid.,* p. 292.

[5]*Ibid.,* p. 152.

[6]*Ibid.*

[7]Mason, *Beginning Teacher,* p. 43.

[8]Ritter, "Answers Given; Opinions Voiced on Education Questions," *C.T.A. Journal,* Feb. 1959, p. 36.

[9]*San Francisco Chronicle,* April 1, 1960.

[10]*Ibid.,* April 2, 1960.

[11]Anderson and Davies, *Patterns of Educational Leadership,* p. iii.

[12]*Ibid.,* p. 1.

[13]*Ibid.,* p. 2.

[14]*Ibid.*

[15]*Ibid.,* p. 28.

[16]*Ibid.,* p. 29.

[17]*Ibid.*

[18]*Ibid.,* p. 34.

[19]From a conversation with the author.

[20]*Ibid.*

[21]N.E.A., *Public School Teacher,* p. 91.

[22]*Ibid.,* p. 49.

[23]U.S. Bureau of the Census, *Historical Statistics . . .,* p. 210.

[24]N.E.A., *The American Public School Teacher,* p. 85.

[25]U.S. Bureau of the Census, *Statistical Abstract of the U.S., 1963,* p. 117.

[26]In the second place in 1919 was physical education, taken by sixty-nine percent of all secondary pupils. Music was third with thirty percent; algebra and industrial arts tied for fourth place with twenty-seven percent each. Home economics had twenty-four percent and United States history twenty-three percent (U.S. Bureau of the Census, *Historical Statistics . . .,* p. 210).

[27]*Ibid.*

[28]Anderson and Davies, *Patterns of Educational Leadership,* pp. 176-77.

[29]U.S. Bureau of the Census, *Statistical Abstract of the U.S., 1963,* p. 117.

[30]N.E.A., *The American Public School Teacher,* p. 56.

[31]*Ibid.,* p. 57.

[32]*Ibid.*

[33]*Ibid.*

[34]Davis, "Where Does the Time Go?," *California Journal of Secondary Education,* Oct. 1953, p. 349.

[35]N.E.A., *National Elementary Principal,* Sept. 1958, p. 98.

[36]N.E.A., *The National Association of Secondary School Principals Bulletin,* Nov. 1951, p. 28.

[37]*Phi Delta Kappan,* Nov. 1959, p. 56. Even Max Rafferty, California's conservative superintendent who campaigned on a platform of greater emphasis on academic studies, decried "the myth that an above-average teacher will necessarily or even probably make a good administrator" (*Ibid.,* p. 51).

[38]N.E.A., *National Elementary Principal,* Sept. 1948, p. 138.

[39]Thorndike and Hagen, *Ten Thousand Careers,* pp. 152-53.

[40]N.E.A., *National Elementary Principal,* Sept. 1958, p. 113.

[41]N.E.A., *Profile of the School Superintendent,* p. 33.

[42]Stiles, *Teacher's Role,* p. 37.

[43]Swift, *The Public School Principal in California,* p. 44.

[44]*Ibid.,* pp. 36-37.

[45]This trend toward specialization in administration rather than in the basic operations of the organization is not limited to education; it is found in many other lines of work. For example, businesses often recruit managers with little or no experience in the activities they supervise. This is true even at the lowest levels of supervision. C. Wright Mills observes, ". . . the foreman is chosen for his skillfulness in handling personnel . . . rather than because of his length of service or mastery of the particular operation in his charge" (*White Collar,* p. 90).

[46]Brukman, "The Educational Leader as a Scholar and Man of Culture," *School and Society,* April 1957, p. 147.

[47]*Ibid.* This belief has also been observed by Lieberman. For example, he refers to ". . . the widely accepted premise that the school administrator is supposed to be the instructional leader responsible for the quality of instruction in the school program" (*Education as a Profession,* p. 492).

[48]Swift, *Public School Principal,* p. 7.

[49]This assertion is made directly (for example: "I'm a teacher, too.") and it is implied by statements in which the principal includes himself with teachers (e.g.: "As teachers, we must dedicate ourselves to the advancement of education."). Finally, and perhaps most frequently, it is taken for granted (e.g.: When teachers vote on matters primarily concerning themselves, such as a proposed change in their salary schedule, administrators often cast a ballot, too).

[50]Pierce, *Public School Principalship,* pp. 153-54.

[51]The male principal was in charge of the school while female principals served under him as heads of various departments (*Ibid.,* p. 12).

[52]*Ibid.,* pp. 153-54.

[53]This is not limited to school administrators. For instance, in speaking of union leaders, Lipset *et al.* observe, "Once high status is secured, there is usually a pressing need to at least retain and protect it. This is particularly true if the discrepancy between the status and the position to which one must return on losing status is very great" (*Union Democracy,* p. 10).

[54]Hughes, "The Study of Occupations," in Merton *et al., Sociology Today,* p. 453.

184   DIFFERENTIAL SUPPORT

[55]Beslie and Sargent, "The Concept of Administration," in Campbell and Gregg, eds., *Administrative Behavior in Education*, p. 84.

[56]From a conversation with the author.

[57]The following newspaper report is typical: "A 2.5 percent wage increase for 3,600 employees of the Oakland school system was recommended to the Board of Education last night by School Superintendent Selmer Berg. Berg estimated the wage raise would cost about $674,000. It would increase basic teacher pay from $4749 to $4830 and advanced teacher pay from $9165 to $9399. Oakland's 2700 teachers have asked for a 5.5 percent raise. The board will meet next Tuesday to consider the recommendation made by Berg" (*San Francisco Chronicle,* May 4, 1960). This article does not explicitly state that the entire $674,000 went to teachers. However, since no other employees are mentioned, readers are likely to draw this erroneous conclusion. The article does not state that the former maximum for principals was $13,299, nor does it say that they also received salary increases which would raise this figure even higher.

[58]Statements concerning budgets are based upon Ben Rust, *Study on Costs of Classroom Instruction*, pp. 11-12.

[59]Information up to 1957 was summarized in Berry's *C.T.A.: An Interest Group in California Politics,* pp. 40-41. Information after that time was obtained from the *C.T.A. Journal.*

[60]From a conversation with the author.

[61]For example, examinations in subject matter, required for the principal's certificate, as described in Pierce, *Public School Principalship,* pp. 153-54.

[62]Anderson and Davies, *Patterns of Educational Leadership,* pp. 6-7.

[63]From a conversation with the author.

[64]In discussing modern managers, Mills commented, "... their skills have become less and less material techniques and more and more the management of people" (*White Collar,* p. 86).

[65]Alvin and Helen Gouldner, *Modern Sociology,* p. 415.

[66]Bendix, *Work and Authority,* p. 335n.

[67]*Ibid.,* p. 335.

[68]*Ibid.,* p. 304.

eight

CONCLUSION

PROGRESSIVE EDUCATION MAY BE VIEWED AS AN IDEOLOGY WHICH, ALONG
with its other functions, contributed to the survival and development of
the American public school system. It had characteristics similar to
those of other ideologies and it found fertile soil in the breakdown of
traditional education. As Chinoy observed:

> Social disorganization and strains in the social structure often
> leave people uncertain and disoriented, without an adequate or ac-
> ceptable conception of the events going on around them. They are
> therefore likely to be receptive to an ideology that provides a mean-
> ingful version of what is happening — one that links individual and
> group troubles to institutions, value systems and social structures.[1]

But ideologies may provide more than an explanation:

> In addition to their interpretations of man and society, ideologies
> also offer a program to deal with the problems for which men are
> seeking solutions.[2]

The stated goals of progressive education provided a sense of purpose, a framework for what might otherwise have appeared to be lack
of direction on the part of the school. Progressive education's concern
for the pupil, rather than for the subject matter, stated in doctrinal terms
what had already become a living reality for the public school. Its call
for adaptation to changing environmental conditions encouraged the experimentation necessary for finding solutions to the schools' urgent prob-

lems. Above all, the broad goals of progressive education facilitated the freedom of action needed for this experimentation.

Along with these broad, general functions, progressive education contributed to the solution of the school's problems in a number of specific ways. First, *it facilitated the establishment of harmonious relations with the community, encouraging public relations directly and indirectly.* While the concept of local public control suggested that the school should keep the public informed, the idea of community-centered education provided further justification for communication between the school and the community. Public relations did not have to be a marginal activity, operating in the shadows. It was a legitimate and even mandatory aspect of the school's program. From informing and educating the public, it was only a minor step to propagandizing on behalf of the school and its personnel.

Second, *progressive education alleviated custodial problems created by an extremely varied student body.* By orienting the pupil's learning around his experiences, this educational trend aroused his interest and thereby enlisted his willingness to remain in school and obey its rules. In addition, extra-curricular activities, ranging from hobby clubs to athletics, further involved the student in the school and could be rationalized under the *whole-child* approach. Moreover, the shift in emphasis from subject matter to the pupils themselves reduced the academic demands which would frustrate the many students who are not academically inclined. Finally, human relations skills enabled school personnel to win at least a modicum of cooperation from the majority of pupils.

Third, *progressive education helped to legitimize the numerous non-academic activities performed by school personnel.* It broadened the scope of the school's aims to such a degree that many kinds of work could be interpreted as contributing to education. In fact, it became difficult to rule out any specific activity as not being connected in some way with the pupils' total welfare. This justification was especially valuable for personnel who had little apparent connection with academic education: administrators, vocational instructors, physical education coaches and the like. Their job security, as well as their self-esteem, could be strengthened by the assertion that their activities were an integral part of the school's operation.

Fourth, *progressive education deterred attacks upon the competence of the public school and its personnel by shifting the school's emphasis from subject matter to pupils.* It established a special field over which the school asserted exclusive jurisdiction, and it obscured standards by which others might evaluate the school's effectiveness. Although parents, college professors or businessmen might claim to be judges of scholastic achievement, and might criticize the school for inadequate intellectual training of pupils, they were less able to disprove the public school's contention that it was successfully developing the whole child, and that it alone had competence in this field.

Fifth, *progressive education increased the versatility of personnel.* By reducing the differences between courses and by providing universal methods of teaching them, it supplied non-specialized teachers who were more interchangeable than were the traditional subject matter specialists. This versatility was especially useful administratively, in matching teachers to the fluctuating demand for classes, and in providing a means of controlling teachers.

Finally, *progressive education suited the modest educational abilities of public school personnel.* Many teachers and administrators lacked the requisites for successful teaching in the traditional subject-oriented curriculum. Progressive education assisted them in four ways. First, it reduced academic demands by de-emphasizing subject matter and by substituting development of the whole child as the goal of education. Secondly, it increased the number of non-academic jobs within the school system by establishing new positions which did not exist in traditional schools; driver training, senior problems, home economics, and similar courses provided jobs for many teachers. Third, progressive education supplied an easily acquired, generalized method as a substitute for extensive teaching experience and thorough knowledge of subject matter. This was especially helpful for administrators, many of whom had little or no experience in teaching academic courses, but who were still expected to be experts in education. Finally, progressive education led to a more realistic occupational image, in which the scholar was replaced by the educator.

Progressive education's contribution in any one of these areas may have been small, but its overall assistance in coping with the many problems facing the school was considerable.

However, the fact that progressive education offered a potential solution to problems does not really explain how it came to be adopted by American public schools. We cannot assume that people or institutions will necessarily choose the path which leads to success; they may be quite unaware of possible solutions to the difficulties confronting them. Therefore, rather than looking for conscious attempts to apply progressive methods to nonpedagogical problems, it may be more fruitful to think in terms of natural selection, analogous to the Darwinian theory. Individuals vary. Some are better able than others to cope with the problems posed by their environment. As new problems emerge and old practices lose their effectiveness, new responses become necessary. Individuals who cannot adapt themselves to the new conditions will fail.

After 1870, a traditionally oriented teacher or administrator became increasingly obsolescent, an anachronistic knight in academic armor, attempting to apply medieval solutions to the problems of an industrializing society. His tasks were no longer limited to maintaining order by force or fear, and bringing enlightenment to a homogeneous, relatively select student body. Conditions in the public schools had changed. Discipline could not be handled by the harsh direct methods of old, and public relations and paperwork became as important as education itself. Those who were able to cope with these new requirements succeeded; the others did not.

Often the process of elimination was direct. Many scholarly men and women were totally unprepared for the harsh realities found in schools in the ghettoes, where "keeping 'em quiet" required more than a master's degree in history. Pressures in better neighborhoods were generally more subtle, but could be just as devastating to the teacher or administrator who failed to perceive soon enough the necessity for getting along with members of the P.T.A. And, in all areas, neglect of paper work could be hazardous to one's career. In hiring, tenure, firing and promotion, considerable attention was paid to personality, relations with the community, prompt submission of written reports, and control over pupils. Knowledge of subject matter was hardly considered.

This selective process operated not only through elimination by others — by unruly pupils, angry parents or dissatisfied superiors. Self-selection also played an important part. There were undoubtedly many traditionally oriented people who might have considered education under a more academically oriented regimen but, knowing of the schools' disinterest in scholarship or of other conditions in the schools which they considered objectionable, they chose some other career instead.

In short, progressively oriented individuals were more likely to enter teaching and remain there. It was not necessarily that those who succeeded were deeply committed to progressive education, but rather that non-academic people with progressive training were better able to adapt to the situations they encountered in the schools. In contrast, the academically inclined individual would tend to be frustrated by the many non-academic demands confronting him and would be more likely to leave. Therefore, those who used progressive principles were more apt to remain in the public schools. Like the early Protestants whose adherence to ascetic Calvinist practices brought them success in business, educators who adopted progressive methods were better suited to survival under the new conditions than were their traditionally oriented colleagues. Of course, failure or success was an individual matter. But year after year, this selective process gradually reduced the proportion of traditionally oriented teachers in the public schools and increased the percentage of those who were progressively inclined.

Although not crucial to this explanation, it is relevant to consider the extent to which school personnel themselves recognized these latent functions of progressive education. It is one thing for us to make these observations today, looking back upon the past from the perspectives of history and sociology; the awareness of the participants themselves is something else. Did they perceive the nonpedagogical problems confronting the schools? To what extent did they look to progressive education as a method of handling these problems? There is evidence that men like Dewey and Cubberly were cognizant of some of these points, but the awareness of classroom teachers and administrators is less certain.

For instance, some recognition of the difficulties which compulsory education caused for the schools occurred early in the century. The *1904 Report of the Massachusetts State Board of Education* observed:

> By steadily raising the age of compulsory attendance, the schools have come to contain many children who, having no natural appetite for study, would under the old regime have left school early. Compulsory attendance laws do not create brain capacity nor modify hereditary tendencies; they only throw responsibility for doing both upon the schools and create expectancy in the public.[3]

Cubberly also recognized these problems, in 1922, and went on to state that, as a result of compulsory education laws, "special adjustments"[4] were necessary to meet the needs of the new types of pupils. In considering these special adjustments, he mentioned several facets of progressive education, although he did not describe them as such:

> The whole question of compulsory attendance is tied up closely with the problems of flexible promotion, adjustment of instruction to individual needs, provision of special type schools, reorganization of the work of the upper grades, increasing the opportunities for vocational training, . . .[5]

A few years earlier, in 1915, Dewey had commented upon the efficiency of progressive education in reducing delinquency. He discussed a school in the Indianapolis slums which had previously been characterized by an ". . . attitude of hostility and unwilling attendance:"[6]

> The percentage of truancy was high and a large number of cases were sent to the juvenile court each year. The children took no in-

terest in their work as a whole, and cases of extreme disorder were not infrequent; one pupil tried to revenge himself on his teacher for merited punishment with a butcher knife . . .[7]

Then a new program was introduced, focused around three old tenements which the pupils remodeled under the direction of the manual training teacher. The buildings were used for such classes as carpentry, sewing, shoe repair, tailoring and cooking for boys as well as girls. The third building was made into a boys' clubhouse.[8] Dewey reported:

> The work has made over the relations between the school and the pupils. The children like to go to school now, where before they had to be forced to with threats of the truant officer, and their behavior is better when they get to school. . . . With improved attendance and discipline, the number of cases sent to the juvenile court has decreased one-half in proportion to the number of pupils in school.[9]

Dewey also indicated some awareness of the public relations function of progressive education, even if he did not state it in one precise sentence. The relationship was suggested, for example, in his remarks about vitalizing pupils' school experiences through closer ties with the community:

> This closer contact with immediate neighborhood conditions not only enriches schoolwork and strengthens motive force in the pupils, but it increases the service rendered to the community. No school can make use of the activities of the neighborhood for purposes of instruction without this use influencing, in turn, the people of the neighborhood.
>
> Pupils, for example, who learn civics by making local surveys and working for local improvements, are certain to influence the life of the locality, while lessons in civics learned from the purely general statements of a textbook are much less likely to have either applicability or application.
>
> In turn, the community perceives the local efficiency of the schools. It realizes that the service rendered to welfare is not remote, to appear when the pupils become adults, but a part of the regular, daily course of education. The statement that the schools exist for a democratic purpose, for the good of citizenship, becomes an obvious fact and not a formula.
>
> A community which perceives what a strong factor its school is in civic activities, is quick to give support and assistance in return, either by extending the use of its own facilities (as happens in Gary) or by the direct assistance of labor, money, or material when these are needed.[10]

Thus, leading educators of the day had at least some awareness of the non-pedagogical functions of progressive education. How deep their recognition went or how many others shared it is uncertain. At any rate, by the time Dewey and Cubberly were putting their observations into print, it was unnecessary to emphasize these functions. Progressive education was so well on its way to gaining acceptance that pronouncements of its non-pedagogical benefits, even if they had been recognized, would have served no useful purpose.

As it was, progressive education could be advocated on a higher, more generally acceptable level than that of crass ultilitarianism. This is important because ideologies may be legitimated on various levels, ranging from exalted, humanitarian ideals down to base self-interest. If an ideology could be effectively established by linking it to a higher, more absolute value, there would be little to gain by publicizing its mundane functions. Few ideas have more appeal than that of the well-being of our children. Most Americans would be more likely to accept a new form of education if they believed it would benefit their children than if they thought it would merely make things easier for principals and teachers. This continues to be the rationale used in American schools: in order to gain public support for salary increases, new administrative positions, or the construction of additional buildings, link them to the welfare of the pupils.

Why did progressive education become established in the United States to a greater degree than in other countries? The intellectual roots of progressive education, as we have seen, were largely of European origin, stemming from Rousseau and other Enlightenment thinkers. By the early years of the nineteenth century, progressive principles had been embodied in Pestalozzi's schools in Switzerland and were officially adopted by Prussia, a century before their emergence in the United States.

An explanation can be offered in terms of the four organizational problems discussed in this book. To begin with, the United States made the first and most ambitious attempt to educate children on such an enormous scale. Our goal was nothing short of universal compulsory education. We did not stop at making education available to all who wanted it — we made it mandatory. It is one thing to offer services; it requires more energy and greater resources to compel people to utilize these services.

This task was complicated by the American dream of equality. Not only must every child be educated; he should also receive the same quality of education as everyone else. Even pupils who seem obviously unsuited for college must be given a chance to stay in the running. This inhibited the establishment of separate schools and made it difficult to introduce distinctive curricula for the various types of pupils. The point of final elimination from the college program has been increasingly delayed. First, it came at the end of grammar school, later it was put off until high school and now it has been extended still further, into junior college. Prussian primary education in the early-nineteenth century may have embodied some progressive principles but the schools were not operating in an atmosphere of equalitarianism. Horatio Alger was an American legend, not a European one.

Still another unique factor was the nature of the American population. Between 1800 and 1960, more than forty-three million immigrants came to the United States.[11] This was the greatest immigration during a period of similar length in the history of the world.[12] Although Europe also experienced a rapid rise in population, from 140 million in 1750 to 270 million by 1850, and doubling again a century later, this was more a matter of natural increase than of immigration.[13] Consequently, even if Europe had attempted universal education, the schools would have been less likely to be inundated by pupils from completely alien cultures and the task of socialization would not have been as overwhelming. The polyglot character of the American population presented more difficult problems.

Administrative problems also contributed to the adoption of progressive education. The size and complexity of American public school systems were unprecedented, and further pressures arose from the development of a managerial orientation originating in the business world. The industrial magnate was a national hero, and business practices provided models for operating the schools. This was more than merely a voluntary adoption of a particular administrative style. Principals and superintendents were under pressure from the public and from their own governing boards to operate their schools in an "efficient, businesslike manner," often to the point of putting costs before all other considerations.

Still another factor in the emergence of progressive education was the school's precarious position with respect to the local community. In this regard, the American experience seems unique. Education here is organized and maintained primarily at the local level, with only the weakest elements of centralization. Not until the last few years has any substantial share of the schools' financial support come from the federal level and, as far as the actual operation of the school is concerned, there still is probably less governmental control here than in any other industrialized nation. There are no enforceable national standards for admittance, promotion or graduation from public schools. The federal government does not certify teachers and administrators, nor does it regulate curricula, textbooks, supplies or buildings. The belief that the ordinary citizen has a legitimate voice in the school's operation is also unusually pronounced. Consequently, American schools, both by their structure and their values, are exposed to local pressures and must expend proportionately more effort to maintain a modicum of autonomy.

Finally, we may consider school personnel. Progressive education would probably have won their support even if its benefits had been limited to facilitating the tasks of the individual teacher or administrator. In addition, however, it may have been welcomed as a means of improving their occupational status, a matter in which American educators seem especially ill at ease. At least part of their concern arises from ideologies extolling the United States as *the* land of opportunity and equality. Although recent studies of occupational prestige indicate that teachers in a number of industrial nations hold about the same rank with respect to other occupations,[14] it is possible that America's emphasis upon social mobility and an open society has made our teachers less satisfied with their position, especially when some blue-collar occupations are surpassing them in salary, working conditions and so forth.[15] Moreover, egalitarian-minded laymen in the United States are less inclined to show deference, even to those in high positions, and so the American teacher receives fewer overt indications of respect from pupils, parents, and the public than do his foreign counterparts. It is not surprising, therefore, that teachers in the United States would be particularly receptive to an educational philosophy which offered to strengthen their claims to professional status.

Any one of these pressures by itself would pose difficulties for an organization and its personnel. Taken together, they constituted an overwhelming force which shattered the traditional structure of the school. Progressive education fitted the particular needs of American public schools as they struggled with the problems confronting them in the late-nineteenth and the first half of the twentieth century.

But what of the present and, for that matter, the future? Does the relative absence of references to progressive education by school personnel signify that the practice has disappeared from the public schools?[16] A brief glance suggests that the answer is "No." Although it is no longer fashionable for educators to proclaim themselves "progressives," and terms such as *life adjustment* have fallen from favor, progressivistic practices are still very much a part of the American public schools.

For example, concern for each pupil's physical and psychological well-being is as high as ever. More attention is given to tailoring curricula to fit a wide range of needs. There are special materials, special programs, and special classes for culturally disadvantaged, mentally retarded, physically handicapped, emotionally disturbed pupils, as well as for the gifted, the "over-achievers" and the "fortunate deviates."

Programmed learning utilizes the prime progressive principle of individualized instruction, allowing every pupil to advance at his own rate. Materials now being developed for this "new" system call to mind the self-teaching materials developed and distributed by San Francisco State Normal School before the First World War.

The accent on the new is nowhere more pronounced than in the teaching of science and mathematics. Yet, both areas employ progressive approaches. Instead of concentrating upon mastery of specific facts, the courses are concerned with a generalized method applicable to a variety of situations. The "new math," for instance, in minimizing the learning of specific facts and attempting to develop more general concepts, is reminiscent of Francis Parker's approach to arithmetic in the 1870s.

Another indication of the persistence of progressive education may be found in the attitudes of public school personnel. Many, if not most educators still believe in its principles and encourage it whenever they can. For example, in the fall of 1965, a California principal, at a meeting on the education of Negro children, exhorted his audience to ". . . get rid of the idea of drill, drill and drill. We've got to make school interesting for these kids." At another meeting a few days later, a board member proclaimed that ". . . we are not providing a program for only one type of student; we are trying to provide equal opportunities for all." Thus, new names may be used, new approaches tried, but the basic concepts of progressivism persist.[17]

One reason for this is that some of the problems which originally led to the adoption of progressive education are still present. A few examples may emphasize this point. Trouble with pupil control was suggested by the mass resignation of seventy-nine teachers from a Bronx junior high school in protest against student assaults on teachers.[18] Such attacks are not simply a problem with teen-age toughs: Chicago reported 1065 assaults on teachers during 1968, and 71 percent of these were by pupils in the first six grades. The president of the East St. Louis school board reported that a majority of his system's 1900 teachers were carrying guns; women, he said, packed small pistols in their purses. The national president of the American Federation of Teachers stated, "There is an increase in violence in the schools and teachers get the brunt of it."[19]

The continuing necessity of maintaining local community support was indicated by a report headlined TAXPAYERS' STRIKE ALARMS THE EDUCATORS:

> SACRAMENTO — (UPI) — California school officials mixed fear and anger today as they reviewed an apparently unprecedented

number of defeats last week for local school bond and tax override proposals.

A preliminary report from the California Association of School Administrators counted only 34 victories in 100 school district elections held with the June 7 primary. According to performance over the past 10 years, voters should have approved about double the number.

Officials could find little comfort in passage of the state's $275 million school construction bond that appeared on all ballots.

Authorities who allocate the bond funds said this year's measure received 61 percent of the vote, well below the average 73 percent these bonds have been receiving since they first appeared on the ballot in 1949.

"I don't think there's any question but that you have a taxpayers' strike," said Max Rafferty, state superintendent. "This is the most serious crisis in school finance since I've been in this business and I'm scared stiff."

Dr. Arthur Corey, executive secretary of the California Teachers Association, called the situation "critical." He said that only school districts — among all forms of government in the state — had to seek voter approval for a tax increase and therefore took the brunt of all dissatisfactions.[20]

In the area of administration, federal funds, though welcome in some ways, can also complicate accounting procedures to the point where additional clerical and managerial personnel may be required. Nor does federal funding solve the problem of public relations at the local level, for angry citizens may threaten to protest directly to Washington over alleged irregularities or discrimination in the use of government money. In California, for instance, local citizens' groups called for a boycott of the Richmond junior high schools because the Board of Education refused to abolish ability-grouping or to integrate the schools completely. One speaker announced that, "Demands of this type are the only things that elected boards understand," and he warned the board president that she and other board members "better shape up, because you can be replaced." He also threatened to have all federal funds withheld from the district.[21]

To the extent that progressive education was initially adopted by public schools because it helped them to cope with urgent practical problems, we may expect it to continue as long as these problems persist. As it is, there are indications that a number of these pressures are still present: local control, large-scale organization, non-voluntary heterogeneous clientele, and non-academic personnel. If anything, these conditions make it as difficult as ever for the school to limit its attention to strictly educational considerations. School systems are growing still larger, enrollments are rising and there is an insistent demand for equal educational opportunities for all. Previous patterns of personnel recruitment continue and, while some government control may accompany the advent of federal aid, there is little indication that drastic changes will occur in the present pattern of local control. In fact, pressures for even further decentralization are coming from the bottom and the top. Ghetto blacks and segregationist whites both want more control over their neighborhood schools, and some federal officials are trying to dodge the politically explosive issue of integration by giving more freedom to the individual states.

In addition to the persistence of these problems, however, there is another factor to consider: institutionalization. Progressivistic education has become so firmly established in American public schools that it would be likely to continue even if the problems which originally encouraged its adoption were to disappear. It has become an integral part of the school, the standard mode of thinking and acting, around which personnel have been recruited and procedures developed. Therefore, it cannot be eliminated simply by a policy directive from the board or the superintendent. Teachers and administrators have become accustomed to it and many would resist attempts to get rid of it. The motives for their resistance are similar to those of employees in a variety of organizations. At the least, learning new procedures may require some effort. There is also the more serious possibility that innovations would render existing skills obsolete, threatening employees' status and jobs. Consequently, many people prefer to let things continue as they are.

But institutionalization involves more than merely avoiding the new. There is also a positive valuation of the present way of doing things. Through long usage, the existing procedures have been accepted as proper, desirable and "professional." American teachers are indoctrinated into support for these procedures through education courses, practice teaching, methods textbooks, curriculum guides, in-service training, and by administrators who, in addition to their formal authority over curricular matters, have the power to hire, fire, evaluate and promote teachers. For this reason, most people who remain in the schools have some commitment to progressivistic education.

This does not mean that no changes will occur, but rather that innovations are likely to remain superficial unless the problems of the school and its personnel are also considered. There are, in fact, various reasons for expecting moderate changes in the schools. For example, administrators may view experimentation as a method of minimizing public interference, by suggesting that the schools are keeping up with the latest pedagogical developments and are well ahead of laymen in determining what is best for the pupil. In other instances, individuals within the school may support a particular innovation because they believe that it will benefit the pupils or that it will further their own careers. Ultimately, however, it is the classroom teachers who must put most innovations into effect. Unless they are really convinced that it is worth their effort to adopt the new system, it is likely to remain superficial.

An illustration of this is provided by the current controversies over reading. If, for example, influential citizens demand more phonics, the superintendent may agree that phonics is indeed desirable. Subsequent publicity releases may assure the community that phonics is being included in the curriculum, and the schools may purchase books which emphasize phonics. But, if the teachers are skeptical about this method of instruction, the books may remain on the shelf unopened or they may be used only once in a while, being brought out primarily for visits by a supervisor or parent who advocated their use. Or, teachers may introduce some phonics, but only after the pupils have already learned to rely upon the word-recognition method. In sum, there are many ways in which recalcitrant personnel can resist innovations imposed upon them without their consent.

If there is one lesson to be learned from the fate of progressive education it is this: in order to introduce changes into an organization, the needs of the organization and its personnel must be kept in mind. Otherwise the desired results may not be achieved. The innovation may be rejected outright, it may be modified so that it loses much of its effectiveness, or it may be so drastically transformed that its consequences are the opposite of those originally intended. Thus, it is not enough merely to introduce a new idea, a new method, or a new technique into the schools. No matter how worthwhile the innovation might be, the schools will try to adapt it to suit their own purposes. The education of ghetto children, team teaching, new math, programmed instruction, or anything else that comes along may all be influenced by non-pedagogical considerations.

It is imperative, therefore, to keep in mind the distinction between the school's stated goals and its actual needs. Too many reformers have overlooked the latter.

REFERENCES

[1]Chinoy, *Society*, 2nd ed., p. 395.

[2]*Ibid.*, p. 396.

[3]Martin, in *Report of Massachusetts State Board of Education 1903-04*, p. 98, in Cubberly, *Public School Administration*, p. 366n.

[4]Cubberly, *Public School Administration*, rev. ed., p. 365.

[5]*Ibid.*, p. 367.

[6]John and Mary Dewey, *Schools of Tomorrow*, p. 153.

[7]*Ibid.*

[8]*Ibid.*, pp. 153-58.

[9]*Ibid.*, p. 158.

[10]*Ibid.*, pp. 150-51.

[11]U.S. Bureau of the Census, *Statistical Abstract of the U.S., 1961*, p. 93.

[12]Thomlinson, *Demographic Problems*, p. 78.

[13]*Ibid.*

[14]Inkeles and Rossi, "National Comparisons of Occupational Prestige," *A.J.S.*, Jan. 1956, pp. 336-38.

[15]As De Toqueville observed over a century ago: "Evils which are patiently endured when they seem inevitable become intolerable when once the idea of escape from them is suggested" (Quoted by Davies, "Toward a Theory of Revolution," *American Sociological Review*, Feb. 1962, p. 6). See also the concept of *relative deprivation* in Merton, *Social Theory and Social Structure*, rev. ed., pp. 227-34.

[16]Recalling the statements made in the opening chapter, that few truly progressive schools have ever existed, it might be more accurate to apply a term such as *progressivistic* to the form of progressive education that was actually practiced in the public schools.

[17]See, for example, the "new" concept of the *open school*, tried experimentally in New York's P.S. 84 and P.S. 123 (*The Center Forum*, May 15, 1969). John Dewey would be pleased to hear that the open school ". . . emphasizes differences among children . . . sees knowledge as uncompartmentalized, and teachers as problem posers rather than solution givers. Its pedagogy allows for exploration of principals (not merely the memorization of standard operations): hence, its boundaries seem ever flexible" (*The Center Forum*, p. 2).

[18]*Honolulu Star Bulletin*, March 15, 1967.

[19]*San Francisco Examiner*, October 26, 1969.

[20]*San Francisco Examiner*, June 15, 1966. For reports of similar problems in other parts of the United States, see *Time*, June 2, 1967, p. 44.

[21]Association of Richmond Educators, *Report*, May 16, 1966.

BIBLIOGRAPHY

Anderson, Vivienne and Daniel R. Davies. *Patterns of Educational Leadership.* Englewood Cliffs, N. J.: Prentice-Hall, Inc., 1956.

Archambault, Reginald. *Dewey on Education.* New York: Modern Library, Inc., 1964.

Association of Richmond Educators. *Report,* vol. 1, no. 32. Richmond, Calif.: May 16, 1966.

Bailyn, Bernard. *Education in the Forming of American Society.* New York: Random House, Inc., Vintage Books, 1960.

Beard, Charles A. and Mary Beard. *A Basic History of the United States.* Philadelphia: The Blakiston Co., 1944.

Becker, Howard S. *Role and Career Problems of the Chicago Public School Teacher.* Unpub. Ph.D. dissertation, Department of Sociology, University of Chicago, 1951.

Bendix, Reinhard. *Work and Authority in Industry.* New York: John Wiley & Sons, Inc., 1956.

Berger, M. I. "John Dewey and Progressive Education Today," in William W. Brickman and Stanley Lehrer, eds., *John Dewey: Master Educator*. New York: Society for the Advancement of Education, 1959.

Berk, Bernard B. "Organizational Goals and Inmate Organization," *American Journal of Sociology,* LXXI, March 1966.

Berry, Daniel A. *C.T.A.: An Interest Group in California Politics.* Unpub. M. A. thesis, Department of Political Science, University of California, Berkeley, 1958.

Beslie, Eugene L. and Cyril Sargent. "The Concept of Administration," in Roald F. Campbell and Russell T. Gregg, eds., *Administrative Behavior in Education*. New York: Harper & Brothers, 1957.

Bestor, Arthur. *Educational Wastelands.* Urbana: University of Illinois Press, 1953.

Blau, Peter. *The Dynamics of Bureaucracy.* Chicago: University of Chicago Press, 1955.

———— and Richard Scott. *Formal Organizations, A Comparative Approach*. San Francisco: Chandler Publishing Co., 1962.

Boone, Richard G. *Education in the United States.* New York: D. Appleton, 1890.

Bowman, Howard A. "Promotion, Retention and Acceleration in the Los Angeles City Elementary Schools," in *Educational Research Projects Reported by California County and District School Offices 1960-61,* Research Bulletin 153. Burlingame, Calif.: California Teachers Association, April 1962.

Brim, Orville, Jr. *Sociology and the Field of Education.* New York: Russell Sage Foundation, 1958.

Brookover, Wilbur A. *A Sociology of Education.* New York: American Book Company, 1955.

Broom, Leonard and Philip Selznick. *Sociology,* 2nd ed. Evanston, Ill.: Row, Peterson and Company, 1958.

Brukman, W.W. "The Educational Leader as a Scholar and Man of Culture," *School and Society,* vol. 85. April 27, 1957.

Butts, R. Freeman and Lawrence Cremin. *A History of Education in American Culture.* New York: Henry Holt and Co., 1953.

Caldwell, Otis W. and Stuart A. Curtis. *Then and Now in Education: 1845:1943.* Yonkers-on-Hudson, N.Y.: World Book Co., 1925.

California Teachers Association. *C.T.A. Journal,* vol. 54, no. 5. May 1958.

Callahan, Raymond. *Education and the Cult of Efficiency.* Chicago: University of Chicago Press, 1962.

Center For Urban Education. *The Center Forum,* vol. 3, no. 6. New York: May 15, 1969.

Chinoy, Ely. *Society,* 2nd ed. New York: Random House, Inc., 1967.

Clark, Burton. *Adult Education in Transition.* Berkeley: University of California Press, 1956.

————. "The 'Cooling-Out' Function in Higher Education," *American Journal of Sociology,* vol. 65. May 1960.

————. *The Open Door College.* New York: McGraw-Hill Book Company, 1960.

Conrad, Richard. *The Administrative Role: A Sociological Study of Leadership in a Public School System.* Unpub. Ph.D. dissertation, Department of Sociology, Stanford University, 1951.

Cordasco, Francesco. *A Brief History of Education.* Paterson, N.J.: Littlefield, Adams, & Company, 1965.

Corwin, Ronald. *A Sociology of Education.* New York: Appleton-Century-Crofts, 1965.

Cremin, Lawrence A. *The American Common School.* New York: Bureau of Publications, Columbia University Teachers College, 1951.

————. *The Transformation of the School.* New York: Random House, Inc., Vintage Books, 1964.

Cubberly, Ellwood P. *Public Education in the United States.* Boston: Houghton-Mifflin Company, 1919; also revised 1934.

————. *Public School Administration,* rev. ed. Boston: Houghton-Mifflin Company, 1922.

————. *Readings in Public Education in the United States.* Boston: Houghton-Mifflin Company, 1934.

Curti, Merle. *The Growth of American Thought,* 3rd ed. New York: Harper and Row, Publishers, 1964.

————. *The Social Ideas of American Educators,* rev. ed. Paterson, N.J.: Littlefield, Adams, & Company, 1959.

Dahlke, H. Otto. *Values in Culture and Classroom.* New York: Harper & Brothers, 1958.

Dalton, Melville. *Men Who Manage*. New York: John Wiley & Sons, Inc., 1959.

Dewey, John. *Experience and Education*. New York: Collier Books, 1963.

————. "My Pedagogic Creed," in Frederick Meyer, ed., *Introductory Readings in Education*. Belmont, Calif.: Dickenson Publishing Co., Inc., 1966.

———— and Evelyn Dewey. *Schools of Tomorrow*. New York: E.P. Dutton & Company, Inc., 1962.

Davis, James C. "Toward a Theory of Revolution," *A.S.R.,* vol. 27, no. 1. February 1962.

Davis, H. Curtis. "Where Does the Time Go?", *California Journal of Secondary Education,* vol. 27, no. 6. October 1953.

Dworkin, Martin. "John Dewey: A Centennial Review," in Dworkin, ed., *Dewey on Education*. New York: Columbia University Teachers College, 1961.

Eby, Frederick and Charles Flinn Arrowood. *The Development of Modern Education*. New York: Prentice-Hall, Inc., 1934.

Fowler, Burton P. "President's Message," *Progressive Education,* vol. 7. 1930.

Freeman, Ruth S. *Yesterday's Schools*. Watkins Glen, N.Y.: Century House, 1962.

Good, H. G. *A History of American Education*. New York: The Macmillan Company, 1962.

Gouldner, Alvin W. and Helen P. Gouldner. *Modern Sociology*. New York: Harcourt, Brace & World, Inc., 1963.

Greene, Mary Frances and Orletta Ryan. *The Schoolchildren*. New York: Signet Books, 1967.

Gross, Edward. *Work and Society*. New York: Crowell, 1958.

Gross, Neal. "The Sociology of Education," in Robert K. Merton, Leonard Broom and Leonard S. Cottrell, Jr., *Sociology Today*. New York: Basic Books, Inc., 1959.

————. *Who Runs Our Schools?* New York: John Wiley & Sons, Inc., 1958.

Handlin, Oscar. *John Dewey's Challenge to Education*. New York: Harper & Brothers, 1959.

Hansen, Donald A. and Joel E. Gerstl, eds. *On Education: Sociological Perspectives.* New York: John Wiley & Sons, Inc., 1967.

Herndon, James. *The Way it Spozed To Be.* New York: Bantam Books, Inc., 1968.

Hollingshead, August. *Elmtown's Youth.* New York: John Wiley & Sons, Inc., 1949.

Horton, John E. and Wayne E. Thompson. "Powerlessness and Political Negativism: A Study of Defeated Local Referendums," *American Journal of Sociology,* vol. 67. March 1962.

Hughes, Everett C. "The Study of Occupations," in Merton *et al., Sociology Today.* New York: Basic Books, Inc., 1959.

Inkeles, Alex and Peter Rossi. "National Comparisons of Occupational Prestige," *American Journal of Sociology,* vol. 61, no. 4. January 1956.

Johnson, Clifton. *The Country School in New England.* New York: D. Appleton and Company, 1893.

—————. *Old Time Schools and Schoolbooks.* New York: The Macmillan Company, 1904.

King, Edmund. *Other Schools and Ours.* New York: Rinehart & Company, Inc., 1958.

Koerner, James D. *The Miseducation of American Teachers.* Baltimore: Penguin Books, 1963.

Learned, William S. and Ben Wood. "The Student and His Knowledge: A Report to the Carnegie Foundation on the Results of High School and College Examinations of 1928, 1930 and 1932," Bulletin No. 29. New York: The Carnegie Foundation for the Advancement of Teaching, 1938.

Lieberman, Myron. *Education As a Profession.* Englewood Cliffs, N.J.: Prentice-Hall, Inc., 1956.

—————. *The Future of Public Education.* Chicago: University of Chicago Press, 1960.

Linn, Robert A. *A Comparison of the Mean Test Scores and Standard Deviations on the Department of Education Test Battery and Student Teaching Grades,* mimeo. Berkeley: University of California School of Education, Student Personnel Services, n.d.

Lipset, Seymour M., *et al. Union Democracy.* Glencoe, Ill.: The Free Press, 1956.

Littlefield, George Emery. *Early Schools and Schoolbooks of New England.* New York: Russell and Russell, Inc., 1965.

Lynd, Robert S. and Helen Merrell. *Middletown.* New York: Harcourt, Brace and Company, 1929.

————. *Middletown in Transition.* New York: Harcourt, Brace and Company, 1937.

Mallinson, Vernon. *An Introduction to the Study of Comparative Education.* New York: The Macmillan Company, 1957.

Mannheim, Karl. *Ideology and Utopia.* New York: Harcourt, Brace and Company, Harvest Book Edition, n.d.

Mason, Ward S. *The Beginning Teacher.* Circular No. 644. Washington, D.C.: U.S. Office of Education, 1961.

Mayer, Frederick. *Introductory Readings in Education.* Belmont, Calif.: Dickenson Publishing Co., Inc., 1966.

Merton, Robert K. *Social Theory and Social Structure,* rev. ed. Glencoe, Ill.: The Free Press, 1957.

————, Leonard Broom and Leonard Cottrell, Jr. *Sociology Today.* New York: Basic Books, Inc., 1959.

Mills, C. Wright. *White Collar.* New York: Oxford University Press, 1956.

Muzzey, David. *The United States of America,* vol. 1. Boston: Ginn and Co., 1933.

National Education Association, Research Division. *The American Public School Teacher 1960-61,* Research Monograph 1963-M2. Washington, D.C., 1963.

————. *National Association of Secondary School Principals Bulletin,* vol. 35. Washington, D.C., November 1951.

————. *National Elementary Principal,* vol. 28, no. 1; vol. 38, no. 1, Bulletin of the Department of Elementary School Principals. Washington, D.C., September 1948, 1958.

————. *Profile of the School Superintendent.* Washington, D.C.: American Association of School Administrators, 1960.

————. "The Teacher's Role in American Society," *NEA Research Bulletin.* Washington, D.C., February 1952.

National Opinion Research Center. "Jobs and Occupations: A Popular Evaluation," in Reinhard Bendix and S.M. Lipset, eds., *Class, Status and Power.* Glencoe, Ill.: The Free Press, 1953.

New York. "Fifth Annual Report of the City Superintendent of Schools of the City of New York," 1903, cited in Pierce, *The Origin and Development of the Public School Principalship.* Chicago: University of Chicago Press, 1935.

Oakland Tribune. Oakland, Calif., June 1, 1960.

Otto, Henry J. *Principles of Elementary Education.* New York: Rinehart and Co., 1949.

Parker, Samuel Chester. *A Textbook in the History of Modern Elementary Education.* Boston: Ginn and Company, 1912.

Pavalko, Ronald M. *Sociology of Education.* Itasco, Ill.: F.E. Peacock Publishers, Inc., 1968.

Phi Delta Kappan, vol. 41, no. 2. November 1959.

Pierce, Paul R. *The Origin and Development of the Public School Principalship.* Chicago: University of Chicago Press, 1935.

Rafferty, Max. *Suffer Little Children.* New York: Devin-Adair Co., 1962.

————. *What They Are Doing to Your Children.* New York: The New American Library, Inc., 1963.

Reisner, Edward H. *The Evolution of the Common School.* New York: The Macmillan Company, 1930.

Richey, Robert W. *Planning for Teaching.* New York: McGraw-Hill Book Company, 1952.

Richmond Federation of Teachers. *Newsletter.* Richmond, California.

Richmond Independent. Richmond, California.

Richmond School District. *Board Bulletin 6-B.* Richmond, Calif., February 28, 1961.

Riesman, David *et al. The Lonely Crowd.* New Haven: Yale University Press, 1950.

Ritter, Ed. "Answers Given; Opinions Voiced on Education Questions," *CTA Journal,* vol. 54, no. 2. February 1959.

Rust, Ben. *Study on Costs of Classroom Instruction.* Sacramento, Calif.: Senate Special Committee on Governmental Administration, Senate of the State of California, 1959.

Ryans, David G. *Characteristics of Teachers.* Washington, D.C.: American Council on Education, 1960.

Stiles, Lindley J., ed. *The Teacher's Role in American Society.* New York: Harper & Brothers, 1957.

San Francisco Chronicle. San Francisco, California.

San Francisco Examiner. San Francisco, California.

Selznick, Philip. *Leadership in Administration.* Evanston, Ill.: Row, Peterson and Company, 1957.

Spero, Sterling D. *Government As Employer.* New York: Remsen Press, 1948.

Swift, David W. *The Public School Principal in California.* Unpub. M.A. thesis, Berkeley, Calif.: University of California, 1960.

Thomlinson, Ralph. *Demographic Problems.* Belmont, Calif.: Dickerson Publishing Co., 1967.

Thorndike, Robert L. and Elizabeth Hagen. *Ten Thousand Careers.* New York: John Wiley & Sons, Inc., 1959.

U.S. Bureau of the Census. *Historical Statistics of the United States, Colonial Times to 1957.* Washington, D.C., 1960.

_____. *Statistical Abstract of the United States.* Washington, D.C., 1961, 1963, 1966.

U.S. Bureau of Education. *Biennial Survey of Education 1918-20,* Bulletin 1923, no. 29. Washington, D.C., 1923.

U.S. Commissioner of Education. *Annual Report of the Commissioner of Education Made to the Secretary of the Interior for the Year 1870.* Washington, D.C., 1875.

U.S. Department of Health, Education, and Welfare. *State Legislation on School Attendance and Related Matters,* Circular 615. Washington, D.C., January 1, 1960.

U.S. Office of Education. *Statistical Summary of Education, 1951-52.* Washington, D.C., 1955.

Wagenschein, Miriam. *Reality Shock.* Unpub. M.A. thesis, Department of Sociology, University of Chicago, 1950.

Waller, Willard. *The Sociology of Teaching.* New York: John Wiley & Sons, Inc., 1965.

Weber, Max. *The Protestant Ethic and the Spirit of Capitalism,* trans. Talcott Parsons. New York: Charles Scribner's Sons, 1958.

Whyte, William H. *The Organization Man.* New York: Simon and Schuster, Inc., 1956.

Wolfle, Dael. *America's Resources of Specialized Talent.* New York: Harper & Brothers, 1954.

INDEX

Rickover, H. G., 24
Riesman, David, 61, 62
Ritter, Ed, 182
Rousseau, Emile, 16, 17, 193
Rust, Ben, 184
Ryan, Orletta, 61
Ryans, David, 158, 165, 182

Salary, administrators', 174
Salary, teachers'
  progressive era, 135-36
  traditional era, 129
  transitional era, 133-34
Schools, types of
  academy, 105
  charity school, 106
  dame school, 104
  district school, 104
  divided school, 104
  double-headed school, 71, 75
  elementary school, 166-68
  free public school, 108
  high school, 161-62
  infant school, 70
  junior high school, 165-66
  lancastrian school, 70, 130
  latin grammar school 104-05
  monitorial school, 70
  moving school, 104
  normal school, 130, 131, 133
  private school, 105
  religious public school, 105
Selznick, Philip, 9, 67, 94
Smith, Mortimer, 24
Spaulding, Kenneth, 84
Spears, Harold, 62
Special services, 24
Spero, Sterling D., 96
Stiles, Lindley, 125, 139, 155, 183
Stout, James, 20

Taxes, 69, 74, 99, 102, 105, 109

Teachers
  academic high school, 161-62
  certification of, 129-30, 131-33,
    134-38
  characteristics of, 141-45
  elementary, 162-68
  non-academic secondary,
    162-68
  progressive era, 15, 46-49
  relation to administration, 110
  substitute, 93
  traditional era, 13, 33-41,
    128-30
  training of, 25, 39, 129-30,
    131-33, 141-45
  transitional era, 131-34
team teaching, 199
tenure, 101, 134, 135, 136, 180
Thomlinson, Ralph, 200
Thompson, Wayne E., 124
Thorndike, Edward, 19, 22, 183
Toqueville, Alexis de, 200
Traditional education, 6
  administration, 67-72
  aims of, 12
  appearance of classroom, 13
  autonomy, 101-08
  classroom control, 33-41
  curriculum, 12
  methods of instruction, 13
  personnel, 128-31
  role of pupil, 13
  role of teacher, 13, 33-41
  social factors, 33-41
Transitional education, 6
  administration, 72-80
  autonomy, 108-09
  classroom control, 44-46
  personnel, 131-34
  social factors, 41-46

Unions, 79-81